The Great Gelatin Revival

the great
GELATIN
REVIVAL

Savory Aspics, Jiggly Shots, and Outrageous Desserts

KEN ALBALA

**UNIVERSITY OF
ILLINOIS PRESS**
Urbana, Chicago, and Springfield

Library of Congress Cataloging-in-Publication Data

Names: Albala, Ken, 1964– author.
Title: The great gelatin revival: savory aspics, jiggly shots,
and outrageous desserts / Ken Albala.
Description: Urbana: University of Illinois Press, [2023] |
Includes bibliographical references and index.
Identifiers: LCCN 2022022431 (print) | LCCN 2022022432
(ebook) | ISBN 9780252086816 (paperback) | ISBN
9780252053764 (ebook)
Subjects: LCSH: Cooking (Gelatin) | LCGFT: Cookbooks.
Classification: LCC TX814.5.G4 A44 2023 (print) | LCC
TX814.5.G4 (ebook) | DDC 641.86/42—dc23/eng/20220729
LC record available at https://lccn.loc.gov/2022022431
LC ebook record available at https://lccn.loc.gov/2022022432

Contents

Author's Note

This is a book about gelatin in its many forms. It is part history, part explanation of why gelatin has had such an intriguingly meteoric rise in some eras and such a precipitous fall in others. My intention is also to serve as a herald, to usher in a new age of aspics, to inspire and delight and terrify you in a way that only gelatin can. Jello has been derided for many decades, and it's time for a serious comeback. I hope to enrich the complex story of gelatin, to seduce you back to its many charms, to help you appreciate the marvelous forms jello has taken, and to inspire you to experiment with your own fabulous creations. This book will help you understand how I went from a detractor to a passionate lover of all things jiggly.

Introduction

I never choose a topic for a book—it chooses me. This is the truth without exaggeration. A year ago, I would have bet any amount of money that I would never write about jello. So let me explain how this came to pass.

As a boy growing up in the '60s and '70s, I was systematically tortured by my Weight-Watching parents with Jell-O brand desserts, artificially sweetened, colored and flavored, laden with canned fruit cocktail and topped with dollops of diet Cool Whip. The experience was permanently scarring. My only escape was a sudden declaration one day when I was about 10 that I had figured out the origin of gelatin: calves' feet. I feigned a repugnance so deep that I would have to abjure forever my mother's Jell-O parfaits.

I never looked back. In fact, jello was the only food on earth I would not touch. Apart from a few lapses in college for sickeningly sweet lime-flavored jello shots laced with Everclear that would leave you drunk on the front lawns of frat houses, I went for about 40 years without so much as a spoonful of jello. This closely coincided chronologically with the dramatic decline in Jell-O sales in the US.

I had seen many gelatinous recipes in my work as a food historian. Most were thoroughly disgusting mid-20th-century aspics, brightly colored and packed with canned seafood, hot dogs, and other unspeakable ingredients, served on a bed of lettuce with mayonnaise. It never occurred to me that someone with rational sensibilities would consume such things.

However, casting a glance toward the past, it's obvious that aspics were nothing new to the post-war era. In Victorian times, they were the height of fashion, and famous chefs proudly displayed their architectural creations, which required enormous skill. It seemed as if only in the 20th century did the aspic reach ordinary households through the advent of little packets of powdered gelatin including the Jell-O brand itself, which came presweetened, brightly colored, and flavored. Technology had democratized the once elite aspic, or at least this was the narrative proclaimed in the ads.

Medieval cooks had actually invented the aspic; they had a penchant for colorful layers of translucent jello. Some would be at home on a table of the 1950s. Scanning the broad swathe of history, there appears to have been a cyclical pattern in the taste for aspics and gelatin molds. Periods that embrace the jiggle are always followed by periods of disgust sometimes so intense and visceral that entire generations lose the skill to make them. The pattern is clear: In periods that favor technology in the kitchen, inventiveness, novelty, and foods that shock and surprise, aspics become wildly popular. In those that favor tradition, homey simplicity, local ingredients, and straightforward honesty in cooking, aspics are seen as too fussy, a hodgepodge of extraneous ingredients, even repulsive. There is perhaps no other food type in history that has experienced such wild swings in fortune.

Aspics are in a sense the bellwether of modernity. Technologically savvy periods in history, like the mid–20th century, the late 19th century, the late Middle Ages and Renaissance, all looked favorably on aspics. We have been for the past few decades in a period that has practically no interest in them, except perhaps as a joke. Now that may be changing. So too is our attitude toward science in the kitchen. Homemade hipster pickles and hoppy craft beers are gradually giving way to industrially made impossible burgers and spiked seltzers. I predict that we are on the threshold of a new aspic forward aesthetic.

After many years of pickling and DIY projects, my own awakening as a gelatarian was recent, fierce, and bizarre. A friend had dared me to make an aspic and post it in a Facebook group called "Show Me Your Aspics." I assumed from the name that it would be ribald and I declined. A few weeks later, I took a peek. It turns out, there are serious jello enthusiasts on social media: people running businesses making flowers in clear gelatin, others experimenting with elaborate molds, there are deep discussions over viscosity, headcheese, and spiked gummies. I was somehow lured in. I started playing with jello and was soon converted—and I became the most ardent advocate of everything gelatinous. How did this happen? Here is a passage I wrote directly inspired by the spirit of the jello:

> Consider the many properties that constitute the exquisite appeal of gelatin. Its translucence, the way it draws light within and disperses it with added radiance. The irresistible jiggle, threatening collapse with every twist and turn. The thrill of the spoon smoothly cleaving its slick glossy flesh. Then in the mouth, that bounce, the subtle firmness that first resists then gently yields to the pressure of the teeth. Followed by gelatin's disintegration as it

begins to melt at human body temperature, transforming into cool liquid, trickling down the back of the throat and rendering its subtle perfume up into the olfactory cavities and directly triggering the limbic brain into a state of primordial bliss. The experience is ecstatic.

My first foray into this world was made of ouzo that consisted of perfectly clear globules set on pita bread with feta and olives. I posted it, for kicks. The acclaim was overwhelming. I made another, a Negroni with a hemisphere of charred Cara Cara orange within, salami, blue cheese, and polenta crisps. Every few days I would try a different drink in a new jello, even making a few historic recipes. A spiced chicken and white wine aspic from a 1549 cookbook was extraordinary. I had never really looked closely at jello recipes in the past—there are many. To my surprise, the Aspics group (over 40,000 members at the moment) proclaimed their adoration for my creations. They eventually named me as their tutelary deity, their *kenpai*. Most people in the group call me Jello Daddy or Jiggle Daddy. I was even featured in a few international news stories.

Over a year and more than 175 aspic experiments later, I began writing in earnest, and what follows is more or less a faithful account of this remarkable journey, with a hefty dose of history. But let me explain the sort of things that excite me and the internal logic of these recipes. Many are quite straightforward and simple, but most are intentionally challenging, keeping with the theme of ushering in a new interest in aspic. I have no intention of bringing back anything from the past, except as a matter of research.

I should also point out from the start that practically everything in this book contains alcohol. Some in fact pack a wollop. If you choose not to drink alcohol, just substitute juice. For those who can, I contend that gelatin in the past almost always contained wine or another spirit. Jello Shots are nothing new. It is only since the infantilization of the Jell-O brand that a boozy jiggler seems dopey, but it is long established and I insist does make jello much more interesting. Also note: the recipes here are for a single serving unless otherwise specified. That makes it much easier to multiply. Now, to my ulterior motive.

The Sublime

Food can serve many varied purposes. There is the familiar and comfortable, the titillating and new, and even the joy of tasting an extraordinarily complex and quirky dish. Simplicity definitely has its place. Consider the perfect slice of pizza or a sandwich made with acute precision and skill. Or the perfect scrambled egg. There is much to be said for the immaculately simple, familiar, and comforting in food. Like chewy udon in a bowl of delicate broth.

But when food aspires to the level of art, it should ride that very fine line between attraction and revulsion. These are not opposites. You should be both disgusted and compelled to look, sort of like passing by tragedy. Edmund Burke, known for his political theory, but equally talented as an aesthetician, understood art that paradoxically both horrifies and delights simultaneously. He called it the Sublime. Think of the painter J. M. W. Turner's gathering storms in swathes of bright yellow or Caspar Friedrich's wind-swept figure teetering at the edge of a mountain precipice. Or the Frankenstein monster—all products of the early 19th-century Romantic notion of the Sublime.

I recollect a plate of andouillettes in Paris with a friend. They smelled exactly like pig shit, and the appeal was not daring each other to eat something vile; it was precisely because they were horrible and delicious at the same time. Art that is merely pretty is forgettable; that which disturbs may stick in the mind, but it hits one note, not a full chord of resonance within. It is only when you are drawn to something full of dread, and it bothers you to think about, but you enjoy it all the same—that is the Sublime. It's like kinky sex. It's like Stockhausen or Jimi Hendrix setting fire to his guitar. It is not art you understand, because it has no internal logic. It is because it is.

Think of this as you gaze upon the bizarre gelatin constructions here and ideally try them yourself. They are not here merely to please. Have a hamburger if that's what you're after. They are here to rattle your very understanding of what food can be, to expand your senses, to embrace the terrifyingly delectable and coax the most gastronomically frightening urges that lie within us.

On the other hand, never take yourself too seriously. Everything here is made for fun—pure and unmitigated. And there's a lot in this book that's just pretty and good to serve to the most squeamish of guests. A jello for all seasons.

What This Book Will Not Include

Since there are so many recipes available in books and online that use pre-flavored gelatin, I decided not to use them here. In the US, that means almost exclusively the Jell-O brand. It might mean Hartley's in Britain, Dr. Oetker in Germany, or many different brands elsewhere. In my limited experience with these various products, I have found them to be basically the same: artificially flavored and colored. I am not saying such things never enter the temple of my body, but as long as I was going to eat a whole lot of jello while researching this book, I thought I'd stick to natural ingredients when possible, so that's what I offer you. Incidentally, many people have asked about the state of my hair and nails, and yes, everything you have heard is true. They grow like mad if you eat large quantities of gelatin, and that is not necessarily a good thing.

I have seen a few brands of instant, all natural, kosher and halal gelatin, and a few without sugar as well, but the latter doesn't sound like fun to use. As for the historic recipes, those before the late 19th century rely on natural ingredients and for the few historic ones thereafter that use preflavored Jell-O, I have given you the primary source material to satisfy historical interest. I will also explain the use of hartshorn and isinglass if you would really like to go fully historical. Just be careful, the hartshorn you can buy today is a baking ingredient, ammonium chloride, not the raw shaved antler of deer that was used in the past. Isinglass is a fining agent in beer today, but not usually today derived from the sturgeon swim bladder or Russian isinglass, used in historic recipes. That is, you have to search very persistently online to find the original forms of these ingredients. See pages 69–71 for a full discussion of these.

I have used several brands of plain unflavored powder and sheet gelatin, and honestly, I haven't noticed a great difference among them, either in terms of ease of use or strength in setting, clarity, or dependability. I've given you a few alternatives in the recipes when a different kind of gelatin works better. On an industrial scale, the sheets are graded according to setting strength—platinum being the preferred. Knox gelatin powder is rated at a bloom strength of 235, and the gelatin sheets I used are 230. In the small amounts called for here, I don't think it will matter which you use, despite what professional chefs say.

There are organic brands of gelatin and if that's a priority, by all means use them. I stuck with Knox unflavored gelatin for consistency and because it's universally available in the US. I received no promotional consideration or renumeration for using their product. I went through a large box about every month, each of which cost about 18 dollars for 32 envelopes. I suppose it's worth saying that I paid for all the ingredients here and using any particular brand is in no way an official endorsement. There are other brands you can find online if you're after perfect clarity.

There are many other things I will not include here, mostly because there are experts elsewhere and directions you can easily find in print or online if you are so inclined. There are remarkable people who make beautiful gelatin art, delicate flowers, plants, and delectable scenes in clear gelatin or agar. I bought the tools to try it and you can see the results. It takes a lot of practice to get really good at it. There are also neat tricks you can do with layered jello, sparkles made with edible mica—essentially eye shadow—and other neat tricks. The directions are all easily found online, so I saw no reason to repeat them. The same goes for alginate, which I have played with before. Now that you can buy a kit and make your own little spherical "caviar" at home, I don't see any reason to explain it. Everything in this book came out of my own kitchen and as far as I know is my own invention. Any similarity to jello real or fictional is purely coincidental, or the original source is cited.

Terminology

In this book I use the term *jello* in the generic sense common in American English. This will always be distinguished from the brand *Jell-O* spelled as trademarked and which I refer to in the narrative but do not use in my recipes. I have consciously avoided the term *jelly,* which in the US means a clarified fruit juice thickened by means of pectin and spread on toast. In Britain they use *jelly* more broadly, but it appears here only in historic recipes or when quoting British sources. More confusingly, the British also refer to starch-thickened desserts made with wheat, corn, tapioca, sago, and the like as jelly—while these would only be thought of as a kind of pudding in the US. I have not covered these here. Nor are gums included like locust bean, guar, xanthan, and the like; they serve as thickeners but almost never as bases for jello on their own.

Gelatin is the specific universal term, but normally excludes similar products based on agar agar, carrageenan, glucomannan, etc. *Gel* is the only scientific term that encompasses all colloidal suspensions, but in the US that term conjures images of a hair product. Aspic is the much more elegant moniker and need not be savory; there are fruit and vegetable aspics. But in practice, we speak of jello for sweet desserts and aspics for meaty combinations and in general, that's how I've used these terms. *Gelée* in French, *Gelo* in Italian both derive from *Gelu, Gelum* in Latin which means ice, strangely enough. Presumably when the first proper translucent jello was presented sometime in the Middle Ages, this was the only term they could think of to describe the mysteriously clear jiggly substance.

Properties and Uses for Gelatin

Gelatin is described by scientists as a thermally reversible hydrocolloid. A colloid is one substance that is dispersed among another at the molecular level, and hydrocolloid means that it's spread through water. Some are irreversible, and others can come apart chemically or with heat. That means that they can melt when cooked and become stable at room temperature, which makes them an ideal stabilizer, thickener, and to prevent crystals forming in ice cream. They also have specific properties in the mouth affecting not only the texture of foods but even their flavor. Gelatin melts around body temperature, so the flavor can disperse in your mouth as you eat it. But a tougher gelatin will lock in flavors, so to speak. This is why a very loose gelatin with a high percentage of alcohol will taste hot in the mouth, a firmer one with a greater concentration of gelatin will taste more mellow—and that's one reason my recipes tend toward the firm side.

The source for hydrocolloids in the food industry is often seaweed (as in carrageenan and agar) so vegetarians, and those keeping halal and kosher diets, can use it. Gums like gum Arabic and locust bean gum from carob are another source, as is pectin in apples and other fruits. Xanthan gum is chemically formed, as is methylcellulose, which is an emulsifier and the base for laxatives. It comes from the cell walls of plants and people can't digest it, which is why it's often described as fiber.

Animal gelatins are made from connective tissues in animals and fish, from the collagen-rich skin and joints, tendons, ligaments, especially in the feet, which is why calves foot jelly and chicken feet have been among the preferred sources of gelatin. Likewise, the swim bladder of fish, especially sturgeon, which is used to make isinglass. As a protein, it contains many amino acids such as glycine, glutamic acid, proline and hydroxyproline, arginine, alanine, and aspartic acid. Once the gelatin is rendered from the collagen-rich tissues, it takes solid form when dried, as the amino acid chains line up, twist together, and tighten. When it's heated and in the presence of water, those chains loosen and get tangled up with the water molecules, forming spirals and other shapes that hold the water, and when cooled, form a gel. Bromelain in pineapples and papain in papaya prevent those chains from linking up, which is why you can't use those fruits raw in gelatin.

When a gel leaks moisture or weeps, it's called syneresis, which will happen over time but also with freezing, which forms crystals and pushes the water out of suspension. So remember if you use the freezer to quickly bring down the temperature of a gelatin, don't leave it in too long. Likewise overheating will destroy the gelling properties, so never boil powdered or sheet gelatin. This is why any liquid added is heated separately, or the gel mixture is only gently warmed in a double boiler. This applies to homemade gelatin as well, so if you boil the bones hard or very long, it will actually lose the ability to set. A long slow simmer is ideal for this reason.

Some gels can be heated and then reset—animal-derived gelatin is one. Pectin won't, though, which is why if you heat your jam it won't set again. Another important factor is the pH; the lower (i.e., the more acidic), the weaker the bond to set the gelatin. Alcohol will also weaken the tight coils of gelatin, so the more you use, the more gelatin needs to be in the mixture.

It is also important to properly hydrate your gelatin first. Ingredients like alcohol and sugar will cause the gel to clump up, so be sure to break up any lumps before adding the hot liquid. So too will the temperature of the water and/or alcohol. The only time I have had real problems with hydration is pulling booze straight from the freezer and pouring it over the gelatin powder. A little room temperature water or vigorous whisking will prevent that.

In this book we'll be talking mostly about animal and fish gelatins and sometimes about agar and carrageenan as food. You've probably never thought much about the other uses for gelatin. Capsules for medicine come both in the two-sided version that fit together encasing a powder as well as the soft capsules that look like little football shapes that can hold liquids. The advantage is that they go down smoothly and the gelatin dissolves in the stomach, releasing the medicine. There were various types of gelatin-coated pills in the past, but the capsule we are familiar with was invented and patented in London by James Murdoch in 1847. Robert Pauli Scherer invented the soft gelatin capsule. Obviously vegetarians would prefer to eat plant-based capsules, but they're more expensive to manufacture and harder to find.

The density and properties of gelatin are remarkably similar to the human body. It jiggles in much the same way we do. In fact, an electroencephalogram will register jello as technically and legally alive. Dr. Adrian Upton in the early '70s showed that the machine can measure alpha waves in a bowl of lime jello that are similar to those produced by the human body when at rest. His point was not that jello is alive of course, but that the EEC was a limited tool for testing life. But the practical application of jello's human-like qualities are that it absorbs the force of ballistics much the same way we do. That is, they shoot a human-shaped jello with guns to see if they can kill it. More importantly, they can use these human-shaped jellos to test ultrasound equipment since its density and viscosity is so similar to ours.

Not surprisingly then, the collagen in gelatin being similar to our own, it is used in skin care products, shampoo, sunscreen. If you purchase bulk gelatin online, you'll notice too that high-protein paleo and keto dieters use it not just for skin care, but as a nutritional supplement.

In food products other than jello, gelatin is used most frequently in commercial baking to stabilize frostings, thicken fillings, and to help set cheesecakes and the like. It's rarely used in home baking, but rather in industrial products that need stability and long shelf life. Unless you're making panna cotta. Marshmallows and circus peanuts also use gelatin, as do a wide range of confections that have creamy fillings.

Where you might not expect to find gelatin is in your drinks. It is basically a clarifying agent, causing particles to precipitate in liquids that might be hazy, such as fruit juices and wine. Isinglass is still a popular clarifying agent in home brewing, though most commercial breweries use substitutes that are free of animal products nowadays.

Lastly, gelatin has been used in photography since the 1870s. It disperses the silver halide crystals used in standard black-and-white film. Color photography is quite different, and of course now digital photography has made photographic prints a rarity. But in the heyday of gelatin, and still among professional photographers, making *gelatin prints* was essential.

te to the final texture of gelatin and so
, that it only makes sense to conduct an
the ideal ratios of gelatin to alcohol by
t a firm texture so it doesn't fly apart.
t's like goo and can't hold its shape or
be expected, the higher the concen-
ı of gelatin must be used. Acidity also
sing a standard packet of supermarket
ate bloom strength, so they're a little
one teaspoon, so three sheets equal
vays use gelatin sheets, and they are
this book, it didn't make a difference.
ı'll have to test as you go, reducing the
cated by heat. Again, for consistency,
Jard packets of unflavored gelatin.

The first experiment was designed to test whether the 1 cup liquid to 1 packet rule followed through much of this book always makes sense. It is ideal for an alcohol strength between 30–40% ABV, which is either a stiff cocktail or straight booze. As you'll see, wine at 13% alcohol and fortified wines, sake, and weaker, diluted cocktails around 20% will set up perfectly fine with 2 tsp of powdered gelatin. Let me explain the entire experiment so you can decide exactly what you prefer texture-wise.

I began with a rosé wine at 13% alcohol, 1 US teaspoon powdered sugar, and 1 teaspoon lemon juice. Those were for flavor since wine on its own without other ingredients can be a little sharp. With this in mind, I should explain that alcohol in liquid form passes over the tongue quickly and enters the throat before the full flavor of the alcohol sets in, and the more sugar is in a drink, the more your taste buds register the sugar rather than the booze. Acid acts the same way, which is why a whisky sour or daiquiri goes down smoothly. In gelatin form, however, the alcohol sits on top of and seeps into your taste buds longer and so tastes more intense, despite its being cold. So in general, alcohol has to be tempered by sugar and acid in gelatin. That explains their addition in this experiment, and in my recipes in the book.

There were four variations: #1 had 1.3 tablespoons of powdered gelatin (or 1 tbsp and 1 tsp); #2 had 1 tbsp to one cup wine, which is the standard proportion in much of this book; #3 used 2 teaspoons of gelatin (.66 tbs) to a cup of wine, and lastly #4 used 1.5 teaspoons (.5 tbs) to 1 cup. Each was poured into a clear plastic cup, allowed to set in the refrigerator for 2 hours, and then each was unmolded (successfully) by dipping for 30 seconds in hot tap water, overturning into my hand, and then placing on a small plate. Some of the melted gelatin from unmolding affixed the jello to the plate, especially when placed back in the refrigerator to reset for 10 minutes.

I decided to judge each jello based on four criteria that were fairly objective and could be measured. First was the jiggle, which was described in terms of frequency and amplitude. Second was the ability to bear weight in pounds per cubed inch. Each cup bore 14.44 cubic inches of gelatin on which was placed a 1 pound jar to see if it could hold together. Third was the shear, or ability to cut with a sharp knife. Did it take some effort or did the knife pass through easily? Lastly was the "bite," or what it felt like on the teeth. There are scientific instruments to measure such things; I relied on my own chompers and will describe the physical properties as best I can.

When it comes to the jiggle, #1 was almost frigid and immovable. Shaking only created a very short quick wave extending no more than a millimeter despite the force exerted to make it jiggle. #2 was a little staid but created a nice wobble, respectable, but moving a good inch or so when shaken. #3 created a lovely fetching jiggle, very cute. The jiggle went on a good few seconds after shaking. #4 was extremely loose, a wild erratic floozy of a jello. It flung itself all over the place in every imaginable direction with the slightest encouragement. If it's just jiggle you're after, this is your jello.

Not surprisingly, #1 could hold a pound weight with no problem. Remarkable strength in fact. For architectural jellos, this is clearly the preferred proportion. #2 sagged a bit but didn't crack under the weight. #3 was about to split when I lowered the jar onto it, and #4 would have been obliterated with just a few ounces placed on top.

The third criterion yielded unsurprising results. It took some force to cut through #1, and when I picked up the slice, it held together as a good solid wedge. #2 was easier to slice and still held together but squished between my fingers if pressure was applied. This is what Knox calls its "block" and what Jell-O calls a "jiggler." #3 bore an effortless cut. It held together but only barely when picked up. This is pretty much the standard Jell-O texture. You want to eat it with a spoon. #4 you can just show the knife to and it will spread apart. And it will disintegrate completely if you tried to serve a slice. It cannot be held at all. This one is just about the limit before the jello would be unset.

Lastly, and I think most importantly, how does it feel in the mouth? #1 was solid, but slightly rubbery. It was a pleasant chewy texture, but nowhere near a gummy. Again, I think this is the one for difficult shapes you want to come out of the mold and for large pieces you want to slice and serve. What you lose in a little palatability, you gain in structural integrity: a solid dependable jello. #2 was perfect and confirms my use of the 1:1 cup to packet ratio for most alcoholic beverages. #3 was soft and I think perfect for individual jellos, but might be tough to unmold if larger, and might just get messy if you're looking for a jello that looks as good as it tastes. #4 is so soft I would only serve this in its container, a glass goblet preferably. I got it out of the cup and it sure was fun to play with, but this one might just collapse on the way to the dinner table. Use the proportions of #4 just for kicks.

The unscientific conclusion: use the 1:1 ratio and you'll always be fine. In larger complicated jellos and with higher alcohol concentration, you can veer as much as a third more gelatin but there's no reason to. With lighter recipes and with less alcohol feel free to use only 2 teaspoons per cup of liquid if you want a lighter texture. Any recipe in this book can use a little more or less gelatin if you like. In several recipes I've veered from the 1:1 rule, either because it was very potent and needed more structure, or because I wanted it very soft and gentle. If it was served in a glass, I went for a very light texture.

To satisfy my curiosity, I replicated this same experiment with the cheapest rotgut vodka I could find: 40% alcohol. The same proportions and ingredients met my expectations precisely. #1 with the greatest amount of gelatin was pleasantly firm but not yet rubbery. #2 with the 1:1 ratio was perfectly fine. It could be picked up and had good solid form. But then things dropped off precipitously. #3 with 2 tsp to a cup barely held its form. It could not be picked up at all, and I was surprised it even kept its shape when unmolded, but it did barely. #4 was still recognizable as a gel, but on the verge of liquefaction and could only possibly be consumed in a cup.

Please do note, these proportions are for gelatin made with alcohol. The proportions will be different if you substitute fruit juice or another liquid.

To begin your exploration of new jello bases, I suggest starting with some of these very simple cocktails set with gelatin. All are ideal for parties and for nibbling while you watch a good movie.

Gin and Tonic Jigglers

neutral oil such as canola, grapeseed, or vegetable
grated zest of one lime
1 tsp sugar
2 packets unflavored gelatin
½ cup gin

1 ½ cup tonic water (choose a luxury brand with real quinine such as Fever Tree or Q)
juice of one lime

If you can find fun silicone molds in the shape of palm trees, or anything kitschy, all the better, but an ice cube tray works well too. Prepare molds by moistening a paper towel with a few drops of oil and rubbing around the

mold. Sprinkle in a little of the grated lime zest and a fine dusting of sugar. In a large bowl, dissolve the gelatin in the gin and stir well. Heat the tonic water to boiling. Add immediately to the gelatin mixture and stir well until no longer hot. Place your molds in the refrigerator and then carefully pour the gelatin into the molds. There's nothing harder than moving a filled mold into the fridge. Let set a few hours until firm. Unmold and arrange on a platter with other hors d'oeuvres. Then shut all the lights off and shine a black light on the jigglers; they're fluorescent. This jello was set in the bottom of a plastic palm oil bottle, giving it this incredible pattern.

Whipped Mai Tai Jello

I can still picture my mother messing with her lime green electric mixer, frothing Cool Whip and Jell-O brand dietetic gelatin, spooning it into parfait glasses. I thought the stuff was revolting. But this looks so much like it! I've tried to capture the flavor of the original cocktail with fresh almond milk replacing the sweet orgeat syrup. Commercial almond milk is really not the same. You can use curaçao, but triple sec or other orange liqueur is nice too.

1 cup raw almonds	½ cup rum
2 packets of gelatin	Juice of two limes, peel finely
1 tbsp sugar	grated for garnish, save the
½ cup orange liqueur	squeezed out part too

Begin by blanching the almonds for a few minutes in boiling water, strain, then remove the brown peels. Pound the almonds in a mortar, slowly adding a cup of boiling water or whizz the two in a blender. Let cool and then pour this over a fine mesh sieve to drain. The result looks and tastes pretty much like milk. Dissolve the gelatin in the milk with the sugar.

Heat up the remaining ingredients to boiling. Then add to the almond milk and stir thoroughly. Here's the fun part: Get a large metal basin filled halfway with ice. Put the gelatin in a smaller bowl inside the larger one, on top of the ice. Whisk vigorously by hand until the jello froths up and sets.

Take elegant cocktail glasses and run the squeezed-out lime on the rims, then dip in a plate of sugar. Scoop the jello into the glasses and sprinkle on a little grated lime zest. Garnish with a thin slice of lime, too, if you like. Very refreshing.

The Boulevardier

This is my favorite cocktail, but I think bourbon really works best in colder months. In the summer you want gin, or rum in the spring. Basically, just mix good bourbon with equal parts Campari and Red Vermouth. I tend to use more bourbon and less vermouth in practice. Make a cup of the cocktail. Mix one quarter of it with gelatin to bloom and then heat the rest—covered so you don't lose too much alcohol. Then pour the hot liquid over the gelatin, pour into a wide low cocktail glass with a slice of orange or a good candied cherry, and let it set in the fridge. To serve just get a spoon.

CHAPTER ONE

HISTORY

The first aspic was undoubtedly prehistoric. Archaeological evidence strongly supports this, but it would probably not have preceded the invention of ceramics and metallurgy around 10,000 years ago. Although people may of course have roasted meat, thrown it in a hollowed log or leather pouch, and gotten some gelatinous bits congealing after leaving it in the cold, there could not have been the conscious creation of gelatin without a container to cook bones in liquid. That people did this in the Neolithic period is evidenced by clay pots that have rings of fat deposited around the upper lip, pretty fair proof that someone was boiling meat, which more than likely had bones in it. The remains of these exist too, cracked open to extract the marrow. It would have been only one short step from that point to having leftover meaty stock in the pot, leaving it in the cold, and having it solidify. None of this is to say that seaweeds could not have been used at the same time, boiled and strained into vegetable jello, but the remains of these would have disappeared.

It is surprising then that the earliest jello recipes are medieval. Gelatin appears suddenly in the written record around 1300, at least in the Western Tradition. It was probably fairly well known, at least in courtly circles, by the time the first recipes were written down. No author had to explain what it is, and some even assume the cook knows exactly how it's made. So the earliest gelatins probably predate those first recipes by a century if not more.

The word *galatina* or *galantina* in Latin is the etymological root of both gelatin in English and the series of recipes called *galantine* in medieval cookbooks. The earliest recipes are clearly referring to gelatin in the sense we still use it. The Latin *Liber de coquina,* which was written about 1300, perhaps in Naples, has the following recipe:

> On Galantina: For galantine of meat, boil it. And when it is half cooked, add above as well enough vinegar, so that it won't be too strong nor weak. Let it boil until reduced to a third. And if it's in summer, let it boil with the aforementioned broth. (II.41, 406)

The aforementioned broth is made of lamb or veal, sugar, wine, spices.

This is obviously a recipe for a cook already thoroughly conversant with gelatin making, since it assumes almost everything apart from the addition of vinegar and the reduction. Only in the recipe for fish gelatin are we given complete directions.

> Here is taught about fish. And first, on gelatin: For fish gelatin, take good wine and a little clarified vinegar. Boil together and when it boils, cut a large fish into slices with the scales, and cook together with the same. Which, when it is cooked, remove, and the wine that remains, boil so long as a third part remains. Then add saffron and other good spices pulverized, with bay leaves. Then take the fish and clean the scales.
>
> Some, however, pound the aforementioned scales, soaked with the afore-mentioned wine, forcefully in a mortar and strain through a sieve. To which sauce they add more wine, so that it can congeal even more.
>
> And when this galantine is chilled, place in pieces of fish and let it stay aside one day or night or more until the conglutination is complete. And thus many are able to conserve fish. (IV.1, 413)

The very last comment suggests that gelatin served a very practical purpose apart from gastronomic pleasure. One wonders exactly how long fish would last in gelatin without refrigeration, but at least long enough for people to do it without making them sick.

Viandier

Among these early written recipes for gelatin are those in a series of manuscript cookbooks called the *Viandier*, which have been attributed to the famous chef Guillaume Tirel, called Taillevent, who lived from 1326–1395 and served Kings Charles V and VI of France. Most of the recipes appear in manuscripts that are older than Tirel himself, so it would be a mistake to say he invented the gelatin or anything like that, but he certainly did help popularize it. Medieval chefs knew well that the easiest way to make gelatin from scratch is with a boney slimy fish like eel, which you can simply cook and it forms its own gelatin when chilled. Jellied eel can still be found in the East End of London if you look hard enough. Something similar appears to have existed in the time of Chaucer. In a ballade complaining about his love for Rosemounde, the poet exclaims,

Nas never pyk walwed in galauntyne, As I in love am walwed and ywounde

Or in modern English: No pike ever wallowed in jello, as I in love am wallowing and bound

It is clear not only that pike would be served in gelatin, but a person in love could metaphorically be just as intensely captured and immobilized. Pleasure and Pain in equal measure.

Yet even before this, Dante Alighieri in the 33rd Canto of *The Inferno*, line 60, has a remarkable passage that not only suggests the familiarity of gelatin but its gluey properties. Like Chaucer, being fixed in gelatin like a chunk of meat was not an enviable position. For Dante it was downright eternal torture. As he descends into the layer of hell wherein murderers are consigned, he comes across two brothers—Alessandro and Napoleone degli Alberti, who were Counts of Mangona. In an embroiled inheritance dispute, in a kind of *Game of Thrones* move, they managed to kill each other in the 1280s. Their punishment was being placed in hell with their foreheads glued together for all time, stuck in jello.

potrai cercare, e non troverai L'ombra/ Degna piu d'esser fitta in gelatina

You can search and not find the ghost / More worthy of being stuck in gelatin

In the course of the 14th century, gelatin and galantine became more fluid concepts. Galantine actually became two different things in medieval cookbooks; one would be the clear gelatin, but other versions also included bread crumbs, and it was served as a hot sauce.

Taillevent has a clear galentine recipe too, but this other recipe (68) is much more complex and shows that above all else, the clarity of the gelatin was paramount. Here the word used is *gelee* (sans accent aigu), which remains in French and is later adopted in English as jelly, which is still used today in England.

Incidentally, in my translation I have decided to leave the word chair as flesh. I think the author means the flesh of fish, not meat from an animal. Especially because at the end, he has us garnish it with crayfish or loach, a freshwater fish. It would also defeat the whole purpose of fish dishes for Lent if you included meat in it. On the other hand, the words "if it's fish" suggests it can be made with either. Despite the fact that there are no cooking times, the funny comment about not sleeping suggests that the first stage of making the gelatin takes a very long time to gently simmer. The sieve is a long cloth sleeve that first strains out the bones and first set of spices, then more spices are added and it goes into the pot, tied up, with the bits of fish.

Gelee de poisson

Gelatin of fish that contains marsh fish and flesh. Let it cook in wine and in verjuice and in vinegar, and some add in a little water, then take ginger, cinnamon, cloves, grains of paradise, long pepper, and make a bouillon and pass it through a sieve, then let it boil with your flesh. Then take laurel leaves, spikenard, galangal, and mace, and place those in your sieve without washing, on the remains of the other spices, and let it boil with your flesh and cover it as long as it will be on the fire, and when it is off the fire skim it, up until the point that it will be served.

And when it is cooked pour your bouillon in a clean wooden vessel until it's settled and place your flesh on a white napkin. And if it's fish, skin it and clean and throw the skins in your bouillon until it will be strained a final time. And be sure your bouillon is clear and clean, and then arrange your flesh in bowls and replace your bouillon on the fire in a clear and clean vessel and let it boil. And when boiling, throw on your flesh and season your plates or bowl where you have placed your flesh and your bouillon, with cassia buds and cinnamon and with mace, and place your plates in a cold place to set. And whoever wants to make gelatin, he must not sleep.

And if your bouillon is not really clean and clear, strain it though a napkin folded in half or thirds and on your flesh place tails and claws of crayfish, and cooked loach if it's fish.

Martino of Como and Platina

By the Renaissance, gelatin was a well-known dish on the most refined tables of nobility and royalty, and it seems even on lesser tables. Although a simple cloudy meat or fish aspic could be made anywhere with a little time, clarity and brightness was the mark of an expert. Such a person was Martino of Como, chef to Ludovico Trevisan, the Patriarch of Aquilea and Chamberlain to the pope, in the 1460s. His manuscript cookbook survives in the Library of Congress, written in a beautiful humanist hand. Gastronomically, it is essentially a late medieval cookbook filled with the colorful spice laden dishes in favor at the time, as well as the spectacles like peacock skinned, cooked, resewn into its feathers and brought to the table with a lit cotton swab soaked in camphor, so it spews flames. The recipes bear close similarities to those in a Neapolitan cookbook, and some are borrowed almost directly from an earlier Catalan cookbook by Rupert of Nola. So, like all cookbooks of the day, the recipes are similar to those in other manuscripts. But in general, the book is more technically precise than most and even introduces several culinary innovations.

At some point, probably in Rome, Martino met Bartolomeo Sacchi, known as Platina, who became the first librarian of the Biblioteca Apostolica and a historian of the papacy. In his spare time, Platina also took a fancy to food, and so he "borrowed" the recipes of Martino, with very brief acknowledgment, and put them in his own gastronomic treatise *De honesta voluptate,* which was the very first printed cookbook (c. 1470). The recipes were translated from cook's Italian into rather elegant Latin, with some made-up words tossed in. The book was a best seller and went through many editions and translations. Even Leonardo da Vinci mentions it. The book attests to the fact that kitchen procedures, and indeed gelatin, were a topic worthy the attention of scholars. For this reason, I offer you Platina's full version in my own translation.

If you want two platters of that dish which we people call gelatin, place 40 sheep feet, skinned and boned, in fresh water for three or four hours. Wash in a pot wherein you put a jar of the strongest white vinegar, another of white wine, and two of water. Adding enough salt as necessary, then boiling on a gentle fire. Remember to skim very carefully. When it is half cooked, add in the pot crushed rather than ground, round pepper, long pepper, cinnamon, spikenard, and simmer until it is reduced to a third. Remove the feet, and simmer the broth again. Beat ten egg whites until they are foam. They should be boiled together a long time, turning once or twice with a spoon. Pour out of the pot at once and strain through a linen sac two or three times.

Put this broth in dishes with chicken or kid or capon, well cooked and divided into pieces, but not too moist, and leave in a cold and humid place until all the gelatin has become solid. From this dish, my Voconius should eat nothing, lest the bile which disturbs him, in this way increase his illness.

Platina added the information about his sick friend. Voconius was of a hot and dry complexion so this very nourishing dish would, according to the humoral dietary theory of the day, make him even more hot and agitated. Unfortunately, Platina messed up just a few of the interesting culinary points in the original recipe. First, the meat that goes in the aspic is skinned and dried on a white cloth, which is probably what he meant when he said that it shouldn't be too moist—that is, greasy or in a stew. But he also left out the precise measurements of the spices: a quarter ounce each of pepper and long pepper, a quarter ounce of cardamom (which he forgot entirely) and the same of cinnamon, plus an eighth of spikenard, an aromatic oil imported from India. The *boccale* in Italian was a unit of measurement equaling about a liter, which he rendered as *metreta*—a jar.

Of course the most interesting part of the recipe is the clarification with the egg whites, the careful skimming and straining, and the use of broken spices to flavor but not cloud the aspic. This was pretty much the standard gelatin technology until the advent of sheets four centuries later.

Messisbugo

Cristoforo di Messisbugo was the Major Domo of the Este Court in Ferrara in the first part of the 16th century. He was in charge not only of the household budgets but organized every grand meal down to the number of plates used in every course. He recorded the menus in a magnificent book called *Banchetti* in 1549. I've cooked many recipes from the book and they are always surprising, but good. The amount of sugar in this recipe will startle you, but it works. The first time I tried it I used packets of gelatin, cut back on the sugar, and followed my modern instincts with the technique. It looked very pretty but flavor-wise, it was just ok. On another occasion I followed his instructions exactly, and the results were exquisite. Here are his words translated.

To Make a Capon in Jello

Take a capon and the feet of four capons, and place them to boil in sweet white wine, until it is cooked, and when it's cooked, take the flesh, the wings, and whatever you want to cover, and let the rest boil together, and let it cook well, then place in a little spoon of vinegar, half a pound of sugar, or honey, an ounce and a half of cinnamon, a sixth of pepper, and a quarter of ginger, a sixth of mace, a little saffron, then pass this decoction through a sieve, and have your little plates with the reserved capon at the bottom and bay leaves, and pour it over, let it cook and it will be good.

A little further explanation: a capon is a castrated rooster; the procedure makes it grow bigger. It was the preferred fowl, actually the preferred meat in the Renaissance above all others. If you can't find a capon, a whole rooster with the head works well. A modern spring chicken isn't as good. The extra feet are essential. You're essentially simmering the bird, removing it, and taking off the parts you want to set in jello. The breast meat definitely. Renaissance diners loved wings too. Then you're simmering the rest of the bones to make the jello. Half a pound in Renaissance times is 12 tablespoons of sugar. YES, use it all. All the spices should be whole so they don't cloud the broth. The measurements are very roughly a stick of cinnamon, a few peppercorns, a few slices of ginger (they would have used dry, but not ground, fresh is fine), a blade of mace, and a pinch of whole saffron threads, which makes it bright yellow. You place bay leaves and capon slices decoratively on a majolica platter and pour over the gelatin. Remove slices with a cake trowel to serve.

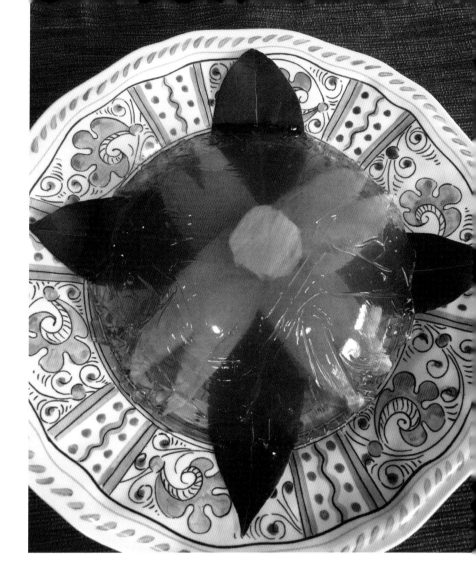

Francesco Berni Burlesque

Renaissance humanist scholars sometimes wrote surprisingly silly things, including making fun of each other in "burlesque" form. Francesco Berni was one such mock heroic poet who penned elevated verse in praise of ridiculous topics, including gelatin. I can't say much for his comedic form, but this is at least good evidence that gelatin was not just the rarefied specialty reserved for kings. I've spared you the entire poem and translated just a few lines.

FRANCESCO BERNI (*OPERA*, 46–47)
Never an evening, nor morning
Nor noon, nor night, do I not contemplate
uttering praises of Gelatin . . .

In each I would express how much is felt
through the nerves, in the belly, in my very soul,
To uncover your immense mysteries.
But I see my wit is not worthy,
For your miraculous nature
Is more profound even than the chamber pot
Yet, nothing dared, nothing done
If I must burst, I feel ready
To say something about it every way I might . . .

Whoever wishes to have good Gelatin
Discern how to give it good color
This is what will bear the crown
Said a certain doctor of philosophy
Its force derives from good flavor
Consisting in a balanced virtue
The strength of the pepper, and of vinegar
What makes a man lick his fingers
I would like to teach my secret
For I don't care if it remains with me . . .

I want gelatin to be quite sturdy
And the meat must be without bones
How many times so near
You must draw them from between your teeth . . .

O gelatin, food of the people
That are lovers of discretion
Blessed are all your parents
That Gelatin of Capon
Of partridge, of pheasant, of good fish
And of a thousand other things that are great
I cannot say, how it upsets me
that I am unable to describe you with my pen . . .

Scappi

Bartolomeo Scappi was chef at the papal court in the middle of the 16th century. Toward the end of his life, he became personal chef to Pope Pius V, which always seemed a pity to me since this pope became a saint for his austerity, including his abstemious diet. Hopefully Scappi had other people to eat his magnificent creations. Worthy of mention is his *Opera*, the most comprehensive cookbook ever written when it appeared in 1570. It included directions for shopping, organizing kitchens, menus, and perhaps most importantly, it was illustrated. For the first time we can peer into a Renaissance kitchen and see the cooks rolling out pasta, turning spits, and straining exquisite sauces. Moreover, this book is clearly written for someone first learning to cook. The recipes are remarkably explicit. One can easily imagine a young novice reading the book and hoping to land a job in a courtly kitchen after having mastered the basic skills.

This recipe is long, but I have to share it for its brilliance and creativity, and to show you how kindred is his spirit. The standard English translation by Terence Scully is excellent, but the last section of this recipe is muddled, so I've retranslated anew for clarity.

Book II Ch 241

To prepare jello with feet of castrated sheep and calves', with which you can fill various molds and eggshells

Take the feet of castrated sheep and of veal, and if it's the month of April and May, in place of the sheep use lamb, clean the skin, remove the bones, and wash well in water, and let boil in a vessel of earthenware or copper with enough white wine so it's covered with equal parts wine and water. Let it cook until the decoction is reduced by more than half, not forgetting to skim, and let it be tested with a cup, gelling the decoction in a way that's stronger than those mentioned above. Remove from the fire, pass through a sieve, remove the fat, and replace in a pot adding strong vinegar, ground sugar, and beaten fresh egg whites. Let it boil, and when the egg white becomes comes to the top, have ready a jelly bag, in which is pepper, ground cinnamon, ground mostaccioli biscuits, and ground ginger, and passing the decoction through many times hot, until it's clear. And if you wish to place in the bag other spices like nutmeg, whole cloves, you can do that. And when it's strained, taste it, because it should be more pleasant than acidic. Let it rest in a clay vessel until no longer hot. And if you want to fill molds of wax or tin, grease the molds with sweet almond oil, freshly made, and fill with the jello that's more cold than hot, because if it's hot it will lift the oil out of the mold and it won't stick there. If you want to fill molds of clay or glass, or tubes, or little squares of white iron, or eggshells, put it in tepid, and when these vessels are filled put them to congeal in a cold place.

If you want more colors in each vessel or in the eggshells, place a part of one color, and let it congeal. Then over that place a little white jello made with water and almond milk, or with starch, and when the white is congealed, place another color, cold on top, because if it were hot, it would liquefy the others. This way you can make all the other molds, except wax and tin. The colors will always be better separated with white in between, because violet and red jelled together will be poorly discerned.

This jello you can pass through a syringe, and when you have many colors mixed together, then passed through a syringe, you can make designs around the plate, and the lines will be of mixed colors. With the syringe, you can make clusters and crosses, and other work following the design of whoever makes it. You can also make the design with a cartoon, which will be cut with various sorts of animals, placing the form above the plate, which when removed, with diligence, it will take the shape of that which landed on the plate with the syringe. This can be done with all soft jellos, and you can decorate any jello made like this with gold or silver.

Apart from the fact that Scappi has mastered so many tricks 20th-century jello enthusiasts believed were their own invention, this final one appears to be completely unique. The cartoon he mentions isn't the kind we watch today, but the original meaning of that term. It was a piece of stiff paper on which was drawn a cartoonish version of a painting. You pricked or cut little holes into it, so that your drawing could be transferred onto a wall, or made into a tapestry pattern, or even just put on a canvas, the dots to be painted over. Scappi has us place the stiff paper over the plate and syringe the pattern through the holes onto the plate below, which means the jello master doesn't have to free-form syringe-paint every plate—and he can make some very complex decorations.

Leaches

There was an entire category of foods defined by the fact that they were set in a rectangular shape and sliced—which is what the word "leche" or "leach" means. In fact, surgery was called lechecraft. Many of these were creamy concoctions made with almond milk or cow's milk cooked until curdled with ale and thickened with bread and sliced. There could also be many colors set in layers, the ancestor of multi-colored jello molds. The introduction of gelatin to the leaches changed them into something quite close to a modern dessert. In modern times these would often be called a blancmanger, but that term originally meant a kind of sweet chicken pudding made with almond milk. Here is a great English recipe for an almond leach.

Sir Hugh Plat, p. 27

To Make Leach of Almonds

Take half a pounde of sweete almonds, and beate them in a morter, then straine them with a pinte of sweete milke from the Cow, then put unto to one graine of muske, two spoonfuls of Rose-water, two ounces of fine sugar, the waight of three whole shillings of Isinglasse, that is very white and so boyle them, then let all run through a strainer, then may you slice the same and so serve it

Banqueting

In the Renaissance and into the 17th century, it became fashionable to throw grand banquets and there were scores of books explaining how to do it. These weren't just large meals with many guests. They were carefully orchestrated extravaganzas, with multiple "courses," each of which included dozens of different dishes, punctuated by entertainment: music, dances, short plays, and elaborate sugar sculptures. The entire event was orchestrated by a manager or scalco, plus an official carver for each table, and many pages scrambling around bringing guests drinks, bowls for washing hands, napkins, and even toothpicks at the end of the meal. Aspics and savory jellos were featured during the cold courses that began the banquet and alternated hot courses. They were organized not by the cook's kitchen but by the *credenziero*—a separate officer responsible for his own brigade of cooks—somewhat comparable to the *garde manger* in a modern French kitchen, but also including anything served cold, like cheese, salami, salads, and cold pies. These cold courses provided an opportunity for the *credenziero* to show off his talents. The sugar sculptures were perhaps the greatest achievements, but gelatins lagged not far behind, especially when they learned how to clarify and concentrate gelatin to make it sturdier.

The word "banquet" also had a narrower sense, especially in England, which meant the dessert course after a meal, taken in the garden, perhaps on the roof of or in a special building devoted to serving fruits and sweets—called a banqueting house. This is where jello, as well as jelly in the sense of fruit conserves, was spotlighted. The more fantastic, the better.

To get a sense of these creations, there are not many images or even recipes in the banqueting books, but there are menus which were a regular feature, and sometimes included in regular cookbooks as well. For example, there were a series of cookbooks published in France, first titled *Petit traicte* in 1539 and eventually expanded as the *Livre fort excellent de cuysine* a decade later. I translated this cookbook with a friend some years ago, and of course totally forgot the remarkable list of banqueting fare in it, until I was googling some strange French culinary terms and came across my own translations! Oddly the entire menu was repeated in Pierre Belon's very popular book on birds, though I have no idea why.

The text states "when you wish to make a banquet, look in this chapter and you will find reminders to make your menu." There are over 100 dishes mentioned, but for our purposes, there are andouilles de gelee, gellee en poinct de diamant, gelee embree, gelee moulee, gelee blanch picques, escusson de gelle, angelots de gelee, gelee dechiquettee, fontaine de gelee, ouflans de gelee, coffres de gellee plain d'escus, fleur de lys gelle. That is, andouille sausages made of jello, jello diamond points, amber jello, molded jello, white spiked jello, escutcheons of jello, angels of jello, chopped jello, fountains, elephants, coffers of jello filled with coins, and of course the fleur de lys, the symbol of the crown.

Many of these could only have been made in a mold, but some are clearly tricks meant to confuse and titillate diners. The sausages made of jello are exactly of this sort, and the chest of jello coins, which would be brilliant for a pirate-themed party.

The heyday of this genre was really in the late 16th and 17th century, though, and the Italians were the real experts, although not without some deference to French expertise. For example, Giovanni Battista Rossetti in his *Dello Scalco* of 1584 mentions a series of jellos that he calls *geladie*. That he's talking about gelatin and not the similar sounding gelato is evident from his discussion of calves' feet (467), which he says can be made into *geladie* and a slew of other dishes. In his list of these jellos, he includes white jello, jello in the shape of prosciutto or salami, with various fruits like peaches, cherries, clear and opaque and finally *di tutte le sorte Francese*. (518) This is not surprising as Rossetti worked at the court of the Este in Ferrara, which had intermarried with the French royal family. If only he had given us a recipe for that salami-shaped jello.

Kenelm Digby

Kenelm Digby is one of the most colorful characters of mid-17th-century England. He was a scientist and founding member of the Royal Society, an ardent Catholic who had to escape to France during the civil wars. He was painted by van Dyck, and perhaps his greatest legacy to posterity is the invention of the wine bottle made of colored glass, with a long neck and depression or punt at the bottom for added strength. He was also an alchemist, botanist, astrologer, and author of a marvelous cookbook filled mostly with recipes for mead, soups, and even jello. It may seem odd today that such a person would dabble in the kitchen, but it was considered partly a branch of medicine and partly a noble pastime for elite gentlemen. Judging from the number of recipes associated with noble figures, it seems like there was a serious *Do It Yourself* movement, with people trading their favorite creations.

To dispel the notion that this was backbreaking labor of the sort left to servants, or that it was disgusting or took days, note the use of hartshorn. It's not exactly an instant gelatin, but one that could be made in a leisurely afternoon while you tinker in your "closet," which meant a kind of secret laboratory with collections of plants and animals, chemistry equipment, and books of secrets.

The Closet of Sir Kenelm Digby Opened (pp. 286–87)

Take four ounces of Harts-horn rasped, boil it in four pound of water, till it will be a gelly, which you may try upon a plate, (it will be so in four or five or six hours gently boiling) and then pass the clear liquor from the horn (which will be a good quart) then set it on the fire again with fine sugar in it to your taste; when that is dissolved (or the same time that you put that in) put half a pound of white-wine or Sack into it, and a bag of Spice, containing a little Ginger, a stick of cinnamon bruised, a Nutmeg quartered, two or three cloves, and what other Spice you like, but Pepper. As soon as it beginneth to boil, put in the whites of three or four eggs, beaten, and let it boil up gently, till the eggs harden into a curd. Then open it with a spoon, and pour in the juyce of three or four good Limons; then take it presently off the fire, letting it not boil above a walm: then run it through a Hippocras bag, putting spirit of Cinnamon, or of Ambergreece, or what you please to it.

Digby has several other "gelly" recipes using hartshorn and some with chicken or meat. Interestingly he has one that indicates a gelatin that is boiled first then chilled, the fat removed, and anything settled at the bottom discarded. Then it is reheated and clarified with egg and strained.

Denis Papin

The Royal Society in London attracted other food scientists, if we can use that term without anachronism. At the time, Robert Boyle was testing his theories on the relationship between volume and pressure—the first of the gas laws. This work attracted the French Huguenot Denis Papin who was partly glad to escape the new restrictions on Protestants in France, but who also had an interesting device to present to the scientists. It was a large bronze cooking vessel with a lid that screwed down tightly which he called a steam digester. The contraption sometimes exploded, so it was eventually fitted with a steam valve. Observing it, Papin wondered whether the force of the steam causing the valve to rise and fall could be channeled into a kind of engine. He never followed up on the idea, though, because he was far more interested in jello. The steam digester (invented in 1679) was of course the first pressure cooker.

Papin was amazed how bones placed in the cooker came out soft. Meat could be cooked in a fraction of the time it would normally take. The long time it took to extract gelatin from bones could be drastically reduced. His interest in this, surprisingly, was not really to rescue beleaguered housewives, but to feed sailors. Papin believed that salting meat robbed it of its essential nutrients—or as he put it, the volatile and spiritous parts, which causes the blood to thicken and leads to scurvy. So he tried putting beef bones into his digester to make a cheap and convenient gelatin. "I may say, that having seasoned it with Sugar and Juyce of Lemmon, I did eat it with as much pleasure, and found it as stomachical as if it had been Gelly of Harts-horn." That is, it was clear, tasty, and easily digested. Best of all it could be made cheaply—"it will be as convenient to be able to make easily for one penny more than we could buy for a shilling."

Papin continued his experiments with beef, mutton, bones, and gristle and made an important discovery—that it is the glue of the connective tissues that forms the jelly and that from this could even be made actual glue to repair broken glass and pottery. He also insisted that if people were just to save all the gristle and tendons and feet from various animals, they could be reduced to gelatin in his machine and the result could be used to supply English ships.

Papin's interests were also directed toward confectioners and cooks, and he experimented with cooking not only various meats, but fruit for preserves, beans, and other foods that normally take a lot of time and firewood to cook. Although he never explicitly envisioned his digester in ordinary households, I think he would be very pleased to see the proliferation of the Instant Pot today.

On April 12, 1682, the diarist and author of a great treatise on salads called *Acetaria*, John Evelyn, went to the Royal Society to check out Mr. Papin's new invention. A philosophical supper caused great mirth to taste "A jelly made of bones of beef, the best for clearness and good relish, and the most delicious I had ever seen, or tasted." "I sent a glass of the jelly to my wife, to the reproach of all that the ladies ever made of their best hartshorn." (168)

The Social Meaning of Gelatin in the Early Modern Period

In a very class-oriented society, such as Europe in the early modern period, food was a powerful tool for expressing status. It was also useful for those aspiring to rise socially, through imitation of their superiors. Fashion, modes of speech, and personal possessions are also powerful markers of class, but somehow the stuff you consume, that which actually becomes part of you, seems to function on a higher level. For example, if spices are very expensive, then using them is not only a way to signify extraordinary wealth and power, but it is a way to incorporate the qualities, literally. For the person of middling rank who emulates the mighty, a splurge on some spices in some measure ennobles you, precisely because you can live like the rich for a brief moment. Of course, once a commodity like spice becomes more available or cheaper, it loses its value in conferring status, and the elites move on, always looking for something new to maintain their distinction. This is the engine that drives changes in fashion. When anyone can make jello at home, as happened in the early 20th century, a chef would look rather foolish serving it in a fancy restaurant.

For earlier centuries, it's a little more difficult to tell exactly what foods were clear status symbols—unless we look at the cookbooks to see what ingredients were hot, and when they go out of fashion and become common or even vulgar. But rarely do we have an author tell us right out that a dish is for the rich while another is for the poor. Surprisingly, medical literature offers more clues than the culinary.

One superb source is Philibert Guybert's *Le medecin charitable* (The Charitable Physician 1659, 379) which was written in Paris and published in 1623. It went through many editions through the century. Guybert's intention was to make available pharmaceutical recipes to the poor so they wouldn't be gouged by the Apothecaries (the equivalent of big pharmaceutical companies). Philibert actually offers explicit recipes for the rich and others for the poor, the cost to make them, including a whole section on jello.

The jello for the rich costs 40 sols to make. It involves a capon, calves' feet, and the hocks of the veal, an ounce of hartshorn. It's skimmed with a silver spoon, stained many times, reduced. Then after much clarification some saffron is used to color it, cinnamon for aroma, half a pound of good sugar, then clarified again with egg white and shells, strained though a bag and then let chill on plates or other vessels. Obviously, this takes a great deal of labor, but as for cost, it seems like it would only be the spices and the sugar that would have been expensive. Actually, not so.

Then he offers a gelatin for the poor which only costs 10 sols. It includes neck of mutton, calves' feet, and even some hartshorn if you wish. It also contains saffron and cinnamon, but much less—a half denier of the former and an ounce of the latter. It's not fussed with quite as much, but it seems the real distinction here is in the capon—an expensive fattened, castrated rooster versus the neck of mutton. The former would be lighter and more appropriate for the delicate digestive systems of the inactive rich, the latter darker, more cloudy, and even more flavorful you might argue, but much more fitting for the laboring poor who have powerful digestive systems that can break down iron.

That is, the difference between jello for rich and poor is partly about cost, but it's also a cultural prejudice against dark meat from older animals. This is actually built right into the medical theory of the day. The gelatin offered by pharmacists at the time would have been crystal clear and extravagantly spiced and expensive, so this version, while not so elegant, should serve to cure the maladies of those less well off without those markers of status.

Elizabeth Raffald

Among the women cookbook authors of the mid–18th century, Elizabeth Raffald stands out both for her lovely turn of phrase, vivid culinary imagination, and the very fact that she ran several businesses, published a business directory of Manchester as well as her cookbook *The Experienced English Housekeeper* in 1769, which went through many editions. Its recipes were widely pirated. Food historian Ivan Day has called her the Empress of Jelly, and I'm inclined to agree. Here she offers a fetching tableaux vivant in gelatin. It's two recipes, first a flummery then a jelly.

"Flummery" is among the most pleasant and diverting words in the English language. At first, it meant a kind of oat starch-thickened pudding, apparently flavorless, because the word came to mean an empty compliment or nonsense. Whenever I hear the word, I picture the grimaced face of lexicographer Samuel Johnson being offered a bit of etymological frippery and his growing angry and frothing at the mouth exclaiming *Flummery! Flummery!*

By the 18th century, it was sort of a cross between an almond milk blancmanche and a gelatin. In these two recipes, Elizabeth Raffald offers us flummery fishes in a clear gelatin pond.

To make Flummery

Put one Ounce of bitter, and one of sweet Almonds into a Bason, pour over them some boiling Water, to make the Skins come off, which is called Blanching, strip off the Skins, and throw the Kernels into cold Water, then take them out and beat them in a Marble Mortar, with a little Rose Water, to keep them from Oiling, when they are beat, put them into a Pint of Calf's Foot Stock, set it over the fire, and sweeten it to your Taste with Loaf Sugar, as soon as it boils strain it thro'a Piece of Muslin or Gawz, when a little cold, put it into a Pint of thick Cream, and keep stirring it often, 'till it grows thick and cold, wet your Moulds [with] cold Water and pour in the Flummery, let it stand five or six Hours, at least before you turn them out; if you make the flummery stiff, and wet the Moulds, it will turn out without putting it into warm Water, for Water take off the Figures of the Mould, and makes the Flummery look dull.

N.B. Be careful you keep stirring it 'till cold, or it will run in Lumps when you turn it out of the Mould.

Two recipes down, Raffald has us make four large flummery fish and six small ones. These are set in a china bowl with successive layers of clear gelatin into which the fish are set. The whole thing is then turned over into a large salver, and she specifies that the gelatin must be stiff and clear. Now just imagine the look on the faces of your average 18th-century dinner party guests, men and women in stiff white wigs, bound up in their tight coats and dresses. It is enough to make one gasp.

Jelly Houses

London's Covent Garden immediately conjures images of Eliza Doolittle selling flowers among the costermongers with their crates of fruits and vegetables. Today it bustles with touristy shops and restaurants. But in the 18th century, the area was a little unsavory—or rather savory if you had a penchant for jello. Young rakes—or "macaroni's" as they were called—renowned for their outrageous coifs and flamboyant attire would come here for a bit of fun. You remember Yankee Doodle with his feather? That was a pathetic attempt at fashion. In any case, there were theaters, then as now, gaming houses, coffee houses, public gardens, but also a curious structure called a "Jelly house" where one could find a young woman for a price. In a 1766 play called "Neck or Nothing," a young Jenny was assumed to be an innocent girl fresh out of the country but was actually a "Covent-Garden-bred Wench, who had lived at a jelly-house, and had two children."

There is even a delightful image titled "The Jelly-House Maccaroni" printed in 1772 wherein a lascivious fop fondly caresses just such a wench. The image isn't really moralizing, but seems to take luscious delight in the sordid situation. *The Complete Modern London Spy* of 1781, a kind of guidebook to the city, tells us that a jelly house is

one of those places whither effeminate beaux sometimes resort of a morning; and rakes and girls of the town meet at night. There was formerly a greater number of these; but as there is a fashion in all things, so the taverns, bagnios and genteel night-houses, have taken away great part of their business; there are enough of them left, however, for people to spend their money in knick-knacks, or pick up a wench, upon occasion.

You might think the jelly is some kind of lewd metaphor, but in fact these houses did indeed serve jelly. Jelly in elegant little glasses, scooped out with a spoon, was all the rage in Georgian London, along with coffee, tea, and tobacco from a long clay pipe. It was considered to be refreshing but also a kind of "pick me up" that presumably would aid in exactly the sort of activities one would seek in a jelly house.

The glasses themselves look rather like parfait glasses, elegantly etched with neo-classical patterns. At first such objects were markers of social status, but by this time they were considered "fancy" and an attempt to communicate to customers that the business was high class, when in fact it was anything but. In 2017 a cellar was discovered at a site owned by St. John's College, Cambridge that contained the remains of Clapham's Coffeehouse, which the archaeologists described as an 18th-century Starbucks. Apart from the pipe stems and broken tea pots, there was a whole set of 18 jelly glasses and the remains of calves' feet. Perhaps they were serving more than just jelly?

Although you still find gelatin mentioned in the late 18th and early 19th century, the excitement over them, as well as the jelly house, seems to have waned. The colorful and very fussy creations of the previous generation gave way to more "natural" foods, just as the enormous wigs and tight bustles gave way to flowing hair and loose dresses. People were encouraged to express their emotions rather than dissemble in polite society. Gelatin at the time, much like in the similarly natural late '60s and '70s, was still around, but nothing new. Not, that is, until it was transformed in the Victorian era, whose revival was partly facilitated by technological innovations in the art of jello.

Peter Cooper

If you spend time in Manhattan, the name Peter Cooper will eventually become familiar, either through the Cooper Union in the East Village, a college of arts and engineering he founded, or through the Cooper-Hewitt Smithsonian Design Museum, or the many buildings, squares, and places named for him. He was a great industrialist, inventor, and philanthropist. His Tom Thumb steam locomotive was the first in the US. He was also an abolitionist before the Civil War and an advocate of Native American rights.

But he got his start in glue and gelatin. If you wander today up Park Avenue above 30th street there's little to remind you that in the 1820s there was water here: Sunfish Pond, fed by a brook that eventually emptied into Kips Bay to the east. In the mid-80s I worked for a year as a production editor a block away. In the early 19th century this pond was just a stop along the post road that eventually went to Boston; there was practically nothing else here. A young Peter Cooper paid 2,000 dollars in 1821 for a glue factory on this site. It was an ideal location, just a few blocks from the Bull's Head Market where the slaughterhouses were located and an ample supply of calves' feet.

The process for making glue is more or less the same as making gelatin, so it makes perfect sense that he got US patent 4084 on June 20, 1845. That this was intended for culinary rather than industrial uses is shown by the specific wording of the patent, which includes this recipe:

For every hundred pounds of isinglass or gelatine, four hundred pounds best white sugar, the juice or acid of twelve hundred lemons, or an equivalent of acid of limes, the peal or rind of three hundred lemons, eight hundred eggs, or a sufficient quantity of other linings, one pound peach-pits, one pound cinnamon, one pound mace, one pound allspice, half-pound of cloves, with such other spices and such variations of the quantities of all as will suit the tastes of different persons. To this solution of gelatine, with the various ingredients incorporated with it, a sufficient quantity of water should be added to reduce the Whole mass to a fluid of such consistency as would admit (after being boiled about ten minutes) of being passed through a fine filter.

Cooper remained in the glue business with an even larger factory in Gowanda NY, but clearly he had many other interests. That's probably why he never aggressively capitalized on his gelatin patent nor tried to market the product for retail. The above recipe is clearly intended for large-scale manufacture. It was not until the patents for gelatin were sold to cough syrup manufacturer Pearle Bixby Wait of Le Roy, NY, in 1897 that the full potential of the invention would be realized. But there were other companies at the time.

Rose Knox

The company that still bears the Knox name was founded in 1889 when Charles B. Knox and his young bride Rose purchased a defunct gelatin factory in Johnstown, NY, northwest of Albany. The town had many tanneries, so it was an ideal locale. Their technical innovation was granulating the gelatin sheets into a fine powder. Charles's real talent however was his penchant for gimmicky advertising campaigns, such as using motorized balloons, sponsoring racehorses like "Gelatin King," and filling every available magazine space with ads claiming how the gelatin was pure, healthier for you than pie, and so much easier than rendering bones for hours. It would free the housewife from kitchen drudgery and made elegant desserts routine. The ads even offered to send a packet that would make a pint for free to anyone who wanted to try. Most importantly, there were little pamphlet recipe books like *Dainty Desserts for Dainty People*, the first edition of which came out in 1896.

The trademarked logo of the Knox company was a little calf's head, which made perfect sense. But there was also another image routinely used—a little naked black boy wearing a chef's hat and bearing a huge translucent molded gelatin. As I write these words, the last vestiges of Aunt Jemima, Uncle Ben, and Mrs. Butterworth are finally being stricken from grocery shelves. Good riddance. But I still wonder what was going through the Knoxs' minds when they chose this image. The kid is cute, but the implication seems to be that the little chef is destined to a life of kitchen work because of his color. And if you can't afford servants, then this little box will make your household appear that it has a full-time black chef in the back doing the cooking. The more you look at the ads, the more the racist implications are undeniable. But there were also ads with both a black and a white boy, one for the sparkling white version, the other for the acidulated (i.e., flavored, perhaps colored) version.

I don't think these ads lasted much longer than Charles B himself. Heart failure took him early in 1908, at which point Rose took over the business. She had apparently always been a full contributing partner, but now reluctant to hire a manager who would think of the business as his own, she ran it until her own boys could inherit the company. That took quite a while—she only retired in 1947 and passed away a few years later at the age of 93. The success of the business into the leading unflavored gelatin manufacturer in the world was entirely her own doing. She ran the business for over 40 years, even building a much larger facility in Camden, NJ, in 1936, right in the middle of the Depression.

She was even featured in a *Life* magazine story on November 29, 1937, which pointed out her enlightened business practices: a five-day work week, paid two-week vacation, and sick leave. Most importantly, men and women were treated with absolute equality; the back door through which women once had to enter was permanently shut. And one executive who said he didn't want to be bossed around by a woman was promptly fired. That never happened again. Rose was also on the Board of Directors of the American Grocery Manufacturer's Association.

The company did eventually pass to her children, who ran it until, as had happened with so many family businesses, it was bought out by Lipton in 1972. Today it is a subsidiary of DGS Stoess AG, the world's largest gelatin producer. The Deutsche Gelatin-Fabriken itself goes back to 1875. Through a series of mergers and acquisitions over the course of the next century, providing photographic, medical, and culinary gelatin, the company is now called the Gelita Group, centered in Eberbach, along the banks of the Neckar River.

Jules Harder

Jules Harder was born in Alsace in 1830 and trained in some of the finest restaurants of Europe. He was lured to work at Delmonico's in New York in 1852 and also worked at the Union Club and Union Hall in Saratoga, the great resort in upstate New York and the Long Branch Hotel in New Jersey, another great resort town.

That resort's manager Warren Leland went to California to manage the new Palace Hotel in San Francisco and brought Harder with him to design the kitchens and dining spaces and work as chef de cuisine. That hotel was the five-million-dollar project of the flamboyant Billy Chapman Ralston, founder of the Bank of California, his fortune derived from the Comstock Lode. If you have ever seen a Morgan Silver Dollar, that's where it came from. It was the same silver that financed the North in the Civil War.

That silver also went directly into the massive Palace Hotel at the corner of New Montgomery and Market in San Francisco. It was equipped with elevators, electric call buttons, and bay windows in all of 755 guest rooms. The Garden Court was a magnificent seven-story open space with a glass conservatory ceiling to let in light. Carriages could pull right into the space. Just weeks before the opening of the hotel in 1875, Ralston's bank crashed when his partner dumped all his stock. Ralston's body was found in the San Francisco Bay a few days later. The hotel opened anyway with great fanfare with Leland taking charge. Although the original building was destroyed by the fires in the wake of the 1906 earthquake, a new hotel opened in 1909 and remains to this day as a National Historic Landmark.

It was largely the great restaurant headed by Harder that made the hotel famous. He had served many presidents, including an extravagant banquet for Ulysses S. Grant, costing thousands of dollars. Among Harder's culinary legacies is his tarragon-laced green goddess salad dressing. But he was renowned especially for his grand towering aspics, the jiggling epitome of the Gilded Age. *The Physiology of Taste: Harder's Book of Practical American Cookery* of 1885 reveals his approach to gastronomy; alas only the first volume on vegetables was published, though five were planned. The book nonetheless gives us a glimpse of his fondness for aspic in this recipe for a Vegetable Salad with Aspic Jelly, Italian Style:

No. 1712.—Cut out one dozen potatoes with a round cutter about the size of a twenty-five cent piece, and slice them finely. Then take two pickled beets and cut and slice them the same way. Put them in separate bowls and season with pepper, salt, oil, and vinegar. Prepare the fillet of one or two flounders, scrape off the skin, and put them in a buttered flat saucepan. Season with salt and pepper and add a little white wine. Then cook them, keeping them white, and when done put them on a platter and lay them aside to get cold. When cold cut them in scallops, add the same quantity of fillet of boned Anchovies, and season with pepper, salt, oil, and vinegar. Decorate the mould with Aspic jelly, capers, olives, anchovies and the whites of hard boiled eggs . . . Put the flounders and anchovies in a bowl and add to them double their quantity of potatoes and beets, after they are drained. Also add some capers and a few spoonfuls of Mayonnaise dressing made with Aspic jelly. Mix them gently together and then fill the centre of the mould. Smooth off the top evenly and set it in a cool place until ready for use. When dressing it garnish with hard boiled eggs and chopped Aspic jelly. (Harder, 400)

There is further visual evidence too: in 1874 Harder was painted by Joseph Harrington, bearing his prodigious mutton chops on the sides of his face, a caricatured chef's hat, and bearing a magnificent aspic. Atop the seafood-filled amber dome surrounded by lemons is a defeated lobster with a decorative sword through his heart. The painting hangs in the Oakland Museum.

Mrs. Marshall

Mrs. Agnes B. Marshall was the quintessential Victorian cookbook author, concerned most with primping and coloring with a ton of frou-frou, sometimes even at the expense of flavor. Everything is garnished to the nines. She founded a cooking school in 1883 and sold her own equipment and ingredients. She was a consummate entrepreneur at a time when few respectable women worked outside the home. I can picture exactly the sort of customer who read her books avidly: socially aspirant upper-middle-class women who were expected to entertain either at ladies' luncheons or formal dinners. They might have a cook doing the actual work, but I like to think that making fancy recipes like this one was a matter of self-expression, a matter of pride, so you could claim boasting rights. Above all, it's a really easy recipe.

Leaf and powdered gelatin were new conveniences in the late 19th century. They gave a woman the perception that they could do something grand and beautiful without a lot of skill or experience in the kitchen. Not that aspics and gelatin were ever that hard to make from scratch, but opening a packet was definitely less time-consuming. You could indeed whip this up in no time.

Claret Jelly with Vanilla Cream *Gelée au Vin Rouge et Crème Vanille* (Marshall 1902, 497–98)

Put a quarter of a pint of water into a stewpan with four ounces of loaf-sugar, bring to the boil, and then dissolve in not quite a half an ounce of Marshall's Finest Leaf Gelatine; let it get cool but not set; then mix into it a wineglassful of

brandy, a few drops of carmine, and three-quarters of a pint of claret; pour it into the nest mold, if you have it, or any other fancy shape, with a pipe, and put the jelly away in a cool place to set; then turn out onto a dish, with a compote of French plums, as below. Have some cream whipped stiff, and to each half-pint add two ounces of castor sugar and a few drops of vanilla essence, and by means of a forcing bag and a large rose pipe, garnish between the fruits with this; sprinkle over a little pistachio that has been blanched, skinned, and chopped, and serve for dinner or luncheon sweet.

Compote of plums for Claret Jelly.—Take a half a pound of French plums, put them in a stewpan with two and a half gills of cooking claret, the peel of one lemon, and a strip of cinnamon about one inch long tied up together; sweeten with two ounces of loaf sugar; add a few drops of liquid carmine, let it simmer till the liquor is reduced to creamy thickness, remove the lemon peel, &c., then set aside until cold and use.

A packet of powdered gelatin is ¼ ounce, so use two packets here or two tablespoons. If using leaf gelatin, 3 sheets equals one packet, so you would need 6. A Quarter of an imperial pint is about 5 fluid US ounces of water, and four ounces of sugar is about 9 tablespoons. A wineglassful is not what it seems, but a unit of measurement equaling 2 ounces. ¾ of an Imperial pint is 14 and a half US ounces, so just use two generous glasses of red wine. Liquid Carmine was a standard natural red dye made from cochineal—a small-scale insect. Synthetic food coloring has largely replaced it in the food industry and for home use, but some products still contain it as Natural Red #4. Use a standard red food coloring.

Jell-O

The standard narrative of the advent of Jell-O is fairly straightforward. Pearle Bixby Wait, a carpenter and cough syrup manufacturer in Le Roy, New York, founded the company and the eponymous product name was contrived by his wife May. The connection to the pharmaceutical industry is perhaps not so apparent today, but it was often the same ingredients that went into medicinal nostrums, candies, and gelatin. Their apparent innovation was the addition of flavoring, sugar, and colors to match each variety: lemon, orange, strawberry, and raspberry. There's not much more to say about the couple, because within two years in 1899 they sold the formula to a neighbor, and it seems a relative as well, named Orator Francis Woodward, for $450. Woodward owned the Genesee Pure Food Company and produced a beverage called Grain-O (not to be confused with Drain-O) and thought Jell-O would be a good addition to his lineup. At first, it wasn't, and he allegedly tried to sell the patent to his plant manager for 35 bucks.

There were other companies offering competition. The Plymouth Rock Gelatin Company had been making pink and white phosphate gelatin since 1889. The white required no lemons—the phosphate providing the acid, as it did in soft drinks of the era. The pink was colored for festivity. The English had been making instant gelatin even earlier. Hartley's in 1874, founded by Sir William Pickles Hartley, was one company, though their fame came from jam and what in the US is called jelly. But today they make jelly cubes, which are a concentrated base used to make desserts. The J and G Limited Company of Edinburgh had been making a powdered gelatin since 1842, and this brand was also sold in the US shortly thereafter as Cox's. Their registered trademark was a little Scots boy in a tartan kilt. The product, manufactured in Scotland, was actually not quite so instant. Their "Patent Refined Sparkling Gelatine" still had to be clarified with eggs and strained. Nonetheless, it was recommended in *Mrs. Lincoln's Boston Cookbook* of 1890, along with a brand called Nelson's.

There's a lesson in good branding with another early competitor that appeared in 1895: Bromangelon. It claimed it would transform into a "delicious and wholesome dessert jelly in 2 minutes" and came in seven different flavors. Its creator, an Austrian immigrant named Leo Hirschfeld, abandoned the product but later went on to invent the Tootsie Roll.

For the Genesee Pure Food Company, Jell-O tuned out to be the big money-maker. Twenty-six years after buying the product, the company was sold for 67 million dollars to Postum (a non-caffeinated coffee substitute based on grain). What had happened to turn that oddball product into such a gold mine?

It was Woodward's advertising acumen and nothing else. There were ads in magazines, billboards, and images pretty much anywhere you could plaster Jell-O. In 1904 a cute little "Jell-O girl" became the mascot. This was modeled after Elizabeth King whose father Franklin worked for the Dauchy Agency that created Jell-O's ads. Woodward also was the first to use balloons in advertising. Orator died in 1906 at age 49, at which point his son Ernest Leroy took over the business. Ernest introduced an assembly line to the production facility and continued the aggressive ad campaigns.

Even more important than ads were the recipe booklets that convinced consumers not only that this wonderful substance once only available to the wealthy could now be made at home, but that it is perfectly clean and wholesome. The packages even said "pure"—much more so than the smelly old bones you would have to buy if you wanted to make jello before. The selling point was convenience, cleanliness—remember the influx of malodorous immigrants made white society particularly suspicious of kitchen smells—and eminently affordable. That price was a consistent theme in the advertisements suggests that they were consciously targeting the less than wealthy, including those very immigrants. Woodward apparently arranged to have Jell-O molds handed to immigrants upon their arrival at Ellis Island in New York, replete with recipe booklet.

There were even advertisements in Yiddish starting around 1910. The question of whether Jell-O could be considered kosher is itself fascinating and one the company seems to have skirted consistently. When asked outright in 1935, the ad agency sent around assurance that it was kosher, to which the Rabbinic authorities thundered back that it couldn't possibly be so since it was a product of pigs. See Roger Horowitz's *Kosher USA* for a full discussion. A long chain of arguments ensued with experts taking different opinions since the gelatin was made of bones not the flesh—which is the prohibited part, and is so transformed in the process that is ceased to be the treyf (forbidden) swine in substance.

Another great selling point for Jell-O was the so-called "servant problem." It was not unusual for middle-class households in the 19th century to hire a female maid, cook, nurse, or all three, if they could afford it. Live-in servants were largely replaced by those who would come during the day, a part-time "cleaning woman" or all-around household "help"—often black after widespread migration northward. There were many causes: rising living standards, other job opportunities for women, and the desire of women of all classes to get married and set up their own households. Regardless of the cause, it left many women managing their own household feeling that they were suddenly overwhelmed by a barrage of duties, especially cooking. Any product that offered convenience, whether the consumer was inconvenienced before or not, suddenly seemed very appealing.

In 1923 the company name was officially changed to Jell-O, and in 1925 it was sold to Postum. The management and workers all kept their jobs for the time being. Eventually that company purchased other manufacturers such as Birdseye Frozen Foods, which altogether became General Foods. That in turn became Kraft.

Second Industrial Revolution

What made Jell-O and other brands so successful had very little to do with an invention of powdered gelatin or rescuing housewives from kitchen drudgery. There had been practically instant forms of gelatin for many decades. Think of Peter Cooper's recipe; it was intended for industrial confectionery rather than home cooks. What really brought jello into the home was the confluence of several important inventions that initially had nothing to do with dessert.

First bizarrely enough came from the petrochemical industry, or more precisely coal-tar based dyes. Up until the mid–19th century, colors were derived from plants like madder or woad, indigo, insects like cochineal. Many of these were also used for food, including expensive spices like saffron and alkanet. Most food was pretty dull though. The great breakthrough is credited to William Henry Perkin, a chemistry student who was trying to make synthetic quinine, an anti-malarial drug. Instead he came up with the first aniline dye—a rich purple known as mauve, which became all the rage in fabrics. Britain had plenty of coal tar as a waste product from its burgeoning industries, so there soon appeared bright, cheaply manufactured greens and reds. The latter was developed by German chemists Carl Graebe and Carl Leibermann, who created a dye based on alizarin. Germany took the lead in chemical research in the late 19th century, and synthetic dyes not only revolutionized the textile industry, but they also led to the first chemotherapeutic drugs used to target specific diseases in the body. In 1891 Paul Ehrlich had discovered the so-called magic bullet that would stain and affect only certain cells, leaving others unharmed. Arsphenamine was the first affective treatment for syphilis.

Food dyes followed shortly thereafter and were among the many reasons the Pure Food and Drug Act was passed in 1906, to monitor the safety not only of slaughterhouses of the kind described in Upton Sinclair's *The Jungle*, but also the dazzling array of artificial colors that had suddenly appeared in industrially manufactured foods. Some of these were potentially poisonous, but no one had systematically tested them until chemists like Harvey Wiley and his infamous "poison squad" were fed regular doses to see how it affected their health.

Although it took some time to get lead, arsenic, and mercury out of the food supply, eventually in the US there were only 7 officially approved synthetic food dyes: Red #1 and 2, Erythrosine (another red), Indigotine, Light Green, Naphthol yellow, and orange. Think for a moment how nicely these line up with the early gelatin flavors: lemon, strawberry, orange, lime. It was as much the colors that dazzled consumers as the convenience of little packets.

Not coincidentally, the imitation-flavoring industry arose at the same time. Artificial flavors were first showcased at the famous Crystal Palace Exhibition in 1851. Vanillin was the first to be synthesized by German chemists in the 1870s. By the end of the century there were a good handful of artificial fruit flavors, precisely the kind that could be easily used in candy and desserts. Think for a moment of how difficult it would be to get the exact complex aroma and flavor of a real strawberry or grape into a shelf stable confection. Artificial flavors don't even attempt that. They pick out a few key molecules that the body will register, almost a caricature of the original. Soon the artificial color and flavor become strongly associated in the consumer's mind such that a cherry that tastes almost nothing like a real cherry, but more intense and vibrant, or a concord grape of deep purple hue becomes more real, more desired. The representation of reality replaces the fickle and variable nature of real fruits, which sometimes aren't so sweet or aromatic. Eventually people come to prefer the fake.

It's not entirely clear what the original Jell-O contained, but the Genesee Pure Food Company certainly went out of their way to advertise that they used natural flavors. "Flavor captured from fresh, ripe strawberries" read one ad. The box itself read "Pure Fruit Flavor" in the early 20th century. Perhaps that was simply a marketing ploy; most likely truth in advertising rules eventually made the company include "artificially flavored" on the label.

The third part to this industrial puzzle is refrigeration. Not in the machine we adore today. At first ice was cut from ponds in New England and shipped around the world. There were ice houses long before, but this was the first time you could have some ice on hand for your cocktail or for chilling an aspic quickly. This kind of pond ice and then mechanically made ice was delivered to people's houses by a man on a truck with a big pair of metal pincers and placed in an icebox with a drip tray beneath. My parents in the Depression both grew up with an icebox. It seems, for this very reason, jello packets were not yet the darling of your average household in the early 20th century.

It really wasn't until after World War II that proper refrigerators came into the average home. The early models were expensive, clunky, and sometimes exploded. Freon technology and a booming economy changed that, and that was the real democratizing factor in the popularity of jello, ushering in the great jello heyday of the mid–20th century. People trusted science; we had gleaming kitchen appliances and food technology made products that were safe, saved time in the kitchen, and most importantly were clean and unspoiled by errant germs and the process of decay. Refrigerators are what made jello truly popular in every home.

Jello for Convalescence

You may have wondered why Jell-O is often served at hospitals. The logic is that pure gelatin is 98–99% protein, and therefore nutritious. It is also easy to digest. It is thought of as a refined and concentrated food that requires little chewing, and won't tax a body that has been compromised by surgery or illness. It goes down easily, pretty much like a liquid, though isn't likely to make a mess. I suspect being cheap has a lot to do with it also.

On the other hand, commercial brands contain a lot of sugar and flavoring. Can that be good for recuperation? And is gelatin really nutritious? It doesn't have many vitamins or minerals, apart from calcium and phosphorous. It certainly cannot be classed as a superfood. Although there are studies that show it eases the pain associated with rheumatoid arthritis, there are very few specific therapeutic health benefits associated with gelatin.

So why do we think of it as a good food for convalescence? Is it simply a matter of the consistency? Or is jello somehow comforting to most people, a reminder of youth and something anyone can happily eat? In one of the strangest ironies, Allie Rowbottom in her family biography entitled *Jell-O Girls*, reports that her mother Mary (niece of Jell-O matriarch Edith Woodward) never really liked Jell-O, yet it was the only thing she was allowed to eat while she was dying of cancer.

Maybe it isn't so much a matter of being especially good for you, but that the act of eating itself, getting calories down in whatever form possible, is better than not eating. And with Mary as the exception, jello is a kind of comfort food. Anything that's soft and relatively bland will remind of us of the food we were given as babies; the first things we consumed after mother's milk or formula were rice porridge, soft pasta, foods that were supposed not to upset tender stomachs. Jello seems to fit into this category and thus became logically an ideal food for convalescence.

This idea is nothing new. If we look at medical texts and cookbooks of the past, regardless of the reigning medical theory, we are instructed to feed convalescents soft mild foods that contain easily digested forms of nutrition.

Fannie Farmer's *Food and Cookery for the Sick and Convalescent* published in 1904 has dozens of recipes for starchy puddings and restorative broths, but also a whole chapter devoted to gelatin. They are all made from scratch using unflavored packets, lightly sweetened and flavored with orange or lemon, but some are made with wine, madeira, port, or sauternes. There are others with beef extract, chicken, and veal. Again, the logic of these is that these are all nutritious foods in a form that is sort of predigested, already broken down into its essential parts so your digestive system doesn't have to do much work. As for the wine, unlike today, alcohol was considered nourishing. For many centuries it was believed to be the analogue of blood, easily converted into it, and therefore an ideal form of nourishment. The early 20th century was actually the last time historically that alcohol could be considered medicinal, backed with standard medical science of the day. It was quickly swept aside with the advent of germ theory, but people did order bourbon for convalescents in good faith during prohibition.

The same basic principles were at play in earlier medical systems as well. In John Huxham's *Essay on Fevers* (83) the author has essentially the same recommendations as Farmer. For what he categorized as a slow nervous fever he suggests this: "I think in this View a thin Chicken Broth also is of Service, both for Food and Physic, especially toward the decline of the Disorder, and for the same Reason, thin Jellies of Hart's-Horn, Sago and Panado, are useful, adding a little wine to them, and the Juice of Seville orange or Lemon."

In the *London Pharmacopoeia*, the standard drug reference work of the 18th century, we are even given a medically approved recipe using Cornu Cervi—Latin for Hartshorn. "Boiled in water it gives out an emollient nutritious jelly. An elegant jelly is prepared, by boiling 6 ounces of shavings in water 6 lb to 2 lb, adding to the strained liquor of Seville orange or Lemon juice 1 oz., white wine 4 oz. sugar 6 oz., and then boiling the whole to a due consistence" (Graves 1799, 24).

Although the preparation is much more complicated, we can find comparable recipes even two centuries earlier. Bartolomeo Scappi's *Opera* (432) contains an entire final book on cooking for convalescents. Here is his magnificent recipe for the sick:

To make a jello of chicken finely chopped, and juice of quince

Take four fleshy capons, and not force-fed, killed that day, plucked and their interior cleaned, cut into mouthfuls, with their feet, necks cleaned of blood, and with these 20 kid's feet, cleaned and skinned, let everything boil in a glazed clay pot, with enough clear water, so that it's covered, and with this water add six pounds of clear verjuice, and if it's new it will be better, and boil until it is reduced from three parts to two, having been well skimmed, and remove the fat with a wooden spoon or silver. It can be tested with a little cup in the way it was done in chapter 26 with the broth of veal reduced to jello. Strain the decoction through a sieve and put back in the pot with two pounds of finely pounded sugar, half an ounce of pounded cinnamon, and eight ounces of clear quince juice, four ounces of vinegar, six ounces of white wine, enough salt, three apples cut finely, let everything boil together, with six freshly beaten egg whites, until the egg white comes to the top, pass it then through a jelly bag of white linen, many times, until it is clear like amber. Place in little glasses or on plates in a cold place to gel. Beneath this jello you can put strips of boiled capon, and not having quince, make apple juice, and not having kid's feet take some more capons, and when the jello passes through the jelly bag, you can place in the bag two ounces of fine musk scented mostaccioli whole.

Scappi's trick in chapter 26, and one that works today, is to put a little of the hot jello into a small glass and submerge that in cold water for half an hour. If it gels, then you know the gelatin will be strong enough to set. Verjuice, by the way, is the juice of unripe grapes, so freshly squeezed, this would be in summer. The quince being astringent and sour, and categorized as cold in the system of humoral physiology, it would be a perfect counteractive medicine for the heat of summer, or for fevers. But it is also, just like all the recipes mentioned, a concentrated form of nutrition, like a broth, but in more easily consumed form, appropriate for hot weather.

To see that Scappi's recommendation wasn't purely the product of his own imagination, we need only look to the late medieval physician Marsilius de Sancta Sophia (d. 1405). In the section of his *Opus Aureum* (fol XC vo) on how to treat fevers, he says that "gelatin is easier to eat and digest, put in it vinegar or verjuice, or the juice of something acidic mixed with sugar and cooked long with meat." He also suggests pulverized sandalwood, sumac, or coriander—all considered cold ingredients. "Let this coagulate and give this gelatin to the patient." And if it's necessary to stimulate the appetite, as happens with feverish patients, he suggests boiling with aromatics or chopped pears. In other words, people were thinking of gelatin as a medicinal food just about as long as gelatin recipes have existed.

The Myth of Difficulty and Consequent Deskilling

No single ingredient better exemplifies the conscious strategy to deskill home cooks than the development and marketing of instant gelatin and flavored Jell-O products in the late 19th and early 20th century. Although aspics were seen as time-consuming, they were never considered difficult or impossible for the home cook. As we have seen, cookbooks stretching back into the Middle Ages, many intended for ordinary households, contained aspic recipes that are surprisingly easy to execute. Yet in the wake of advertising instant gelatin as a labor-saving innovation in the early 20th century, within one generation people were convinced that making gelatin at home was impractical if not entirely impossible, horrible-smelling, and inadvisable without industrial scale equipment. A century later this is still the case.

While it is true that the Golden Age of Aspics occurred precisely because these new products were purchased and used extensively in the home, it is also the case that few people thereafter understood how simple an aspic can be to make from scratch. It demands nothing more than cheap connective tissue, skin, feet, and other parts to render gelatin. It can be made on any scale and requires only a pot and a low flame. But 20th-century cooks were convinced otherwise, and instant gelatin became a household staple for much of the 20th century, and the simple process of making it from scratch was almost entirely forgotten. Think of the first season of Julia Child on TV making a duck Montmorency using gelatin packets.

The supposed difficulty of making gelatin has been an assumption made by everyone who discusses it, but it was an idea created by the instant gelatin companies. The instant form is said to have democratized gelatin. The beautiful Jell-O ads made by Maxfield Parrish feature medieval royalty being served gelatin, reading "The King and Queen Might Eat Thereof and Noblemen Besides." But later ads show homespun Americans at what appears to be a colonial kitchen table "Polly Put the Kettle On, We'll All Make Jell-O"—implying that now anyone can make it. But stop and think for a moment: feet are just about the most inexpensive part of the animal. It doesn't require much special attention—you put it in a pot and simmer. It smells like meaty stock, that's all. Clarification is a little more complicated, but it's just an ordinary kitchen skill, not expensive or difficult, just forgotten. Let's look a little deeper at how this came to be.

Perfection Salad

In the early 20th century, there were many new industrially manufactured ingredients advertised as labor-saving, convenient, and liberating for women who spent too much time in the kitchen. Whether such work was really burdensome drudgery as the corporations claimed is beside the point; most people believed they were. So it was that canned products and frozen foods made their way into American households as staples. They promised to be nutritious, hygienic, and perfectly suited for the scientifically managed home. Among these new products was powdered gelatin.

In the United States the unflavored gelatin market was dominated by Knox. Still the leader, and for flavors and bright colors, the Jell-O brand was so successful that the very word *jello* has become a generic term for all gelatin products. These companies promoted their goods not only with advertisements in magazines, newspapers, and on radio but with enticing pamphlets full of recipes that promised the weary homemaker delightful dishes that would please their families.

The Knox advertising team hosted a recipe contest in 1905, and the winning recipe was called Perfection Salad, entered by a Mrs. John E. Cook. Jello as salad was more or less a new invention, and it caught on. It promised, as did the entire Home Economics movement that sought to implement scientific management principles into the home kitchen, that women could be empowered, even perfected with technological advances and labor-saving devices. This jello fit the bill precisely. Laura Shapiro's book with this title is a classic that belongs on every foodie's shelf.

In 1915, *Knox Gelatine: Dainty Dishes for Dainty People* included a recipe for Perfection Salad whose name promised ease and simplicity and more importantly fulfillment through the appreciation of husband and children in an ideal family. The reality was rarely so neat and tidy of course, but for aspirant housewives this recipe promised happiness and, one might say, perfection.

Perfection Salad

1 package Knox Sparkling
  Gelatine.
½ cup sugar.
½ cup cold water.
1 teaspoonful salt.
½ cup mild vinegar.

1 cup cabbage, finely shredded.
2 tablespoons lemon juice.
2 cups celery, cut in small pieces.
2 cups boiling water.
2 pimientos, cut in small pieces.

Soak gelatine in cold water five minutes. Add vinegar, lemon juice, boiling water, sugar, and salt. Strain, and when mixture begins to stiffen, add remaining ingredients. Turn into mold, first dipped in cold water, and chill. Remove to bed of lettuce or endive. Garnish with mayonnaise dressing, or cut in cubes, and serve in cases made of green or red peppers, or turn into molds lined with canned pimientos. A delicious accompaniment to cold sliced chicken or veal.

Since the recipe allows room for creativity in garnishing and gussying up the recipe, of course you can take free rein in adding whatever strikes your fancy. Don't be tempted to use fresh pineapple or papaya, because they will prevent the jello from setting, but canned fruit is fine.

For my own version, I simply substituted rosé wine for the water and added in some grated carrot. Although recipes like this have become almost completely obsolete, the taste is actually refreshingly pleasant and the vegetables keep their crunch encased in jello. To serve this, I put slices on lettuce leaves with a dollop of mayonnaise, exactly as the Knox folks suggested.

Postwar Changes

After World War II there was a dramatic change in the ingredients used in gelatin manufacture. Before, it was mostly bones and connective tissue that were soaked in lye and chemical solvents to dissolve the collagen. This was a lengthy process. But changes in American taste suddenly provided an abundance of pig skins, more than the football makers could handle, I guess. Lard was once a major cooking fat in US households. Pigs were raised to have a large "fat back" that could be rendered and sold for frying, to be used in pie crusts and just about anywhere fat was called for in a recipe. It's both delicious and a completely natural product. But scientists were beginning to understand the difference between animal-derived saturated and plant-derived largely unsaturated fats. The claim, although hardly proven, was that vegetable sources were better for maintaining health. They were neutral for vegetarians, not controversial for kosher consumers, and once they were stabilized with hydrogenation, they were even shelf stable, requiring no refrigeration. Consumers were convinced that Crisco was better than lard. The latter was almost completely stricken from the American diet. You could still purchase it, but it was the butt of jokes.

This shift encouraged pork farmers to grow leaner pigs since there was less of a market for the fat and because people increasingly ate fresh pork products like chops and roasts, which could be transported to market fresh. This again meant that hams, salt pork, cured salami, and the like became a smaller proportion of the pork industry—again leading to an abundance of skin. In 1947 an effective machine for removing the skin made them even cheaper. The gelatin industry was there to buy them up, especially since it's much easier to extract collagen from skin than bones. Gelita runs the largest gelatin processing factory in the world, in Sergeant Bluff, Iowa—not surprisingly, right where the pigs are raised.

Gelatin and Weight Loss

Weight loss diets seem to be a purely modern phenomenon, but the treatment of obesity as a pathological state began to achieve serious medical attention in the early 18th century in a series of German dissertations and then among English authors. Most notorious was George Cheyne who used his own milk and seed diet to lose several hundred pounds. Fashion dictated these trends as much as anything. In certain periods of history, a fulsome figure was popular, in the mid–17th century (think of Rubens) and then again in the Victorian era. In others, slimness was the cultural ideal, especially in the early 20th century, when the narrow flapper figure dominated the advertising space. These swings in fashion mostly concerned women, but men were not entirely left out. Just compare the portly silhouettes of presidents like Taft with the bony frames of Wilson and Coolidge.

Dieting mostly involved getting more exercise, eating less food, and cutting calories once those were discovered in the mid–19th century. There were patent remedies and nostrums and fad diets aplenty in the 19th century, but not until the early 20th century was there a proliferation of mass manufactured foods specifically designed for losing weight. Gelatin, because almost pure protein and containing no fat, was a decent candidate for a dieting food, but not when it was laden with sugar. This changed with the supposedly accidental invention of saccharin by the Johns Hopkins scientist working with coal tar derivatives, Constantin Fahlberg, in 1879. By the turn of the century, companies like Monsanto were selling it as a sugar substitute, and it made its way into commercial products.

The timing for this was not ideal, mostly because pure food advocacy and muckraking had just hit the scene and Harvey Wiley targeted saccharin specifically to be banned under the Pure Food and Drug Act. Apparently it was his uneasy relation with Teddy Roosevelt that prevented that from happening; Roosevelt's own doctor had recommended it to lose weight. It was eventually banned in 1912, but then quickly rescued, ironically, by World War I—when all the foods considered most nutritious—wheat, fat, and sugar— were sent to the front to keep soldiers well fed. At home, the dearth of sugar forced the reintroduction of saccharin. After the war, the timing was perfect. Slim figures were again in fashion, and in 1923 the Genesee Pure Food Company trademarked the name D-Zerta for their new saccharin weight loss gelatin.

There was a product called D-Zerta before this because in 1906 the Attorney General of New York handed down a ruling on the use of the name for three separate products manufactured by a Rochester Company —an ice cream powder, a quick pudding powder, and a jelly powder. It's not clear whether Genesee merely bought the name or the product itself containing saccharin, but in either case, they were the ones who first marketed it widely. Within two years, that company was bought out by Postum, which later became General Foods. The Name D-Zerta lasted all the way until 1984, when "Sugar-Free Jell-O" replaced it.

D-Zerta, like all dieting foods, was aimed predominantly toward women, especially those prone to judging their own bodies against the slim figures depicted in the ads. The ads not only featured "salads for a slim life"—meaning of course gelatin salads—but happy, youthful women who appeared to be fulfilled because of their careful dietary choices. Ads such as these, perhaps even in earnest, promise weight loss, but much more is going on. What they are selling is a promise of transformation, a simple product you can purchase, which will lead partly to a thinner body but ultimately will give you the happiness and love you want from your partner, family, and most importantly the envy of your friends. That is, the ads frightened consumers, making them think that a woman's value in society is primarily a matter of physical form.

This type of dieting ideology as a kind of societal constraint was first envisioned by Jeremy Bentham as a means of prison reform. Bentham (who until recently you could visit at University College London where his stuffed body was unceremoniously on display in a case under a stairwell) believed that a prison should take the shape of a Panopticon—or star shape with a single guard on surveillance in the center. Prisoners had the feeling that they were always being observed, and thus began to monitor themselves. This is analogous to what such advertisements succeed in doing. They make the potential consumer scrutinize their own lives, generating dissatisfaction within, and offer the solution in a box of diet gelatin with only 10 calories per serving—no more than two slices of banana, according to the ads—and 5 cents a serving. In other words, there is no need to starve yourself or go through any difficult regimen or pay a lot for nutritional advice. All you need to do is buy the product, and you will find happiness.

This psychological strategy works the same way in all religions and food ideologies. Following a set of rules will make you fulfilled and complete—that's the true goal. Thinness is merely a means of achieving power. You can imagine how appealing this must have been, especially for women who felt disempowered by the culture's gender expectations.

Although saccharin was the first major artificial sweetener, cyclamates, which were invented in 1937, gradually replaced it in the '50s and '60s, only to be banned itself for concerns over cancer in laboratory rats. Saccharin came back, then it too was found to be carcinogenic, but apparently not enough to remove it from the market. Aspartame had its heyday in the '80s and then Sucralose, primarily in the form of Splenda, followed on its heels. Ironically, none of these have proven that effective in maintaining weight loss long term. It's suspected that they actually trick your body into thinking it's taking in calories, which triggers your body to store fat.

Obviously, sugar-free products are wonderful for diabetics and people who can't eat sugar. But I wonder if specifically the rise of Jell-O as a dieting dessert food, especially in the '70s, didn't coincide with the slump in Jell-O sales in general. That is, did they hit this dieting market hard, just as they had jello for children, precisely because regular Jell-O had begun to go out of fashion?

This is the diet gelatin I remember as a kid. It was called Jell-O 123. It separated on its own into three layers. You poured the mix into a blender with hot water, if I remember correctly, and then add ice water and put it in the fridge to set. Magically you had a gelatinous layer, a creamy layer, and a light spongy layer on top. Somehow my mother made a sugar-free version of this—maybe it was sold under the D-Zerta label? Or maybe she made her own version with cool whip on top? Jell-O 123 suddenly disappeared in the mid-80s when I went away to college. Apparently they kept making it for a few select cities until finally discontinuing the product completely in 1996.

The Jell-O Generation

Jell-O achieved unprecedented popularity in the decades following World War II, and skyrocketing sales were maintained into the 1970s. This offers a unique opportunity to examine this particular generation, even if only impressionistically. There have been excellent studies of the demographics and spending patterns of this era, even as they relate to food, the appeal of instant cake mixes and other convenience foods, as well as household appliances. But I'd like to examine Jell-O in particular and why this product was so appealing, far beyond other supermarket items. In other words, what was going through the minds of consumers—especially middle-class housewives—in the '50s and '60s? I don't mean to suggest that working women or those of color, or even men, never bought Jell-O. But if you look at the advertisements, this was very clearly their target audience: the heterosexual family unit of 2.5 children and perhaps those aspiring to start a family like that. Never mind that this Beaver Cleaver family was never the reality; it was what the dominant culture dreamt could become so.

My ideas reflect the fact that I was one of those children and that my mother was one of those consumers eager to purchase Jell-O. She was born in 1933 and grew up in a family that was surviving the Depression, but just barely. They scrimped and made do with the least desirable cuts of meat and lived in a small apartment in Brooklyn. Like everyone else, they lived with rationing during the war. My mom got married at age 19 and had my brother a few years later. The economic boom of the postwar years sparked middle-class families' desire to own homes—think of the movie *It's a Wonderful Life* and George Bailey's affordable housing development. The culture was hell-bent on social mobility, escaping the city, often with explicitly racist motivation, and living contentedly in suburbia, even if that meant a long commute for the father of the household.

This left the homemaker to raise children, cook, clean, and live out the suburban dream. In this setting, ownership of material possessions were not only markers of status but expressions of identity—the clothes they wore, cars they drove, and even the words that came out of their mouths. They consciously tried to erase their working-class origins and Brooklyn accents. Spending became a way to forget your past and refashion yourself.

On some level, I think all human beings desire to channel their creative energy into creating things or providing services that gain the attention and approval of others. Doing one's job well, making beautiful furniture, raising perfect children. Yet in a society that so valued personal and professional accomplishment, I think homemaking women had a difficult time channeling that creativity and gaining the esteem of their peers. There's only so much approval you can get if everyone is basically living in the same cardboard cut-out houses, driving the same cars, and buying the same stuff. Cooking is one outlet for creativity, but can easily become a chore, especially if you have to feed children, and are trying to save money to send them to college or to go on vacation.

So imagine a product that is relatively cheap and ubiquitous, is eminently malleable in form and function, and allows you to go a little wild with your creative urges. Leftover chicken? A few cans of mandarin oranges in the cupboard? A bottle of soy sauce? Throw them together with Jell-O! The advertisements and recipe booklets got you started, but I think there was no other product that could give you ecstatically sparkling results for so little cost and with practically no labor. Jell-O salads, aspics, and desserts were actually not difficult to make at all. You could collect the molds too. For holidays, company, special occasions like birthdays or picnics, out comes the fantastic Jell-O creation that earns the esteem of your family, but more importantly of your peers and social competitors. Share the recipe? Why of course!

Here's the revealing text from a 1952 ad with a recipe for Molded Maytime Salad. (It's essentially lemon Jell-O with shredded carrot and green pepper served on a bed of lettuce with cottage cheese.)

> Like to add a touch of glamour to dinner tonight? Then make the Jell-O salad above. In the first place, its bright, colorful good looks are sure to suit everyone's fancy. . . . And in the second, third, and fourth places Jell-O salads are economical—ideal for the whole family—and they can be made hours—even a full day—ahead of time without losing any of their shimmering appeal!

The elegantly attired young woman sits confidently at a table for two with candles lit and her husband beaming behind the grand shining yellow Jell-O mold. She and the Jell-O are both objects of desire, and the implication is that the children are out, so both will be dessert as well. And like the Jell-O, she too after a long day has not lost any of her shimmering appeal or good looks. She too is light and refreshing and won't fill you up with a mountain of nagging concerns. Her hair even matches the Jell-O perfectly. https://www.alamy.com/stock-photo-1950s-full-page-advertisement-in-american-consumer-magazine -for-jell-34513481.html

There was another set of ads at the same time that emphasize the importance of weight loss for young women and muscle building for young men. That a product could do both is nothing short of miraculous. A young woman watching an exercise show on TV tries to touch her toes in similar fashion, but her very slightly bulging stomach appears to prevent her from doing so. "Now it's Time for Jell-O." The boy is given the same message as he looks at the muscle magazine and tries to lift dumbbells over his head. The product is all about fulfilling social aspiration—in this case by promising a more perfect physical appearance (see https://americasbestpics.com/picture/now-the-time-for-jello-H36TqH9x8).

One could go on deconstructing ads indefinitely, but my larger point is that sometimes a particular product perfectly matches the cultural desires of a particular era, and this is seized upon by marketing and advertising campaigns. It explains massive swings in fashion and how products once so popular suddenly see sales plummet when a new generation rejects the shallow aspirations of their predecessors. That is exactly what happened in the '70s and '80s. The response was to make Jell-O a children's food, offer new products like pudding cups and jigglers, and hire a new spokesman to sell the product: Bill Cosby—who is said to be the longest-running product spokesman in advertising history. He practically became synonymous with Jell-O.

Tom Lehrer

Among my favorite stories of popular foodlore is about Tom Lehrer inventing the jello shot. That is, before he became the comic genius songwriter of such hits as "Poisoning Pigeons in the Park," a patter song about the Table of Elements, the "Masochism Tango," and my favorite "The Vatican Rag." And before he became a noted professor of mathematics. Lehrer was drafted between 1955–57 and posted on a base in Washington, DC, working for National Security. Naturally, alcoholic beverages were banned at such a facility. Yet reading this dictum as might any Harvard educated wit, it didn't specify that alcohol in some other form was forbidden—say, a semisolid hydrocolloidal matrix (i.e., jello shot). He told this story himself to the *San Francisco Weekly* years later, that they were having a Christmas party and decided to experiment with putting booze in Jell-O. Vodka worked best, and especially with orange flavor, he claimed, which they put in little paper cups and sailed right past the guard on duty.

As we all know, recipes using booze are as old as gelatin itself; in fact you would be hard pressed to find a historic recipe that didn't contain at least wine or madeira. But the Jell-O shot is a little different. It's the extremely loose texture, the burning sensation of undiluted booze, and the chemical afterglow that leaves your tongue stained some lurid color and your head throbbing. And it has to be slurped from a plastic cup, which I guess for college-age kids was half the fun. Or better yet, scooped from the plastic and tossed across the room into your mouth. I've had my share, though I have no intention of ever tasting that classic version again.

Children and Jell-O

Whenever a food falls out of sync with consumers, the manufacturers and ad executives start thinking of ways to sell their product to a different audience. This might mean expanding overseas, seeking a different demographic, or slightly changing the product to seem new and improved. This falling from favor can happen for any number of reasons: changing societal values overall, the turning tide of fashion as people get tired of a product, or simply because consumers are scared by an ingredient—like red dye #40 or something suspected of being carcinogenic. All these various scenarios apply to the story of jello, generically speaking, and the brand Jell-O.

We might assume that this is a modern phenomenon, restricted to mass-produced packaged goods that are not staples but luxuries. These were products that people were only convinced to buy in the first place through aggressive advertising campaigns and astute marketing. But almost all foods experience a relative rise and fall in popularity, driven partly by medical opinion—think of how beef fell in popularity when associated with heart disease and obesity. Or think of how kale, once so lowly, suddenly became a supermarket staple for health-conscious consumers. Sometimes it is simply a matter of price and availability. Spices were once exotic luxuries, but when direct trade routes made them more available and the price dropped, they were no longer so special and were relegated to the end of meals.

Jell-O was one such product that matched the mid-century ideals of convenience and affordability, and as I have argued, was spectacular in a way that middle-class families approved. But then people began to look twice at the amount of sugar, the calories, the artificial dyes, and probably no single product dropped so precipitously, so quickly that the next generation found those darling perfection salads laughable if not disgusting.

Kraft, who owned Jell-O by this point, had two very distinct strategies for reviving the product. One was to push their diet gelatin line; the name D-Zerta was deserted and Sugar Free Jell-O with NutraSweet replaced it in 1984. The other new target audience was children. Bill Cosby became the spokesman in 1974 and appeared in TV ads with children. Jigglers was the first new way to use jello. This was basically just the same jello with half the amount of liquid, so it could be poured into little molds or set in a large sheet and cut out by children with cookie cutters—then best of all, it could be eaten with fingers.

Cutlery is a tool of social control. People who know how to use it can pass in certain social circles, but uncouth and lower-class people reveal themselves immediately by their lack of table matters. The more socially anxious a society becomes, the more obsessed it becomes with the proper use of cutlery. Victorian England was the worst. Egalitarian-minded Americans in certain periods fell sway to proper etiquette but by in large we dislike cutlery—we prefer hot dogs and hamburgers that can be eaten with your hands, or pizza. They are great equalizers. For the very same reason, children abhor cutlery. Not only because they're sick of their parents yelling at them to hold the knife properly, but because it reminds them that they are subordinate, inferior, and cannot pass in polite social circles because of their heathenish manners. Cutlery singles them out as undeveloped, incomplete. And along come jigglers, a food they are encouraged to play with. Bright and subversive. It was brilliant, and children bought it.

Other products helped out. No one of my generation can hear the words "Jell-O Pudding" today without wincing. Bill Cosby is now a name no one wants to hear anymore, for very good reason. But when I was young, he was the epitome of the upwardly mobile African American man. Doctor Huxtable had a great wife and children, a beautiful house, and a rewarding job. He made people think that somehow race relations were headed in the right direction and that black folks would eventually be economically well off. One generation knew him as a comedian and detective, and their children knew him as all the voices on the cartoon "Fat Albert." It was not surprising then that Jell-O chose him as a spokesman because he got along with kids so well and he was so admired by people of every color.

There were new ways to make Jell-O, too—pudding pops, plus individual cups that kids could take to school—although I think that made people think Jell-O was more of a portable snack than a proper dessert. Bright new flavors appeared—all of which successfully captured an entirely new demographic. If Jell-O before was for families, now it was for kids.

But this was at the cost of infantilizing the food entirely. Whenever a food becomes so strongly associated with children, no adult in their right mind would eat it, for fear of being thought childish or having stunted gastronomic senses. This is what happened to most candy, especially the super sugary kind. An adult might eat candy out of nostalgia or for kitsch value, but to admit to seriously liking it, one risks social devaluation. So the cost of becoming associated with kids meant that Jell-O became more and more distant from mainstream adult taste and would never under any circumstances be served in a respectable restaurant.

Sales figures are not readily available, but one I have seen repeated many times is that between 2009 and 2014, Jell-O sales declined from 932.5 million dollars per year to 692 million. I don't know if these figures are true, but they at least reflect the popular perception that Jell-O is simply not in fashion anymore, except among children, dieters, as hospital food—although even that is changing—and the unique favorite of Utah and the so-called Jell-O belt of Mormons.

Mormons and Jell-O

At first glance you might suspect that the connection between The Latter-day Saints in Utah and Jell-O molds is just a matter of quaint backwardness or maybe the result of not being able to drink, smoke, and indulge in other vices. Jell-O may serve then as a Freudian displacement, into which Mormons can channel their deviant urges and release them cathartically by sinking their teeth into green jello salads, releasing that primal angst and helping them cope with the many moral demands imposed upon them in a restrictive culture. Jell-O is a palliative, an opiate without the sting, and a respectful, conservative way to express family values in sharing a common traditional dish. It is what you bring to church suppers, to potlucks at friends' houses, what you serve at home, as a way to redirect the psychological discontents engendered by civilization's constraints.

Actually none of the above. People have eaten a lot of Jell-O in Utah, but just about as much as they did in Iowa. That is sort of where the present obsession across the so-called "Jell-O Belt" originates. Marketers at Kraft thought that they could sell more product by promoting it heavily in family-centric communities in the 1990s, like Utah. And they proudly announced that the state consumed more than any other in the union, something the people embraced partly because it was a little silly, but also it was fun. Then in 1999 it was announced that Des Moines, Iowa, consumed more than Salt Lake City. Was this intentional jello-baiting by the manufacturers? Who knows?

In response to the crisis, the chef at what is a really swanky upscale restaurant called Bambara in Salt Lake City (I had an exquisite meal there a few years ago) decided to sponsor a "Take Back the Title" contest. This was Scott Blackerby. I offer you the specifics because it's hardly a restaurant that would serve Jell-O, but this was a matter of state pride, and they did put some jello on the menu for a while. Honestly, I think this was all really just tongue-in-cheek, or green Jell-O-spoon-in-cheek, silliness. When someone makes fun of you for something, a way to diffuse that is to embrace it, ironically. Then the accusation is made to look more ridiculous.

Why else would they make a green Jell-O pin for the 2002 Olympics in Salt Lake City? Why else would they declare it the official state food? Bill Cosby even came to make an appeal in support of the bill singing J-E-L-L-O! But in fact it is not just a joke; it would only resonate if there were a kernel of truth in it, it would only be funny if Mormons really did love Jell-O—and they do. They won the title of biggest consumers again shortly after the campaign, and I think still hold it to this day.

Jell-O is indeed a marker of identity. It is something to embrace precisely because it is mocked by outsiders. It serves as social cement, gluing the community together in a way that kosher laws do for Jews or halal restrictions for Muslims. Not that anyone is constrained to eat it, but when you show up at a function and people bring bright Jell-O salads, it's a way to perform your identity, a way to confirm your status as a member of the group, and a way to proudly remind yourself of who you are.

Bompas and Parr

For the past 25 years I've been attending the Oxford Symposium on Food and Cookery. It's a gathering of food writers, scholars, chefs, and crazy people that involves serious papers on food history, culture, science, anything to do with food, and also exquisite meals. The best by far gastronomically was 2009 when the theme was Food and Language. One meal was prepared by Raymond Blanc, the other by Fergus Henderson, the two most renowned chefs in Britain. The latter meal was a tribute to Samuel Pepys, the 17th-century diarist who happened to write a lot about food and also witnessed the city of London burning in 1666. Notoriously, he buried his wheel of Parmesan cheese in the garden rather than lose it to flames.

Henderson's courses included ox tongue, anchovies, bottarga, venison pie, quail, rabbit fricassee, mutton legs, beef shins. Among the most delicious things I have ever tasted. The Banqueting Course of that meal featured "St. Paul's Cathedral Aflame"—an enormous structure with dozens of buildings representing the moment Pepys described, made entirely of gelatin by the impresarios Sam Bompas and Harry Parr. The little houses in red and orange were made of natural fruit juices and wobbled their way across the grand dining tables, one per diner.

Bompas and Parr were the sole practitioners in the early 21st century of an art several centuries old. They humbly referred to themselves as Jelly Mongers and made fantastic spectacles, mostly for industrial clients, state functions, and special events around the world. Their work blossomed into a full-scale studio in London that still pushes the boundaries of food as art in many different directions. The pair also published several books that scaled down their gelatinous creations for the domestic cook. At the time their work was very much in the British tradition of molded jellies with fruit flavors and sometimes alcohol, though now they seem to be doing more ambitious conceptual art on a grand scale.

What follows in the rest of this book is my attempt to revive the art of gelatin making and reframe it in bold new ways that will appeal to the next generation.

TECHNIQUE

Some Essential Tools

Molds are the ubiquitous vessel in which practically all historic aspics were made in the past. The shape of the unmolded jello was in some ways even more important than the flavor, since these were grand presentation pieces meant to be gawked at as masterful decorative creations showing off the chef's talent. An enormous quivering jello supporting its own weight is indeed a marvelous thing to behold.

Molds were originally made of ceramic, the moist clay itself having been pressed or poured into a plaster mold form, so that countless numbers could be mass manufactured without the use of a potter's wheel. But there are examples of a bundt cake shape with a hollow tower down the middle that indeed are thrown on a wheel. The original logic was presumably for increased air circulation and quicker setting. Theoretically, the filled mold could be placed in a basin of cold water for increased surface contact and a quick chill before the advent of refrigeration.

The tin-lined copper or tin mold has a few advantages—mostly light weight and durability. You drop a pottery mold once and it's done for. The copper does need to be polished, and it can dent too, but there are cheaper metal molds that resist stains and corrosion. These molds became decorative items on their own, often adorning the upper reaches of 20th-century kitchens, along with other kitsch.

Silicon molds appeared in the later 20th century by which time jello molds had gone out of fashion, so these were mostly for baking cakes or small muffins, though there have always been plastic molds for novelty brain shapes and other obscene forms. The advantage of these is not only indestructibility, but flexibility, which is a boon for those difficult shapes that need nudging out of tiny crevices.

I have never been much into molds, mostly because after you've used it once, the thrill seems to evaporate. But if you're a collector, then I am certain they will give you hours of joy. I think it's much more fun to use whatever you find around. The bottom of plastic soda bottles is beautiful; so are many containers you would just throw away without thinking twice about. Plastic take-out Chinese food containers were remarkably useful as molds, and so too surprisingly were plastic bottles that vegetable oil comes in. Once you start looking, you'll find yourself trying everything in sight. The only rule is that the base must be narrower than the rim for unmolding. On the other hand, you can cut thin plastic Solo cups away with scissors. Balloons likewise, though for some reason they don't expand and fill up the same way they do with water. A disposable glove works well. The most exciting mold I discovered was a blown-out egg shell. And of course any fruit or vegetable that can be hollowed out can serve as your edible mold.

Whatever mold you use, the standard procedure for unmolding is once the jello is fully chilled and set, gently pry the upper edges with your fingers to break the seal, very carefully without tearing the jello. Then dip the entire mold into hot water—either your sink, a large basin, or bowl will do. Don't let the hot water pour into the mold, of course, or you're ruined. About 30 seconds should be enough; metal conducts heat much quicker than plastic, so bear that in mind. Cross your fingers, say a Hail Mary, or whatever you need to do to evoke the mercy of the jello Gods. Place a plate over the mold and turn it upside down. It might take some vigorous jiggling or even a good thump. Or a few more seconds in hot water for the truly recalcitrant colloid.

There are numerous tools designed specifically for poking colors into your jello to make flowers, bunnies, or myriad jello art decorations. Most look like little spears and darts that hold a dollop of colored jello that plunge into the interior leaving behind a clean trail of pure flower petal, leaf, or bird wing. I gave it a shot for fun, and the results were ok, but I think with practice anyone could get really good at it.

The surprising tools I have come to use all the time in jello making are perhaps unconventional, but almost indispensable I now find. First are tweezers. I was once giving a keynote lecture at a huge conference at the Culinary Institute of America in which I made fun of effete chefs who arrange ingredients meticulously on a plate with tweezers. There was an audible gasp in the audience. Not 20 minutes later I found myself in the gift shop, buying culinary tweezers. I love them. You want to remove or add something tiny, they are perfect. I have one set maybe 10 inches and another smaller offset pair about 6 inches long. Serving much the same purpose, *moribashi* are long Japanese chopsticks, usually one end stainless steel and pointy, the other end wooden. They are tricky to use but once you get the hang of it—I assume it takes a decade or longer—you will be able to pick up and plate a single sesame seed. I'm definitely not there yet, but I like the idea so much and apparently am so profligate in my spending on kitchen tools, that I am willing to invest in such things. Long wooden chopsticks, which are designed for cooking, do not work with the same precision. In any case, many of the delicately plated ingredients you see here were handled with tweezers or sometimes the moribashi.

Even more useful is a blowtorch. I shopped around and ogled lovely culinary blowtorches for several decades, always promising myself that one day I'd find use for one, beyond crème brûlée. Well now I found it. But I never did buy the little handheld model, mostly because they didn't come with the gas cartridge. Instead I spent 50 bucks on a huge honking blowtorch from the hardware store. I use it to give a beautiful sheen to any jello by briefly passing the flame over. You can even sculpt with the intense flame. And if you have little air bubbles, a crack, or any surface defect in your finished jello, just get out the blowtorch.

For true sculpting, however, I prefer a cheap old steak knife, heated up over the gas range until glowing bright orange. When it cuts into the cold jello, it emits a high-pitched squeal and sizzles as it passes through. This itself is thrill enough, but even if you want a simple touch-up or a full-scale sculpting session, use a searing hot knife. Just don't use a good knife—it will be ruined, blackened, stained, misshapen forever. But if you don't mind, a sharp knife that was otherwise destined for the trash heap can be used to cut decorative patterns into your jello, which is as simple as it is fun.

A paintbrush is also very useful for touch-ups, applying color to the exterior of a jello creation. I keep them in a big ceramic jar with all my chopsticks, next to the stove.

A whisk is necessary for our whipped jello. I have found a metal mixing bowl is really useful too. I usually dissolve powdered gelatin in mine and then pour in hot liquids after. But if you need to, you can place a metal bowl right over a pot of boiling water to gently dissolve sheet gelatin or just to reheat a gel that's gone a little too thick. It's much easier to move around than a ceramic bowl.

There are also many possibilities for extruding jello, either using a plastic syringe, a piping bag fitted with a metal tip, or even an extruder designed for pasta. You can also have a lot of fun with a ricer, which is a kind of extruder, to make thin vermicelli-shaped jello.

Apart from these, everything you need should already be in your kitchen: spoons, platters, serving utensils. Look around and whatever you see that might be fun to use, give it a try.

Making Silicone Molds

There are two different types of silicon bases from which you can make molds that will capture a great amount of detail. One is a kind of putty, very easy to

use, fairly inexpensive, and comes with very clear assurance that it is food safe. The brand I tried is called EasyMold, which says you can even bake with it. You just mix the two little containers of putty and get this cheery purple silly putty. You roll a ball of it, flatten, and then press a little object into it. I used a few seashells. The downside is that it firms up in a few minutes, and if you try to do an object in 3-D or with various projections, it would be impossible to get it out of the putty. It becomes pretty hard. So it works on shallow objects in 2-D like scallop shells. But something like a plastic dinosaur would be embedded in it permanently. Coins would work well or even a pyramid shape. With children I think this is the better choice.

The other type of silicone base is a liquid, or rather two liquids you mix together and stir. It comes with many warnings, not to use wood to stir, or latex gloves or various other things. It's a bit scary. But unlike the putty you can put basically anything into a plastic container and pour over the liquid. And when set, it is very flexible, so even something like a little toy can be extracted from the mold later, assuming there's a hole cut out at the base that's big enough. It captures the finest details. The downside, at least the one I bought here in California (Tap Platinum Silicone), which is described as "an RTV silicone rubber which vulcanizes at room temperature," is that it costs fifty dollars a batch. And the lady from TAP plastics couldn't assure me that they had gone through all the FDA tests to make sure it was food safe yet. I think she was just surprised that I was going to use it for jello and wanted to make sure I wouldn't come back and sue them. I pass the store every day on my walk to work, so I didn't mind supporting them. I buy all my buckets and squirty bottles there.

You make the choice. The latter makes a very sturdy mold that will last a long time if treated well. I used two beautiful little conch seashells, the inhabitants of which I ate many years ago. I bought them at a market in Rome, and the lady explained exactly how to cook them. So they conjure up very fond memories, and I can use them to make a little sea-flavored snack anytime.

For using this particular mold, I suggest either a rich seafood stock made with white wine, or a dashi stock with sake. For even greater depth, try something like an XO sauce that uses dried scallops as the base with garlic, chili peppers, shrimp shells, and ham, all simmered together and strained. But if you want clarity, a nice rosé is beautiful and delicious.

Colors in Gelatin

Brightly colored gelatin is nothing new; only the source has changed—now they come in little plastic vials. In the past, cooks would have used natural colors from ordinary food, plus a few unusual ingredients. Medieval chefs favored above all else parsley juice for green and saffron for yellow. Sandalwood was used for a reddish-brown color. In the past they also used calendula flowers or tansy for yellow and turnsole (*Chrozophora tinctoria*) for a purplish blue. Here's a recipe from the 1540s, in the anonymous English *Proper New Booke of Cokery*. It was served at a talk I gave at the Getty Museum in Los Angeles, to great acclaim, though we used purple pea flower for the dye, which is much easier to find.

To make clere jelly

Take two calves fete and a shoulder of veale & set it upon the fire in a faire pot with a gallon of water and a gallon of claret wyne & than let it boyle tyll it be Jelly & than take it up and strayne it and put thereto Sinamon, Ginger & Sugre and a lyttel turnesole to colour it after your discretion.

Here are some ways you can make natural food colorings:

Most of the gelatin in this book has been colored by the alcohol that went into them, but sometimes you do want a bit more pizzazz. Using synthetic dyes is the easiest way to color your gelatin. It's cheap and the colors are bright. But making colors at home is not difficult.

Red

Peel three little beets and chop into slices or quarters. Your hands will immediately reveal the powerful potential of the beet, so wear disposable gloves if you are concerned about that. Put the pieces in a pot and cover with water. Bring to a boil, then simmer until the beets are soft. You can of course eat the beets too. The liquid can be used as a base for any gelatin, or reduce it further until thick, and it will be a kind of concentrated coloring. It will keep in the fridge for a week or so. But you're better off just making enough to use as you need it.

Yellow—Orange

A decade ago fresh turmeric was not available anywhere but Asian grocery stores, but now it's everywhere. Peel and cut the turmeric and use exactly as the above. It's kind of an earthy orange color. You can also use dried turmeric, but it can be a little bitter in quantity, and you'll want to strain out the powder if you want a clear jello. Although very expensive, saffron steeped in hot water gives you the cheeriest bright-yellow color. In the end, they don't look terribly different in a jello though.

Green

You can get this color with any green plant such as parsley, spinach, kale, etc. Just blanch the leaves in hot water to preserve their color. Maybe 10 seconds in the boiling water, then right into an ice bath. Then pound the greens in a mortar or, better yet, put in a blender to puree completely. Place the puree in a cloth dishtowel and squeeze and twist so you wring out all the liquid. This can be used directly in any jello for a bright green color.

Blue

Blueberries or blackberries pressed are the easiest way to make blue. Let the skin soak with the crushed berries for a while, since in blueberries that's where all the color is. Dark red grapes, likewise, need to sit on the skins to extract color in the "must"—and they will probably start to ferment too. Purple cabbage boiled will also give you a nice cheery purple, but tastes like cabbage. The brightest blue comes from the purple butterfly pea flower or *Clitoria ternatea*. (Look at the flower if you want to see where it got its name. Yes, botanists have a sense of humor too.) It comes in petals or powdered form and is perfectly edible, and can be mixed right into a jello recipe. It's easily found online. The coolest thing about it is that it turns purple in acid, the more you add, the more the color changes.

Mixing the blue and yellow will give you green and you can keep combining colors to get what you're looking for. White is most easily found with milk or coco-nut/almond/soy but it will also make your base opaque. Black is a little more elusive, though squid ink is pretty useful. A drop can darken your natural food coloring.

Having made a range of colors, the thing to do with them is a layered rainbow jello. You can get the spectrum of ROY G. BIV if you plan it well. Beet, Turmeric, Saffron, Parsley, Pea Flower, and then Pea Flower with Acid to get lighter violet shades. Though it might be better to contrast dark and light colors so you can see them better. Keeping the vessel level is key, especially if you're impatient and put the mold or plastic container in the freezer to set quickly—it may come out tilted. Also unmolding with hot water may cause the colors to run on the exterior, so you might want to cut the jello to show off the colors.

Calf's Foot Jelly (Escoffier)

When I embarked on this project in earnest, I kept my eye out for calves' feet, knowing that I'd have to learn how to make gelatin from them eventually. My regular butcher never carried them and the Asian butcher insisted that they don't eat veal—though they had enormous beef hooves if I wanted. Pig's feet were easy to find, and chicken, but no calf. I looked online, nope. Then one day I became a grandfather and decided I would make an array of meals to freeze for the happy new parents, only to realize after shopping I had forgotten a key ingredient. No ricotta for the lasagna. And the kids would be home from the hospital in a

few hours. In desperation and a hurry, I went to the local *really* crummy grocery store a few blocks away. When I say really crummy, I mean that I had set foot in there 20 years ago when I first moved into the neighborhood and never again.

The décor was still late 1960s with original signage in the aisles and a floor beaten into ruts by the feet of shoppers. Yet, it was much nicer than I remembered—apparently a change in ownership. They didn't have ricotta, but I'd use cotija instead. Then, I spied my heart's desire: dainty little calves' feet wrapped in a yellow Styrofoam tray.

The great champion of classical French haute cuisine Auguste Escoffier, writing in 1903, which was just before instant gelatin would make this art obsolete, offers a succinct recipe in his typical terse style. It is recipe 2651 Gelée de Pieds de Veau.

Take some fine soaked and blanched calves' feet, and set them to cook in one and three-quarters pints of water apiece. Skim as thoroughly as possible; cover, and then cook very gently for seven hours. This done, strain the cooking-liquor and clear it of all grease; test its strength, after having cooled a little of it on ice; correct it if too thick with sufficient filtered water, and once more test it by means of ice.

He then adds sugar, lemon juice and rind and cinnamon. It's exquisitely simple. The clarification is pretty easy too. 1 ½ egg whites are whisked with a glass of white wine in a pot. The gelatin is poured in while whisking, and the pot is placed on the fire. Then simmered gently for 15 minutes and then strained. The egg whites create a raft which captures all the debris which would cloud the gelatin. Escoffier also offers variants which include liqueurs like kirsch, maraschino, rum, anisette or wine like champagne, Madeira, Sherry, Marsala. This is the ideal base for any fruit jello made from scratch.

Aspic Base

Now if you want a savory base for an aspic, then you'll have to add more ingredients to make a rich stock. Normally I save chicken carcasses and wing tips, bones from pork or beef, basically anything that would otherwise be tossed, and wrap them tightly in plastic and put in the freezer. Lamb neck bones are great, as is oxtail, though it has become expensive lately. You don't want to use marrow bones, because that will mostly render fat. You want cartilaginous joints, tendons, skin, and nubbly bits.

About once a month I do a freezer dive and take out all the bones and put them in my biggest stockpot, simmer all day with aromatics. Normally I would strain and freeze the contents in plastic containers. I get maybe 4 or five quarts, which lasts a month or more. For an aspic base, however, you don't necessarily want to freeze it, and you need some other ingredients to make it gelatinous. If you can find chicken feet, they are great, but so are pig's feet. Note also you can use any combination of bones—there's no reason to stick to one type.

Unlike stock making, you don't want to roast the bones, which creates more color and flavor but will lessen the power of the gelatin. Rather, you want to do as Escoffier and blanch them. This means just put into water, brought to the boil for just a minute, and then everything dumped out and the bones rinsed in the sink. I find this gives you a much clearer base and prevents the need for skimming constantly. You can skip the blanching and just skim the pot more vigilantly, which is rather relaxing to tell the truth—good mindless but useful labor.

Next, return the rinsed bones to the pot and cover with fresh water and a quarter cup of white wine vinegar and at least two glasses of white wine or vermouth. Sometimes I use a whole bottle. Bring just to the simmer. If you boil it hard you will get deeper flavor but also ruin the power of the gelatin. Gelatin must not be boiled. The gentle simmering allows the collagen to melt slowly and retain its strength. Six or 7 hours is good, but you can let it go longer. Sometimes I put the pot in the oven on low and leave it there overnight.

For the final hours of simmering, add a few stalks of celery, carrots, onion, parsley, parsnip, leeks, whole garlic cloves, pepper corns, and about 2 tablespoons of salt. Sometimes I throw them in at the beginning though. Any combination of the above is fine.

Then pass the liquid through a cheesecloth-lined conical fine-mesh sieve into another smaller pot. I use a ladle to do this, so as not to disturb the debris too much. Then I transfer the stock to plastic containers and put in the fridge. After thoroughly chilled, the fat will rise to the top—which you remove, and a little grit will sink to the bottom. So scoop out the gelatin and put into a fresh pot. Discard the gritty muck at the bottom of each container.

At this point you can proceed with any aspic recipe, or if you want to further clarify it with egg whites as Escoffier directs, or if you want to reduce it further, this would be the time to do it. Also taste for salt at this point, unless you're reducing it, in which case taste after reduction.

With this aspic base you can simply throw pieces of meat or vegetables into a mold and pour over, or you can add other flavorings, basically anything except fruit.

Alternatively, you can just make a good rich homemade stock and then bloom a packet of gelatin in it and add hot stock in the proportion of about 1 tbsp to 1 ½ cup liquid. And the simplest of routes is to buy the consommé in a can and turn it into gelatin—which takes just a few minutes, but the taste is inferior and it's hardly any fun to prepare—and that really is the purpose of doing it yourself.

Pig's Feet

If you are keen to make a simple gelatin from scratch, pig's feet are the easiest, most readily available, and most tasty ingredient to use. They are traditional in most places where pigs are common and you will find gelatinous dishes throughout Central and Eastern Europe, from British brawn and Jamaican souse to Georgian Mujuji, and even similar recipes in China made from pork rind. Although many versions will use a clear gelatin base, it's hardly necessary, but you also don't want it completely boiled to smithereens. For this I used an instant pot set on slow cooking. You want to disturb the contents as little as possible, so if you decide to use a regular pot, you'll get the best results by putting the pot in the oven on low for about 7–10 hours.

---

1 large pig's foot about 1.5 lb, sawed into sections
1 shallot
sprigs of fresh thyme, sage
a few peppercorns, cloves, coriander, mustard seed whole

1 tbsp salt
1 tsp sugar
2 cups white wine
½ cup white wine vinegar
1 cup water

Put all the ingredients in your pot or cooker; they should be just covered with liquid. Cook very slowly as long as you can, without disturbing the contents at all. When done, carefully remove the meat and let cool. Remove the bones from the feet and place the meat and shallot in a rectangular container. Strain over the stock to cover. Let the gelatin set in the fridge overnight. In the morning scrape off the layer of fat and save for cooking. Remove the gelatin from the mold and slice, present on a platter with cornichon pickles, mustard, and hearty brown bread.

Isinglass

In every account of the advent of instant gelatin, authors write that before the 19th century gelatin was only eaten by the rich, mostly because it took hours of laborious and filthy preparation and only those with servants could possibly afford it. Tell that to every European peasant that ever made a chilled meat aspic—kholodets or head cheese or p'tcha. Then they say, well, maybe but a clear aspic took hours of boiling and straining, and fat removal, and clarification with eggs and straining again. Yes, but none of those actually take more than a few minutes and cost practically nothing.

Both of these competing narratives omit that there were two particular, almost instant forms of gelatin popular from the late Middle Ages through to the 19th century. Both have almost completely disappeared today, or have changed form so dramatically that they deserve a full explanation.

First is isinglass, which is the swim bladder or sound of several species of fish, but most often of *Acipenser huso*, the same sturgeon that gives us caviar. The swim bladder is a sac along the back of the fish, under the spine, that helps it maintain buoyancy, sink and rise, and keep its balance. Sturgeons rise to the surface and gulp air to fill it. These bladders are removed, opened up, and the inner membrane removed. Then they are dried and sold as sheets or folded up, but also shredded to make dissolving them easier, which is done in simmering water.

This was known in ancient times as *Ichthyocolla*, the Latin term for isinglass borrowed directly from Greek, which literally means fish glue. Pliny mentions it in his *Natural History*, book 32, where he says that it is the name of a fish and the glue extracted from it. It comes from Pontus (the northeast coast of modern-day Turkey on the Black Sea) and is used for pains in the head and tetanus. That's solid evidence that people ingested it, but it almost certainly was never eaten in the form of gelatinous food. Galen also mentions it, as used for leprosy and to remove wrinkles from the face. "It extends the skin and makes it splendid." Dioscorides in Book II chapter 88 says much the same about facial lotion. Until the early modern period it seems to have been exclusively for medicine and as a glue for artists.

How and why does it begin to be used as food? That appears to have happened in many places around the world at different times. China has had a long tradition of using similar products. But Western Europe appears to have learned its use from Russia. As Europeans began to explore in every direction for trade in the 16th century, Russia was a particular point of interest. This was partly an attempt to find a Northeast passage to China—which would have been shorter than the northwest passage up above Canada. England had a Muscovy company as early as 1553. Early in the 17th century explorers to Russia were sending back vivid descriptions. Giles Hobbes in 1619 described the process of making caviar and isinglass along the Volga, the "isinglass is made of the string taken out of the Sturgeon's back" (see Purchas' Pilgrims, 731).

However, the big winners in the Muscovy trade were the Dutch via the Baltic Sea, which is precisely why the Dutch word *huysenblas* (sturgeon bladder) was corrupted to the English *isinglass*. And it was the Dutch who became major suppliers to the rest of Europe.

Isinglass doesn't become a common culinary ingredient in cookbooks until the 17th century. Take for example John Bate's recipe for white jelly published in *The Mysteries of Art and Nature*. I'm not sure what makes this a mystery, but it certainly doesn't sound very difficult or laborious.

> *Take two pound of Almonds, and make creame of them, then boyle three ounces of Isinglasse in a quart of faire water, to a pinte, then mix with your creame, adding to them one pound and a quarter of refined sugar, and a quarter of a pinte of rosewater; boyle them all together a little while, and then strain it, and it is done.*

From the mid–17th century to the early 19th, isinglass was the preferred source of gelatin. Ideally it is completely colorless and odorless, which makes a perfect base for fruit gelatin. It was also important for Lent and fast days in the Catholic church when meat products, including ordinary gelatin, were forbidden. Not surprisingly, well into the 19th century Russia was still reputed to provide the finest and purest isinglass. Lesser forms were made from cod and hake. Isinglass from India was considered almost as good as Russian, and definitely preferable to Brazilian, which was said to have a fishy odor. The Chinese also exported several forms sourced from different fish and it can still be found labeled "fish maw" in Chinese groceries.

Its principal use nowadays is for fining beer and wine, acting as a flocculent, and causing spent yeast cells to precipitate out of solution. Interestingly, this makes it inappropriate for vegetarians. The result is that many products labeled isinglass are actually nothing of the kind, but simply bear that traditional term generically. Manuscript conservators use isinglass also for repairing sheets of paper or parchment, as it is an excellent glue, which is why if you look to buy real isinglass today, that's the kind you're most likely to find.

You might find the line in the musical *Oklahoma* in which a surrey with a fringe on top was described as having "isinglass curtains you can roll right down in case there's a change in the weather." Wouldn't that just dissolve in the rain? Well, real isinglass would, but the term was applied randomly to all sorts of other products, including mica, which is a thin translucent mineral formed into sheets, which is used in lampshades and early carriage windows instead of glass. You may have also heard of eggs stored in isinglass or *waterglass*. This is actually sodium silicate, not the fish-based jello.

Why did this product virtually disappear? Instant gelatin for one, but perhaps more importantly, the relative disappearance of the sturgeon themselves. It stands to reason that this particular part of the fish should become prohibitively expensive, like caviar itself. Yet for those interested, as the American sturgeon industry grows, the swim bladders have become available, albeit in raw unprocessed form. I found them, of all places, online from Walmart, sourced from Marky's caviar supply in Miami. They get the swim bladders from farmed American sturgeon. They were shipped overnight on ice packs. Honestly, I thought I was buying a single cleaned and dried bladder, but for about 50 dollars I got 10 little packages containing two fresh bladders each of *Acipenser stellata*—which is sevruga. Here's how to process them.

Historic descriptions basically only say that they are cleaned, the inner and outer membrane removed, and then split and pressed, and dried. Though there are also various ways they were rolled into quills or folded into book shapes. Drying in the sun seems to be important rather than a dehydrator and thankfully I received these when it was about 100 degrees out—it only took a day to dry on the roof.

I also experimented with some fresh. It was difficult getting exactly the right proportions. I learned that you can't boil them hard, just dissolve in hot water on very low heat, which only takes about 10 minutes. One bladder to one cup of water was way too loose. Four to one was too hard, but worked alright with added wine, lemon juice, and sugar, which weakened the gelatin. To give you an idea of how expensive this is compared to powdered jello, it was about 10 dollars for a cup's worth of jello. For a comparable firm jello, unflavored packets are about 50 cents per cup. But here's the real revelation—it is as instant as anything you will find on the grocery shelf and has been around for about 500 years.

One burning question though remains—was isinglass so expensive and only the preserve of royalty in the past? Clues are left in advertisements. In the *Sacramento Transcript*, grocers *Quereau and Johnson* took out an ad on April 28, 1851, and ran it several times thereafter. Their shop was on Sansome Street near Washington in San Francisco; middlemen would pick up supplies shipped around The Horn, and then resell them to miners in places like Sacramento and Stockton (where I live) and then bring them up to the mining camps. The supplies are completely ordinary: coffee and tea, sugar, beans, vinegar, vermicelli, soap, sherry, madeira, cigars, and then isinglass. Can this have been such an extravagance that it was served to miners during the Gold Rush? Maybe a few struck it rich, but to include among the staples? Maybe it was a luxury item—or appeared to be.

To return to my experiments—isinglass is instant if you want a cloudy thick gelatin. But light and evanescent required a little more work. This was revealed by Ethel S. Meyer's *A Practical Dictionary of Cookery* (no. 345), published in London in 1898. There she tells us how to make claret jelly with isinglass and wine. The trick is to clarify it with 2 egg whites and the shells crushed with ¼ pint of water and whipped, added to the isinglass liquid, and stirred, then gently simmered without disturbing for 10 minutes. The raft of egg collects all the debris that would make the jello cloudy, and with passing through a jelly-bag you get a perfectly clear gelatin.

Now was this really a matter of expense? Certainly not for an egg. Or of a great amount of time demanding servants' labor? Not really; it was a matter of expertise—a very particular skill that appears to have been lost in the past century. I doubt this was a conscious act of deskilling on the part of instant gelatin manufacturers, but that was certainly the effect.

Hartshorn

Hartshorn is the other historical and practically instant source of gelatin. As the name suggests, it does actually come from the antler of a male deer, or "hart" as it was called. If you go online looking for this, don't be confused by the common form today which is ammonium carbonate or baker's ammonia obtained from horn calcined with heat and distilled. That is a different product entirely, a forerunner to baking soda. We are talking about the horn shaved and boiled and strained to make a firm but simple kind of gelatin. Like isinglass, it had many medicinal uses since ancient times.

William Rabisha (The Whole Body of Cookery Dissected, 1682 ed, p. 33)

Take the Brawn of six Cocks, being steept in Water, and shifted for 24 hours, then take a quarter of a Pound of Harts-horn, and boil these together two hours, then strain the Broath out into a Pipkin, and let it be cold, then take off the top and bottom. Return you clear Jelly into a clean Pipkin, and season it as your Chrystal Jelly before; only adding thereto a little quantity of Chainny; if it be too strong, add some Rhenish Wine; if too weak, a small quantity of Ising-glas: You may put herein Majesty of Pearl, or if you please, Corrall after which set it on the Fire again for a quarter of an hour, more or less, according to the strength or weakness and run it through your Bags as aforsesaid, and preserve it in a Glass or Pipkin for your use: This Jelly is a great Cordial, very Restringent and strengthning to the back. It may be taken cold or else dissolved, being heat again, and so drank.

Chainny was possibly *Smilax china* or sarsaparilla. The seasoning before he mentions was cloves, mace, cinnamon, ginger, nutmeg, musk, ambergris, and rosewater.

Louis Lemery in the *Traicte des aliments* (1705 p. 263) clarifies exactly how hartshorn was made into gelatin.

The cornichons or the horns of the deer, newly sprung, and still soft and tender, are used much among the aliments. You slice them easily into rounds and prepare them in many different ways. You can also make a jelly from it, but you use principally for this the shavings of large horns of deer which you boil on a small fire in a certain amount of water, just until the liquid acquires the consistency of a jelly. After which you strain and forcefully press out the essence, then you beat the white of an egg with some white wine and citrus juice. You mix the jelly with enough sugar, a little cinnamon, and let it boil gently to clarify the liquid that you chill and let rest.

He adds that the jelly is nourishing, fortifies the stomach, and stops diarrhea, vomiting, and spitting of blood.

Here is another classic mid-18th-century recipe from one of the best-selling cookbooks of the day:

Hannah Glasse *Art of Cookery Made Plain and Easy* 1747

Boil Half a Pound of Hartshorn in three Quarts of Water over a gentle Fire, till it becomes a Jelly. If you take out a little to cool, and it hangs on the Spoon, it is enough. Strain it while it is hot, put it in a well-tinned Sauce-pan, put to it a Pint of Rhenish Wine, and a quarter of a Pound of Loaf-Sugar; beat the Whites of four Eggs or more to a Froth, stir it all together that the Whites mix well with the Jelly, and pour it in, as if you were cooling it. Let it boil for two or three Minutes, then put in the Juice of three or four Lemons; let it boil a Minute or two longer. When it is finely curdled, and of a pure white Colour, have ready a Swanskin Jelly Bag over a China Bason, pour in your Jelly, and pour back again, till it is as clear as Rock-water; then set a very clean China Bason under, and have your Glasses as clean as possible, and with a clean Spoon fill your Glasses. Have ready some thin Rind of the Lemons, and when you have filled half your Glasses, throw the Peel into the Bason; and when the Jelly is all run out of the Bag, with a clean Spoon fill the rest of the Glasses, and they will look of a fine Amber Colour. Now in putting in the Ingredients, there is no certain Rule; you must put Lemon and Sugar to your Palate. Most People love them sweet; and indeed they are good for nothing unless they are.

What happened to hartshorn as an ingredient? First hunting diminished, making a regular supply difficult and I think illegal to sell in the US, because it's game. More importantly, the meat industry supplied a ready and cheap source of hides and bones, centralized slaughter serving large cities, which is exactly why the gelatin industry began at the same time in the mid–19th century.

Ivory

For a brief period ivory also came into use for gelatin making. Lest you think this was merely an extravagance, it was actually the dust and shavings left over from cutlery manufacture—ivory handles being produced in the shops that went into Sheffield knives and forks that were used throughout the entire British Empire and beyond. African colonies supplied the elephant tusks in the first place. The preparation was long, apparently taking 12 hours or more to boil the gelatin out, and then it also required clarification with eggs, much like other forms of gelatin. The product gradually disappeared as ivory handles became an expensive rarity, and finally when ivory was outlawed in international trade. You might be tempted to boil up some old broken piano keys, as I was, but who would want to eat it, even if it did work!

Agar

Just south of downtown Kyoto lies the Fushimi Inari Shrine. From the train stop you run a gauntlet of tourists and food stalls and then follow a complex of winding paths lined with bright orange-red gates (torii), snaking up a mountainside. The earliest structures were built in the year 711. The shrine is dedicated to the kami Inari (kami is a spirit in Shinto) who assures good rice harvests and clean water. This makes perfect sense in this location; it is reputed to be the best place to make sake—the Gekkeikan factory founded in 1637 is nearby and many others. Around the same time (1658) an Innkeeper in the vicinity named Mino Tarozaemon having served his guests a seaweed soup one chilly night, threw the leftovers away—only to find the next morning that they had set solid. Like so many accidental invention stories, this should be taken with a grain of shio.

In Japan, agar is called kanten and the most common form is a stack of evanescent sheets pressed into a light rectangular bar that kind of looks like cellophane, and there are brightly colored versions too. This is dissolved in boiling water to make the gelatinous base. It also comes in shredded form and as powder, but people say the agar powder doesn't give you the right slippery-chewy texture. This can be used to make tokoroten which is a block of the jelled kanten pressed through a long wooden box with a handle and a plunger called a tentsuki. At the end is a little grate through which the gel passes, emerging as long clear gelatinous noodles. These are served in a cold soup with soy sauce and vinegar and sometimes dashi stock. They can also be sweet with a kind of molasses syrup and fruit, perhaps sweet red beans too. The kanten can also be served as little cubes in a dish called anmitsu with fruit, bean paste, and dark syrup, or made into little elegant confections.

These kanten-based noodles are similar to but different from kuzukiri noodles which are made from kudzu starch and also shirataki noodles which are made from indigestible konjac flour (glucomannan). None of these have much flavor; the appeal is all in the texture.

Agar also spread throughout southeast Asia, and the name *agar-agar* in English comes from Malay. It can set without cold as well, making it ideal for the steamy climate, and offering the sensation of a cool refreshing drink.

In the Philippines it takes the form of *gulaman* which is put into a drink called *sago at gulaman*. The sago are the tapioca balls or boba that you find in bubble tea, combined with cubes of the gel in an iced brown sugar syrup. *Gulaman* can also be used pretty much everywhere gelatin can be used in fruity desserts. It can also be found in halo-halo, another cold mélange of evaporated milk, sweet beans, cubes of *gulaman*, fruit, shaved ice, young coconut, toasted rice—everything mixed up, which is what the word means in Tagalog.

In Burma there is a smooth silky coconut milk jelly called *kyauk kyaw* (pronounced chow chaw), served in little cubes. When setting, the gel separates into two distinct layers, one white and the other clear. Vietnamese *rau câu* is another agar-based dessert that comes in flavors like coconut, pandan, coffee, banana, chocolate—sometimes all of these set in layers. Pandan is a fragrant green juice obtained from the leaves of a tropical plant: *Pandanus amaryllifolius* or screwpine.

Agar can be substituted for gelatin in any recipe, though the texture is quite different. It's good for vegetarians and anyone with dietary restrictions that can't eat pork or beef products. Although it has to be boiled to dissolve, its unlike gelatin in that once its set solid it can't be melted back into a liquid, which of course makes it stable even in hot climates.

How it's made is also fascinating. I was once given a little sample of the red algae called *tengusa* in Japanese. They're in the phylum Rhodophyta and in nature look like a thin lacy red plant—which is what its name means in Greek. You would easily recognize it on the beach—and both edible dulse and laver are in this same phylum of seaweeds. *Gelidium* seaweed is the source commonly used but so is *Gracilaria* which looks like thin strands. In either case the seaweed is cleaned and heated in water for several hours. Then it is strained, set and broken up, and usually bleached. All the water is then removed under pressure and it's further dried in a hot oven. Gracilaria, however, also has to be treated with an alkali to make it strong enough to set. There is also an alternate process of synaeresis used to drive off the water. Traditionally however it was left outside to freeze and thaw, which drove off the water before fully drying in the sun. The sample I had was merely poached in water and it made a pretty decent murky gel.

If you've ever worked in a biology laboratory you'll be familiar with agar as the gel substrate used as a culture medium in little round Petrie dishes. In 1882 Walther Hesse was working in the lab of the famous Robert Koch. Hesse's American wife Angelina (called Fanny) suggested using agar rather than gelatin, because it could remain set at higher temperatures, allowing bacteria and other microorganisms to multiply. Most microbes can't digest the agar either, so it makes an ideal sterile growth medium. With the agar gel Koch was able to isolate the bacteria responsible for cholera and tuberculosis. Fanny never got any credit or remuneration for the idea.

Grass Jelly

Although not based on agar, a sweet dessert similar to these, found in China and elsewhere through Southeast Asia, is grass jelly—xian cao or cincao. It is made with *Platostoma palustre* (formerly *Mesona chinensis*)—the twigs and leaves of which is boiled for hours with potassium carbonate with arrowroot starch and then cooled at which point it sets into a kind of gelatin. It's dark and a little bitter, fragrant and sort of smoky. It's thought to be good to counteract the heat—a yin property. It goes into cooling drinks and can be found in a can in Asian grocery stores. It also comes in powdered form, so you can make the cubes at home. It's especially delicious with condensed milk poured over.

Aiyu Jelly

In Taiwan and Singapore there is a jelly made from the seeds of a variety of creeping fig—called *ogio* or *wan tau long* in Cantonese. Interestingly, although you can find creeping figs even in California and elsewhere, they don't produce edible fruit without the wasp pollinators indigenous to Taiwan.

The large bell-shaped fruit is cut in half, turned inside out and dried and is sold like this, or with the seeds removed. These seeds are washed in a mesh bag, rubbed gently in mineral water for 5 minutes to extract the gelatinous pectin. Strangely, sugar can't be added or it won't set, nor will it work if there's a drop of oil on your hands. So the light brown gel is served cold with honey and lemon juice on top, in a drink, with shaved ice, or even in a hot soup because it won't dissolve in heat. Legend says the jelly takes its name from the beautiful young daughter of a tea businessman who accidentally discovered its curious jelling properties. In 2013 the Taipei Tourist Bureau declared the jelly the most popular summer snack food. In the US you can find the canned jelly in Asian grocery stores and tea shops that serve bubble tea, cheese tea, and the like. They often have aiyu as an add-in option.

Carrageenan

A cousin to agar, carrageenan was traditionally made from another red algae *Chondrus crispus* or Irish Moss. The name comes from the Gaelic word for little rock (the name of a village where it's abundant) and it was the Irish who first dis-

covered its gelatinous properties in the Middle Ages. A carrageen pudding was made from it by soaking the dry seaweed and then boiling it in milk, sweetening with sugar and thickening with egg, and maybe fortified with a dram of whiskey. It came into wider use in the early 19th century as a restorative for invalids and substitute for gelatin in desserts. In 1819 Dawson Turner in *British Fuci* noted that the seaweed "will melt on boiling and afterwards harden into a gelatine, which I do not despair of seeing hereafter employed to useful purposes."

The types sold for use in the food industry today are classified as Kappa, Iota, or Lamba, probably named for a college fraternity. There are actually epsilon and mu grades as well. Each is ranked according to the amount of sulphate it contains; the more it has, the less its gelling power. The first is the strongest and is made from *Kappaphycus alvarezii*. It works more or less like gelatin. The iota is made from a different seaweed, *Eucheuma denticulatum,* and is most often used for soft custardy textures, but sometimes is mixed with kappa to soften it. Lamba is just used as a thickener for products like eggnog. There are many different species used today and harvested all around the world.

Most carrageenan isn't used on its own to make vegetable gelatin but rather as a stabilizer and thickener in other products, so you probably eat it all the time without knowing. It's in ice cream and yogurt, soy and almond milk to create viscosity, in puddings, in diet soda and toothpaste, and as a stabilizer in basically any industrial product.

Carrageenan has been the subject of petitions to the FDA to ban it as a stomach irritant. Scientists on both sides of the issue have presented decent evidence and for some people removing it from their diet has helped with conditions like ulcerative colitis and Crohn's disease. For the moment it remains on the list of ingredients generally recognized as safe and it appears that for most people it is nothing to worry about, though there are many people who insist otherwise.

It can generally be used as a vegan substitute for any recipe in this book but must be prepared slightly differently. Rather than bloom in liquid, carrageenan tends to clump up. Many people use a blender to prevent that, but I've found that if you start with the powder and just add drop by drop of liquid while stirring, it will absorb the liquid—all of which should be added to start. Then everything must be heated to at least 185 degrees—or if you're like me, just bring it to the boil. Then pour it into the mold. As with gelatin, some recipes you want fairly thick, others soft and translucent. These two recipes nicely illustrate the possibilities. Also keep in mind that it won't set in a very acidic environment, under a pH of 4. I intentionally tested orange and lemon juice in a mixture to test this, and it worked fine.

The Simplest Negroni

Mix 2 ounces of gin, 2 ounces of Campari, and 2 ounces of white vermouth. Put 1 teaspoon of carrageenan powder in a small glass mason jar and slowly dribble in the cocktail while stirring. When it is entirely smooth, microwave for 60 seconds on high heat. It should have just come to the boil and stayed there for a few seconds. Then carefully remove, let cool, and then let set in the refrigerator. This is as close to regular gelatin as I've come with a seaweed product. It's still slightly different, but very pleasant. Interestingly, it comes out of the glass jar very easily without dipping in hot water.

The Bronx Cocktail

Usually this is basically a martini with orange juice, but I've switched out the proportions to make it more like a screwdriver with gin. Start with the juice of ½ lemon and 1 tablespoon of powdered sugar. Add 2 ounces of gin. Then put one tablespoon of carrageenan in a pot and slowly dribble in a cup of orange juice until it's dissolved and smooth. Bring to the boil and add in the rest of the liquid, continuing to boil for another few seconds. Then pour this into a rectangular plastic container and let set either in the fridge or even at room temperature. Turn out and cut into little cubes. Serve these in a glass with condensed milk and ice or ice cream. I think this would even be delightful in a poke bowl with raw tuna or salmon.

Cold Set Gelatin

During my research a good friend connected me with people at PB Leiner, a company that had come out with a new kind of gelatin that can be mixed without the use of heat. It's called Textura Tempo Ready. You need to use about 2 tbsp per cup of alcohol-laden liquid rather than one, but otherwise this sounded really great. Imagine all the raw products you could introduce into gelatin, let alone the fact that not heating up alcohol means you aren't letting any evaporate during boiling.

They sent me a few containers to play with. I made a simple jello with a cup of maraschino liqueur and some Ranier cherry halves. Then I made another half with milk, sour cream, and almond extract with some white chocolate chips. Both were set with 2 tbsp of the gelatin at room temperature and whisked, then poured into the bottom of a water bottle, so I got a pleasant little crenellation on top when the bottle was cut off. It looked rather nice, though I got some tiny bubbles, probably introduced while whisking the mixture. Normally these are only on the surface and so I take out my blowtorch and pass it briefly over to restore the sheen.

I was standing over the jello with camera in hand watching the side of the jello dissolve and not understanding what was happening for a good 15 seconds, despite the crackling sounds. This jello was extremely flammable and the flame was invisible. Regular gelatin is difficult to set on fire. It must have something to do with the way the alcohol bonds with the gelatin, or perhaps not in this case. I decided that it spontaneously combusted because I had been listening to KISS that day.

I think the greatest potential for this product, a version of which you can buy online from the Modernist Kitchen, is with fizzy drinks whose carbonation you want to keep in the final jello. Champagne is the obvious choice. The trick is stirring enough to dissolve the gelatin but not so much as to lose the fizz. Otherwise, there's nothing more to it than letting it set in the fridge.

Gelatin Flowers

Professionals in the business of gelatin flowers have created astounding works of art that baffle the mind in their complexity and beauty. Surprisingly, you can make a simple version with a few tools and a steady hand, even as a beginner. Experts use a variety of different gelatin bases for clarity. Carrageenan seems to be the clearest, but others use a very fine pork-based gelatin from Custom Collagen. Many people in Southeast Asia and Latin America use agar which is probably a better choice for the heat. I tried it with gelatin just for the sake of doing something different. Regular Knox gelatin will be a bit cloudy.

The tools you'll need are small plastic syringes and a few metal tips that are designed solely for this task. They come in leaf shapes, ovals, and a wide variety of widths. A full set is pretty inexpensive and they seem sturdy enough to last years. The whole idea is that you made a clear base and then inject lines of different colors into the gelatin, which if done well do look exactly like flowers. You inject a little nubbin at the center, colorful petals all around, and green leaves on the outer edge. With practice I think no species of flower would be impossible. This batch makes three separate gelatin flower arrangements.

Clear Base

6 cups water	6 tbsp powdered sugar
1 cup water	3 drops clear lemon or almond
6 tbsp gelatin	extract

Flower Base

1 cup milk
1 tbsp gelatin
1 tbsp cornstarch
1 tbsp powdered sugar

2–3 drops each of red, yellow, green, and blue food dye, natural if you can find it

Use three separate ceramic salad bowls for your flowers. Heat the water to boiling. As that happens, bloom the gelatin in a large bowl with another cup of room temperature water. Add the sugar to the hot water to dissolve. Mix the two thoroughly and let cool. Add the extract. Pour into the small bowls and let set in the fridge until very cold and firm.

Bloom the other tablespoon of gelatin in ¼ cup of milk and heat the rest. Mix the two. Sprinkle in the cornstarch while hot and stir thoroughly. Pour this into 4 very small bowls that hold about a quarter cup each. Add 2–3 drops of food coloring to each bowl. Let them cool until almost beginning to thicken.

Then dip the end of a syringe into the colored gelatin and pull back on the plunger to fill the chamber. Stick on the tip. And do the same with the other colors. Keep a spoon around and paper towels. Starting in the center plunge the tip right into the center of the gelatin and draw out while pressing down gently on the plunger. Then turn the bowl and do another line, then another until you have the center of the flower. Clean off the excess color that seeps on top, using a spoon and paper towels. Then move on to the petals in the same way, moving around in a circle. Then finish with the leaves in green around the edge. I then used the blue to create a base that accentuates the colors in the clear section. Put in the fridge to thoroughly set. Dip each bowl in hot water for 20 seconds or so. Unmold onto plates.

If you choose to use carrageenan, use one teaspoon per cup of liquid, adding the liquid drop by drop and stirring continuously, then heating the mixture and pouring into the container. You can also see what you're doing with the tools better when it's clear.

CHAPTER THREE

VEGETABLES AND SALADS

Caprese

When the tomatoes are perfect, the mozzarella fresh, and you have basil whose aroma fills the room, it's time to make this simplest of salads. Layer ingredients with a sprinkle of coarse salt, olive oil, and maybe balsamic vinegar. It's a messy dish and certainly not easy to serve as an hors d'oeuvre. If the tomatoes aren't perfect, the cheese wan, the basil not yet up to par, ramp it up as a jello. And if the ingredients are great, the result is better than the original, the tomatoes are pleasantly chewy and align with gelatin and cheese texture perfectly.

6 Roma tomatoes
2 packets unflavored gelatin
2 cups rosato, rosé of pinot noir
   or other type

handful of fresh basil leaves
2 ounces mozzarella (fresh or
   regular low moisture)
salt

Slice the tomatoes cleanly into rounds and place in a dehydrator on high or in the oven at its lowest setting until very crisp. Don't be tempted to add oil or salt. This may take a few days. Arrange the best-looking slices on the bottom of a flat-bottomed glass or ceramic casserole, leaving a half inch between them. Dissolve the gelatin in ¼ cup of wine and bring the rest of the wine to a boil in a pot. Mix the two, stirring well. Let cool down to room temperature. Carefully pour the gelatin over the tomatoes. I find it best to place the casserole in the fridge and pour in the liquid right there. But you can always rearrange the tomatoes if they shift.

When set, place the casserole in a sink full of hot water for 30 seconds. Cut out the tomatoes with a knife or cookie cutter and carefully transfer to a platter. Then take all the jello scraps in the casserole and microwave just until melted.

Roll the largest basil leaves together into a cigar shape and cut into long fine ribbons—a chiffonade. Place in little mounds in the melted jello. Place on top a small thin round of mozzarella or whatever shape you like. On top of that place the tomatoes set in jello. Return the whole thing to the fridge. Then cut out the shapes again and arrange on a platter overlapping. Sprinkle with salt. These can be picked up and eaten by hand.

Mushroom Lamb Aspic and Japanese Barley

Stuffed Mushrooms are classic. In my search for novel forms to contain aspic, big brown cremini mushrooms came to mind. Where else better than a mushroom and barley soup reconfigured? Cooked mushrooms lose their shape and ability to hold ingredients unless bolstered by bread crumbs, so I left these raw, but scooped them out with a tiny melon baller or ¼ tsp metal measuring spoon as thinly as possible. The warm aspic cooked them just enough.

I do call this a proper aspic since you are depending on the natural gelatin in the lamb bones. You can of course use any kind of well-flavored meat stock on hand and if necessary firmed with a bit of unflavored gelatin, but I like the idea of doing this completely from scratch.

For the Aspic:

2–3 lb lamb neckbones, shanks or any other nubbly bits
2 tbsp olive oil

1 stalk of celery
1 large carrot
1 onion

1 clove garlic
1 tbsp salt
1 lamb shoulder chop
3 large shallots
1 cup Old Vine Zinfandel
4 large mushrooms

1 cup Japanese barley
1 tbsp black sesame seeds
1 tbsp toasted sesame oil
pinch of mace
1 tbsp Greek yogurt
1 sprig mint

Brown the lamb bones in the olive oil in a large pot and the add the aromatics (unpeeled). Cover with water and simmer for 3–4 hours covered. Strain the bones and put into a container, let cool, and refrigerate overnight. In the morning scrape off the fat and reserve for another use. This step can be done way ahead and the stock frozen for several months.

When ready to make the aspic, brown the lamb shoulder and pour over the clarified stock, add whole shallots and the wine, and simmer very gently for an hour. Remove the lamb and cool, likewise cool and strain the cooking liquid and refrigerate until firm. The gelatin should be fairly solid. Scrape off any fat. Then heat the gelatin until liquid. (If your gelatin was not firm, add a tsp of powdered gelatin dissolved in the room temperature liquid, then reheat.)

Hollow out your mushrooms and fill them with the gelatin. Top each with a cube of lamb chop. Chill until set. Boil the barley in a lot of salted water until cooked but still firm, and drain. Arrange the mushrooms in a shallow bowl, surround with the barley, sprinkle on the sesame oil and seeds, then mace, garnish with yogurt and mint.

As always, multiply this by the number of guests as a first course, or offer them individually as an hors d'oeuvre, allowing guests to spoon a little of the barley and yogurt on top of each mushroom and eat with their fingers.

Tomatillo Tequila Jello in Tamago Spring Roll

Have you ever considered how many cultures roll things up in starch or a bread-based wrapper? Burritos and spring rolls presumably have no real connection, but the flavors inside and the way they're eaten are so similar. A good example of convergent evolution, two distinct species move toward the same solution, though unrelated. Like hummingbirds and bees sipping nectar from flowers. I decided to throw in another rolled favorite of mine. Though I seriously thought about shredded turkey or cabbage leaves, egg just seemed perfect and in terms of flavor, I think I was right.

6 tomatillos, husk removed
2 whole serrano chilies
2 tbsp olive oil
½ cup tequila
1 tbsp unflavored gelatin
1 egg

½ tsp dashi stock
2 spring roll wrappers
a little chopped cilantro
    slivers of carrot
lime or tomato for garnish

In a pan or on a comal, toast the tomatillos and chilies with a little oil until charred and soft. Remove stems from chilies and put in a blender with tomatillos and ½ cup water and a teaspoon of salt. Blend until smooth. Then fry the mixture in the pan with residual oil. Set aside in a bowl.

Mix the tequila with the gelatin in a small pot, add ½ cup of the tomatillo sauce, and gently heat until it barely comes to a boil. Pour into a greased square casserole pan and put in the refrigerator to set.

Mix the egg and dashi stock and cook in a large frying pan with a tiny bit of oil. Swirl it around so you have one very thin layer of cooked egg. Let cool on a large plate.

Unmold the jello on top of the egg. Roll both into a cigar shape and cut in two, trimming the ends if necessary. Moisten two spring roll wrappers with hot water and place on a board or plate. Sprinkle on cilantro and carrot. Place the cylinders of jello inside, fold in the sides, and wrap up tightly. Chill again until firm.

Then cut each on the bias and arrange on a plate with garnish of lime or tomato or whatever you like. It doesn't need a dipping sauce because the mole verde is already inside. It's spicy, crunchy, chewy, and refreshing—all at the same time.

Ouzo Jello and Greek Salad Deconstructed

This was the jello that launched a thousand ships and burned the topless towers of Ilium. My very first jello. And in truth I just happened to have these ingredients around, so you too should feel free to add whatever you have with store bought or homemade ingredients. I give you explicit instructions just in case you want the same frisson of delight I experienced. Most everything was homemade, so I'll explain how.

Good ouzo is easily found where most liquor is sold. I prefer Turkish rakı only because my grandfather drank it, and the elegant gentleman on the label reminds me of him. Both will cloud up when you mix it with water, so don't do this for this jello. You want it crystal clear. One cup liquor to one cup gelatin. Set the jello in shot glasses or any mold you like.

The olives came from my trees in the front yard. I follow the very ancient Greek method of curing. Throw the olives in sea water or water salted to taste like it. Put in a covered jar and wait about one year. At that point, taste, and if too bitter, change the salt water and wait a few weeks; if too salty, just dilute the brine with water and wait a few weeks.

Pita is made very simply by mixing a packet of yeast in a cup of warm water at about 110 degrees. When it bubbles up, add about three cups of flour and a teaspoon of salt. Make a smooth dough and knead about 15 minutes, then let rise one hour in a bowl covered with a cloth. Cut dough into balls about the size of your fist. Roll one between the palms of your hands vigorously until perfectly round and then on a floured board, roll into a flat round of dough. To cook, heat a nonstick pan on one burner of your stove top to medium and turn on another burner with no pan. The trick of this is that while you're cooking one pita in the pan, you're rolling out the next dough, so it's a continuous smooth process. Flour gets everywhere and you will sweat profusely, but it is so much fun.

Place your first round in the hot pan and while you count to 30, start rolling the next dough ball. Turn the dough over with your fingers and count to 45,

and finish rolling the raw dough. Then with tongs, move the cooked pita directly onto the open flame of the other burner, turning over frequently. Ideally it will puff up magically, but if it doesn't, no worries. Place the charred pita between two plates and start cooking the second dough. Then start rolling the third one. Continue the entire process until all the dough is used up. This will put the flavorless store-bought pita to shame.

Make some hummus with a can of chickpeas, tahini paste, lemon juice, garlic, if you like, and salt. Whiz in a blender. That's all there is to it, but feel free to boil dried chickpeas if you prefer; they do taste better.

To serve you can arrange all the ingredients on a plate with some good feta, cucumber rounds, and your ouzo jello. Or wrap everything in the pita. I made tiny pitas and served the jello as a mini appetizer. You will not be able to resist the urge to listen to a bouzouki and play backgammon.

Rainbow Salad

This is so colorful, crunchy, and delightful that I bet even people who pretend not to like jello will dig in. It's fine for kids too—no booze. Though if you want to add some, why not? You'll need a square baking dish, and fill to your heart's content. The key is making little bridges of celery that fit snugly across the dish so that everything stays in place when you pour in the gelatin. I used cold set gelatin so everything stayed crisp as well.

5 stalks of celery	juice of one lime
1 carrot	juice of half a small orange
1 tomato	2 tbsp sugar
1 small cucumber	3 cups of water
small piece of purple cabbage	8 tbsp cold set gelatin
4 jalapeño stuffed olives	Japanese Kewpie mayonnaise
juice of one lemon	

Place the celery sticks in the dish, trimmed so they fit in tightly, alternating wide and narrow ends. Finely chop each of the other vegetables, except for the carrots in rounds, and fill the celery stalks. Take all the remaining trimmings and mix them and put on the ends of the dish. Mix all the juices and water and add the gelatin, whisking vigorously so it dissolves. Pour over gelatin and let set in the fridge. Then unmold carefully, cut across celery to make long pieces of multicolored jello, transfer to plates, and squirt with mayonnaise.

Sake Jello with Candied Carrot and Seaweed Salad

1 cup dry sake
1 packet gelatin
1 carrot
1 tsp sugar

mix of Japanese seaweeds such
    as wakame, hijiki, red aka
    tosaka
rice vinegar, salt, light sesame oil
1 green onion

Dissolve the gelatin in a quarter of the sake, heat the rest, then mix. Set aside. Peel a carrot so it's cylindrical rather than tapered. Cook it in water with the sugar. Put the sake gelatin in a cylindrical cup and arrange the carrot right down the middle. Keep in place with a skewer or toothpicks extending over the rim of the cup. Cook the seaweeds and season with a light rice vinegar dressing. Unmold the jello and slice into rounds. Serve two with the salad and a green onion for garnish.

Caesar Caesar

This is a mashup of two classic dishes, both named, albeit indirectly, for the Roman emperor. The first comes from Calgary, Canada, and the other from Tijuana, Mexico. Apart from the jello and reconfiguration, they are classic versions of both the cocktail and the salad. This serves two because the dressing requires one yolk. It's an appetizer you might not be surprised to find served in the 1950s, rather refined.

4 Romaine lettuce leaves
1 tsp Dijon mustard
1 egg yolk
3 crushed anchovies or a tbsp of
    paste
juice of ½ lemon
½ cup olive oil
salt and pepper to taste
1 cup Clamato

½ cup vodka
1 tbsp freshly grated
    horseradish
3 drops smoky tabasco
3 drops Worcestershire sauce
1 tbsp lemon juice
1.5 tbsp gelatin (a packet and a
    half)
croutons

Arrange 2 leaves in a plastic container or bowl so they will hold the gelatin. Then make the dressing by putting all the ingredients in a squirty bottle and shaking vigorously. Make the cocktail by mixing all the ingredients. Take about a quarter of it and mix with the gelatin to bloom. Heat the rest and then mix the two. When completely cool, pour over the lettuce leaves, being sure

that the jello doesn't leak through. To unmold, remove the leaves and place on a plate, pull the jello off, and turn upside down. It will have the neat, striated impressions from the leaves. Squirt the dressing around and garnish with the croutons. Make these by cutting cubes of good crusty bread, drizzling with olive oil and salt, a little oregano and baking for about 10 minutes at 350 degrees. Add a grating of Parmigiano cheese and a grind or two of pepper if you like. If you want to make this a Caesar cubed, thrust many knives in it before serving.

Rhubarb Popsicle Jello

Rhubarb is a wonder among vegetables, among the few that are decidedly sour. It was once considered a medicine and was imported from Central Asia to Europe where it went into cooling syrups and electuaries believed, according to humoral theory, to counteract the heat of the summer and especially good to combat fevers. When I see the stalks for sale (the leaves are toxic) I buy it on principle although it rarely makes it as far as a strawberry rhubarb pie. I came up with this recipe while cooking with a friend in the Netherlands, online, both of us with a bunch of rhubarb. Perfect for staving off the doldrums of summer. You need some plastic popsicle molds.

3 stalks rhubarb	1 pack gelatin
1 cup sugar	lavender buds, or rosemary or
a pint of water	sage flowers
1 cup vodka	

Slice your rhubarb stalks into pieces and poach briefly in the sugar dissolved in the water, maybe 3 minutes. You want them soft but not falling apart. Drain in a colander. Place the pieces in the popsicle molds. Depending on the size of your mold you may get 4–6, but don't pack them in tightly, leave a lot of room for the jello. Dissolve the gelatin in ¼ cup vodka, bring the rest to the boil and pour the hot liquid into the gelatin and mix the two. Let cool and then

fill your popsicle molds. Chill until set. Unmold by dipping each into a pot of hot water for about 30 seconds and then carefully sliding out. Then place in the freezer on a plate for half an hour or so until very cold, but not too long or the jello breaks down. These are extremely refreshing. You could also use cantaloupe, berries, just about anything. And if you prefer these sweeter, by all means add some sugar to the mix and a little lemon juice.

Probiotic Gummies

Pickling was a former obsession of mine, that is, before bread and noodle soup, but after beans. A good friend called me a serial monomaniac, which is true, but I never lose interest in former projects. I still pickle. One I make consistently is called şalgam suyu, which comes from Turkey. The pickles themselves are good, but the real reason to make it is the super sour, spicy, salty vegetal brine, which is the most refreshing thing on earth. Vendors sell this in plastic cups by the Galata Bridge in Istanbul.

The proportions are not very important, nor are the contents, but black carrots are best. They usually come in a bunch of various colors, and I just take out the black ones. Get a big glass jar and put in a few peeled carrots. You can add a few pieces of cabbage or cucumber, or even cauliflower is nice. A few green chili peppers sliced open is also essential. Cover it with filtered water and add salt to taste. Start with a tablespoon and at the point that it tastes pleasantly salty to you, stop. Remember, you're going to eat this liquid, so don't go up to 4 or 5% salinity as you might with a regular pickle recipe. Then get a small square of cheesecloth and put inside some stale sourdough bread with the crust, a few dried chickpeas, and some bulgur wheat. Tie it closed and add to the brine. Make sure the liquid comes nearly to the top and screw on the lid. Leave on the counter for 2 weeks without touching, but I've actually left it much longer, even many months. When you open it, it will fizz violently. Remove the cheesecloth bundle and discard. Remove 2 cups of liquid and put the rest in the fridge to sip when you need a boost.

Mix ½ cup of the brine with 2 packs of gelatin. Heat the rest gently—there's no reason to bring to a boil, which would kill all the good bacteria. Mix the two and then fill small silicon molds with the liquid. Let set in the fridge and then remove from the molds and let get a little harder and chewier uncovered on a plate in the fridge for another few days. When to your liking, keep in a plastic bag. The color and flavor is so bright and cheery and the flavor such a surprise in this form.

Soju Shooter

Soju is just beginning to be found regularly in ordinary liquor stores. It comes in many varieties, but you're most likely to find either the kind that's made from rice and similar to sake around 17–18% ABV which is called for here, or the stronger ones that can be around 25%, which are luscious. And there are others distilled to be as strong as vodka. They can also be made of sweet potatoes or barley which are also really good.

4 raw escarole leaves	2 shrimp
¼ cup kimchi	1 tsp sesame seeds
Korean soju	1 piece of yellow bell pepper

Line small metal timbales with bitter escarole leaves to form little cups. Put some kimchi at the bottom to stabilize. Then mix a quarter cup of soju with a tablespoon of gelatin and heat another ¾ cup. Pour the hot liquid over the gelatin and mix the two, let cool, and pour into the cups. Then take shell-on shrimp and char them with a blowtorch or over an open flame using tongs. Peel off the charred shells and place in the jello with the tails hanging out. Sprinkle with sesame seeds and top with another dollop of kimchi. Then slice some yellow bell pepper and arrange the slices in the cup as well. Let it set in the fridge. Unmold by dipping the molds into hot water and sliding out the little shots. This would also work very well with crab or even smoked fish. It makes a pleasant opening to a Korean dinner, 2 per person.

Bourbon and Birch

My love for the flavor of birch goes back to the many summers I spent at sleepaway camp, living in canvas tents that opened up to the bounty of nature. One year I had a tent right on the lake, so I could cast a line from my bed. It was there that I first learned to eat and eventually smoke clover in a corncob pipe. There that I learned rudimentary fermentation with blueberries. One day a week we had "camp out" and the kids were expected to cook the hamburgers or hot dogs ourselves over open fires in the woods. It was better as an opportunity to play with fire, cook the fish we caught, and even more importantly make birch tea. It was just a matter of taking a little branch or two, stripping off the outer brown layer, and then carving off the inner green layer, putting it in a pot with water and a little sugar and boiling it. Sassafras roots were just as good if you could find a small sapling.

Who knew syrup can be made from birch too? It's a specialty of Alaska, and so much more interesting than maple syrup. I bought a few little jugs there, and the timing was perfect—someone had just sent me pecan flour and pecan oil. The heavens shone on this conjunction. I used little star-shaped silicon molds, but you can use anything.

1 cup bourbon	½ cup pecan oil
¼ cup birch syrup	¼ sugar
1 tbsp gelatin	¼ cup powdered sugar
½ cup pecan flour	drizzle of milk

Heat the cup of bourbon almost to boiling, and dissolve the gelatin in the birch syrup. Pour the bourbon over the syrup, stir, and then pour right into the molds. Mix the pecan flour and oil with the sugar and make crumbles like you'd put on a pie. Bake these in a 350-degree oven until crunchy. Let cool. Unmold your little jellos and sprinkle the crumble on top. Then put the sugar in a bowl and drizzle in just enough milk to make a thick pourable glaze. It's much less than you might suspect. Drizzle over the jellos and serve.

Borscht Salad

If cold borscht is such a delight, imagine it a little jiggly as well. What makes this different from the classic '50s beet salads in jello is that all the flavor and color comes from vegetables here, and it has a little kick as well.

1 carrot
1 stalk celery
1 small parsnip
1 small onion
1 beet
½ cup vodka
2 packs gelatin
fresh horseradish root
mustard greens
sour cream
fresh dill

Cube the root vegetables and cut the celery into dice too. Poach all of these in 2 cups of water, lightly salted. Remove them after just a few minutes, so they are still a little crunchy, but not raw. Then peel and dice the beet and cook in the vegetable broth until just approaching softness. Remove them to a separate bowl. Bloom the gelatin in the vodka, then add the hot broth. In a circular mold, arrange the first set of vegetables. Put the beets on top and then grate fresh horseradish on top liberally. Pour over the gelatinous broth and chill. Unmold onto a leaf of mustard greens and garnish with a dollop of sour cream and a sprig of dill.

Mezcal Jello with Blue Corn Pudding

Have you ever gone on a trip and become so enthralled with the cuisine that you couldn't stop thinking about it? Santa Fe was such a place. I went for a food conference and even took a cooking class at the local school. The chilies still haunt me. The alcohol used here is a smoky mezcal, mostly because I had

tasted it there and not long before in Mexico. Put any image of a worm floating in a bottle out of your mind immediately. Mezcal is the more complex cousin of tequila, and while a good aged reposado tequila can be a thing of great beauty and subtlety, mezcal made in the traditional way has guts. You sip it. And it goes so nicely with these southwest ingredients. Teparies are tiny beans grown here, after many years of neglect. They are ideally suited to the dry climate and sudden thundershowers once every few years. They hold their shape with long cooking and have a sweet nutty flavor. After many years of cooking beans in a clay pot, I tried the instant pot and I swear it does a better job than I do. As for the other ingredients, you can find them online or make a visit yourself.

1 cup blue cornmeal	2 packets gelatin
½ tsp salt	2 tbsp agave syrup or honey
1 tsp lard or butter	juice of ½ lime
1 cup brown tepary beans	1 zucchini
1 tbsp olive oil	1 tomato
pinch oregano	sprinkle of dried green Hatch
1 small chopped tomato	chili powder
½ tsp salt	fresh green chilies
2 cups mezcal	smoked salt

Boil water in a small pot and sprinkle in the cornmeal and salt. Stir and add the fat. Turn down the heat to low and cook gently for about 20 minutes, checking now and then to make sure it doesn't burn. You want it very thick.

Cook the beans either in a pot slowly, covered with water, or in your pressure cooker with the other ingredients. The former will take about an hour, depending on the freshness of the beans. The latter will be much quicker.

Scoop out some of the cooked cornmeal and form into an interesting shape with your fingers; I made a star. You can use a cookie cutter, too, if you like. Place the shape in the fridge to cool and set.

Mix ½ cup mezcal with the gelatin, lime juice, and the syrup. Heat the rest and pour over the gelatin, then mix thoroughly. Let cool. Then set your cornmeal shape in a bowl or mold and gently pour over the cooled gelatin, making sure the cornmeal doesn't break. Let chill together.

When ready to serve, turn over your cornmeal and jello onto a plate and surround with the beans, rounds of zucchini, bits of tomato, finely chopped green chilies, and a good dusting of the chili powder and a final touch of smoked salt. The mezcal will be fairly strong, so with each bite, take some of the other ingredients.

Tremella

There is a genus of jelly fungus known as *Tremella,* the name of which derives from the Latin tremor, to shake—so it means quivering or a little shaky. It was named by Karl Fuckel (1821–76) a German mycologist whose name is immortalized in species like *fuckeliana*, *fuckelii,* and the subject at hand *Tremella fuciformis*. It's rare to find in the wild, but in Asian grocery stores, it will be called snow fungus or dehydrated white fungus or silver ear. In Japanese its name means white tree jellyfish. It's a frilly cloud-like pouf with a gelatinous texture used widely in a sweet soup with both medicinal and culinary benefits according to Chinese cuisine. Because it is moist and cooling, it counteracts dry ailments like coughs, dry skin, and thirst.

Remarkably what you purchase is actually two species. The *Tremella* is a parasitic yeast that invades a host species (commercially *Annulohypoxylon*), which looks like a little black blob until the invader causes it to fruit into glorious gelatinous fronds. We tend to think of individual species all competing in nature, the very red in tooth and claw narrative Charles Darwin envisioned, but nature is rife with species that not only live off others, but act as true symbionts, each benefiting the pair. I don't just mean certain insects that pollinate particular flowers; I mean creatures that grow together as one—which is how life began on earth and how it continues with the colony of bacteria that thrive in the human gut.

The dessert soup (a kind of *tong sui*—or sweet soup) includes this fungus along with sugar and fruits like jujubes and longans, goji berries, and lotus seed. But any sweet dried fruits will be tasty, like prunes and dates.

1 cloud of fungus per person	½ cup baijiu or alcohol of
water to cover in a large pot	choice
sugar, sweeten to taste	3 cup hot soup
assorted dried fruit	3 packets gelatin

Rinse the fungus well and soak it in water for about an hour. Drain and cook gently in sweet syrup and dried fruits just until the fungus is palatable— about an hour. Usually people remove the tough yellow core, but I've left it on to make the final jello look dramatic in serving. Place each fungus cloud in a bowl upside down and arrange the cooked fruit around it. Then bloom your gelatin in the booze and add the hot soup, mix thoroughly, and pour over the fungus. If you need more soup to fill your bowl, that's fine, just use a little more gelatin. Let set in the refrigerator. Unmold onto plates and enjoy. One fungus can easily feed two, so don't feel the need to double this recipe.

Nopalito Slider

Like all recipes in this book, feel free to follow my long and laborious procedures that give me infinite pleasure. Or just go the easy route with this and buy a jar. But if you choose the former, I promise you hours of indescribable pain trying to find the microscopic spines stuck in your fingers, plus some incendiary heat a few minutes later when you accidentally rub your eyes with chili pepper hands. It's all worth it, folks.

4 young unblemished nopal	3 tiny Thai bird chilies
cactus pads	1 shallot sliced into thin strands
pint of water with 2	juice of 1 lime
tablespoons salt	½ tsp salt
an ear of corn raw (or better	½ cup tequila
yet, charred on the grill for a	½ cup lime soda or seltzer
minute)	1 packet gelatin

Begin by putting on gloves if you are smart. Or just get the largest tweezers you have—a thick Japanese type used for fish bones is perfect—and pull out all the spines from the cactus. Aggressively. Slice it into thin strips and soak in salted water for half an hour; rinse and repeat a few times until some of the slime is gone. (I told you this would be fun.) Then put the cactus strips into a jar and cover with brine. Close the lid. Wait two weeks. You will see it bubble furiously. Pull out a handful and rinse once more. Keep the rest for salads or tacos; they are deliciously crunchy.

Place these at the bottom of a flat mold and throw on the corn. Marinate the shallot and chilies in the lime juice and salt for about 20 minutes.

Mix your cocktail and dissolve the gelatin in about a quarter cup of it. Bring the rest to a boil and then pour the hot liquid over the gelatin and mix them. Arrange the shallot and chili in the mold and pour on the lime juice, then add the gelatin mix. Let set in the fridge.

When I unmolded, cut, and tasted these, they were very exciting, but actually so hot and intense that I wondered if they could make a good jello on their own, or perhaps something more like a condiment. On a flour tortilla it was ok, on a rice paper wrapper with shrimp quite good, but oh on a small Sweet Hawaiian Roll with a dab of mayo and some pickled herring, it was a smash. Put it on any sandwich, and you will be very happy.

Gỏi Cuốn Jello

When it comes to food, I am so easily swayed by whatever I see or hear. If someone is talking about a recipe, I have to have it. After hearing the incomparable Andrea Nguyen teaching the correct pronunciation of these Vietnamese rice paper rolls on the Spilled Milk Podcast, I immediately started making them. Then throwing in various ingredients like chicken in peanut sauce, leftover ribs, thin rice noodles, and then naturally jello made of the sauce they might be dipped in. The textures and flavors elide perfectly. Add meat if you like or not.

¼ lb thin "vermicelli" rice noodles	1 shallot finely chopped
1 tbsp vegetable oil	2 scallions, chopped
1 small red chili chopped finely	1 tbsp fish sauce
1 small nob of ginger, peeled and julienned	½ tsp sugar
	juice of 1 lime
	¼ cup chopped cilantro
4 rice paper wrappers	juice of 2 limes
2 leaves of escarole finely shredded	dash of sriracha
	1 tsp sugar
2 tbsp fish sauce	1 tbsp gelatin

Boil the noodles for 2–3 minutes or following package instructions. Drain and rinse. Then heat the oil and fry the chili, ginger, shallot for a few minutes, then add the well-drained noodles and the other ingredients in the first list. Stir well, remove from heat, and let cool.

Moisten the first rice paper wrapper in warm water until barely pliable. Lay on a flat surface and fill with the noodles and escarole. Fold up the bottom end over the ingredients, then the sides, then roll up encasing the contents tightly. Set aside, lightly oiling the surface so it doesn't stick. Continue with the other wrappers. Then mix the fish sauce, lime, sriracha, and sugar, adding enough water so you have a cup. Dissolve the gelatin in ¼ cup of the mixture and heat the rest. Then pour over the gelatin mixture, stir, and let cool. Poke a small hole in one end of the rolls and inject the liquid with a syringe. Let cool in fridge until set. Slice on a diagonal and serve. They contain their own sauce.

CHAPTER FOUR

SEAFOOD

Daiquiri Jello with Black Cod Ceviche

When you have impeccably fresh fish, the best way to eat it is raw, or just lightly "cooked" with the acid of lime juice and salt. Pair with a proper daiquiri, not the frozen sickeningly sweet nonsense served in most bars, and you have a splendid combination.

A few ounces of Black Cod
juice of a lime
½ tsp salt
a touch of green jalapeño
    chili, chopped
½ cup light rum
juice of another lime
few tablespoons sugar syrup
1 packet gelatin
¼ of a mango
chili powder and salt
thin slices of chili
sprig of cilantro

Cut the cod into small squares and marinate in the lime juice, salt, and chili for a few hours at least. Mix the daiquiri and dissolve the gelatin in ¼ of the drink, heat the rest, and then mix. Pour into the bottom of a plastic soda bottle. It will give you a groovy flower pattern. Set in the fridge. When ready to serve, cut off the bottle with scissors and serve the jello with the ceviche, mango sprinkled with chili and salt, and other garnitures.

Lobster Tail and Champagne

The only time I ever broke down and just had to buy an antique jello mold was in a shop on my walk to work: a copper lobster. Among aspic aficionados, this is the one to own. Whatever you put into it, the jello comes out looking phallic, and I think the manufacturers of these molds knew it. Incidentally, if you look on the wall in the kitchen of the Golden Girls there hangs the same one. If yours is a bit tarnished, mix some vinegar with salt and give it a good scouring. It will come clean. Naturally the only filling that makes sense is lobster itself.

1 live lobster	1 shallot, peeled and coarsely
2 tbsp butter	chopped
2 cups cream	salt to taste
sprig of fresh tarragon	2 cups rosé champagne
	3 packets gelatin

Most people dispatch the lobster by boiling it, but I assure you much of the flavor is lost that way. It is much better on the grill, but even that scorches the shell a bit. This method, while seemingly brutal is actually more humane and preserves much more of the flavor. First render your thanks to the lobster—seriously. With the lobster facing you, place the tip of your knife right between the eyes, and plunge it directly in and then lever it downward, dividing the lobster's head in half. Turn it around and cut the entire lobster in half, rinsing under water immediately to clean. If there is red coral I save that, but the green tomalley I find distasteful. Remove the tail meat and set aside. Crack open the claws and remove that meat as well.

Take the remaining shells and put them in a pan with butter, cooking them lightly. With a pestle, break the shells up as best you can right in the pan. Add 1 ½ cups of the cream, the tarragon, and shallot, and simmer for about 15 minutes.

Meanwhile cut the lobster meat into chunks and gently cook in some butter, just to cook though but not color. Set aside to cool.

Bloom one and a half packets of gelatin in ½ cup rosé and heat the rest. Pour the hot liquid over the gelatin and mix the two. Pour the wine mixture into your mold and drop in the pieces of lobster. It should come up about half way. Put this in the fridge to set.

Next strain the cream and set it aside. Taste it for salt at this point; it may need a bit or none at all. Mix the remaining cream with the 1 ½ packets gelatin to bloom, then mix with the hot cream. Let it cool completely at room temperature. By this point, your lobster in the fridge should be nicely set, so pour over the layer of cream. Let it all set in the fridge. To serve, unmold on a fancy platter lined with romaine lettuce leaves. And of course serve the rest of the champagne.

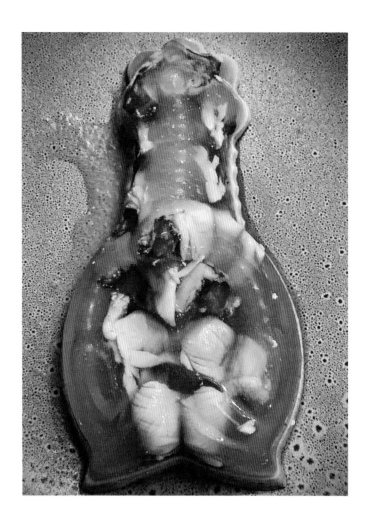

Takoyaki Jello

At the covered shopping street in Osaka (Tenjimbashi-suji), there are stalls where they sell little hot balls of batter cooked in a special pan with hemispherical impressions, each of which contains some octopus, aromatic seasonings, and when served is slathered in mayonnaise and a sweet kind of barbecue sauce. In your excitement you will probably shove them in your mouth and burn yourself while they're still molten inside. It is among the greatest pleasures on earth. I was dreaming of them when I decided to make a gelatinous form of the same.

2 whole baby octopus
1 cup dashi stock
Rice wine vinegar
1 cup sake
1 tbsp gelatin
Kewpie mayonnaise

Bulldog Sauce or okonomiyaki
   sauce
Seto fumi furikake (seaweed,
   egg, sesame seed, shaved
   bonito flakes in a jar)

Poach the octopodes in the dashi and vinegar for just a few minutes. You want them cooked through but tender. Chill them in small hemispherical molds, mouths downward, that are just big enough. Mix the gelatin with ¼ cup sake, heat the rest, mix the two. Pour into the molds to cover the octopus. Chill until set. Unmold—so you can see the legs curled around. Then garnish with lines of mayo and sauce, and sprinkle with the furikake flakes.

Champagne Jello Oysters

Over spring break 2020 (right before the Covid pandemic) I was planning to lecture on a cruise up the West Coast of South America from Santiago, Chile, to San Diego. I got to Chile only to be told upon arrival that the cruise was cancelled, and they would get me on the next flight home. I thought—at least I'll get to tell a story of the time I went to Chile for lunch. I actually spent two days there and vowed to eat nothing but seafood the entire time, three meals a day plus snacks. Clams in the Mercado Central, crab claws in the busy little Puerto Calbuco restaurant, scallops, conger eel, local abalone (locos) in an upscale restaurant, but the oysters were divine. For this recipe they should be small and briny, not big honking chewy beasts. And use a good dry champagne—the effervescence accentuates the brininess.

Shuck the oysters over a bowl, and keep any liquid that spills out. Arrange them on ice. Mix the champagne with the juice and a packet of gelatin per cup and a half of liquid. This is best as a very loose jello. Cool to room temperature and then spoon it over the oysters and return to the fridge to set. You eat them exactly as you would an oyster, slurping down. Garnish with a little lemon zest.

Jello Schmear

No matter what anyone says, there are no good bagels in California. It's not the water, or being boiled, it's the chutzpah with which they are made—and that's not a genetic thing. Some of the best bagels I've ever eaten were made by an Asian family on the Upper West Side. So if you can't get to NY, here's some pleasant diversion instead without the bagel.

¼ stick cream cheese

1 tbsp toasted sesame seeds

a few slices of lox

a few strands thinly sliced red
onion

a few capers

1 cup dry white wine or Dr.
Brown's Cel-Ray celery soda

a few drops of lemon juice

1 tbsp gelatin

Make a small ball of cream cheese, then flatten it between the palms of your hands. Press one side into the sesame seeds. Arrange some of the lox on top. Then add the capers and onion strands. Set this in a petri dish or other shallow round mold. Mix ¼ cup of the wine with lemon juice and bloom the gelatin. Heat the rest, pour it over the gelatin, and mix the two and then let cool thoroughly. Pour over the lox. Put in the fridge to set. Unmold and using an apple corer or paring knife, cut a circle out of the middle and serve on a plate. Something tells me this might be a hit with people avoiding carbs. Or expats from New York like me.

Bouillabaisse Hors D'Oeuvres

The flavors of a proper bouillabaisse have moved poets to flights of ecstasy, inspired great cooks like Julia Child, and have ignited as much gastronomic vituperation as any food on earth. I went to the Old Port in Marseilles to try it and was less than overwhelmed. Nevertheless, I made it myself for many years, without the proper rascasse, grondin, conger, daurade, baudroie—none of which are available in California. You just need a nice combination of shrimp, a light but solid fish like halibut or snapper, actually whatever you find. The more the better. Freshness is more important than specificity.

Likewise with this recipe. The shrimp are chopped so finely that they hold everything together. Thereafter, add whatever fish is at hand. It's not a soup, but it sort of is. Success depends not only on the quality of the fish, but a good strong fish stock. This can be made easily in about half an hour with fish bones and heads, celery, onion, carrots, and a few herbs, simmered and strained.

12 raw shrimp, peeled

4 ounces of fish

½ tsp smoked paprika

¼ tsp salt

½ tsp tapioca or other starch

1 tbsp olive oil

¼ cup pastis

1 packet gelatin

¾ cup fish stock

Toast rounds

1 clove garlic

½ cup olive oil

Pinch of saffron
¼ cup fine bread crumbs

Pinch cayenne pepper
Pinch of salt

Chop the shrimp very finely and add the fish, continue chopping, adding paprika, salt, and starch. Chop until you have a very fine paste. Roll into small balls or press into tiny decorative molds. Fry these in olive oil and let cool.

Combine the pastis and gelatin until dissolved. Bring the stock up to a boil and add to the gelatin. Arrange your fish balls in molds and pour over the gelatin until barely covered. Place in fridge until set.

Toast your rounds of bread. In a mortar, pound together the remaining ingredients, adding more bread crumbs if necessary to get a thick paste. Spread this thinly on the toasts and place the unmolded jellos on top. This will make about 10 small hors d'oeuvres.

Feast of Seven Fishes

Apparently in Italy no one has heard of this, but among Italian-Americans it's a beloved feature of the night before Christmas meal: in Italian, *La Vigilia*. Ironically that means exactly the opposite of a feast. Traditionally, since the early Middle Ages, days were set aside throughout the Christian calendar in which meat, eggs, and dairy products couldn't be eaten. These were fast days, days of penitence in preparation for a holy day. It's not that fish was seen as punishment exactly, but rather that meat was so very nutritious, because of its similarity to human flesh, that it was easily assimilated and converted into our flesh. And according to medical theory of the day, when your body replenished the parts that were spent in the course of daily activity, any excess nutrition (a plethora) would be converted either into fat, or milk in women, or more importantly into sperm in both men and women. Remember their anatomical knowledge was gained without any human dissec-

tion and without microscopes. So men and women had basically identical but inverted reproductive parts, they believed. What does this have to do with eating fish? Fish, because it is cold and watery and so unlike our own flesh, is not very nutritious. Neither are vegetables. So on days of penitence, you eat these so as not to stimulate the libido, remain penitent, and suffer while eating the food of affliction: cold salad and fish. I think fish is usually preferable to all other foods. I would have done fine during the medieval Lent. So I designed this penitent jello. You can tell me if it quells your libido or otherwise.

I chose 7 species prepared in 7 different ways, but of course use what you like in whatever quantity you need to serve your guests. This is a large jello that might feed 7 guests.

Raw sushi-grade tuna	anchovies in oil
boiled shrimp	pickled herring
dried scallops	1 bottle of rosé wine
smoked trout	juice of one lemon
baked salmon	4 packets of gelatin

Slice your tuna into decorative shapes and arrange at the bottom of a large glass bowl. Boil your shrimp, peel, and chill in ice water, then arrange in between the tuna slices. Soak your scallops. These can be found in Chinese groceries and can be hundreds of dollars a pound; buy the smallest inexpensive ones. All the other fish can be bought prepared. Arrange everything in the bowl decoratively. Then dissolve the gelatin in a cup of wine and lemon juice. Heat the rest and mix into the gelatin and stir. Let cool. Pour over all the fish and let set overnight in the refrigerator. When ready to serve, dip the entire bowl in a sink full of hot water for 30 seconds. Remove and place a large platter on top. Say your Hail Mary and turn the entire thing over. It should unmold. Serve festooned with whatever strikes your fancy and serve slices. Now fast.

Jellyfish Jello

Jellyfish don't have much flavor, but the texture is intriguing, especially when set inside gelatin, so you get chewiness, bounce, and crunch all together. It's very much like the tremella recipe in the previous chapter. I've added some nuggets of loveliness to ramp up the flavor and served it with shrimp chips. Incidentally the name in French is much better: Meduse. Don't worry, this one will not turn you to stone.

Handful of Salted Jellyfish
1 small piece of fresh tuna,
    about 2–3 ounces
small pat of butter
½ cup cream
salt and pepper to taste
handful of smoked oysters
2 cups sake
2 packages gelatin

Soak the jellyfish in water for several hours until no trace of salt is left. Cook the tuna in a pan with butter over high heat just until cooked and a little pink inside. Let cool and then pound in a mortar, adding cream little by little until you have a smooth and light paste. Season to taste. In a bowl or mold, place some smoked oysters and then the jellyfish on top. Put the tuna last in the center. Then bloom the gelatin in ½ cup of sake and heat the rest. Combine them and let cool. Pour gently over the mold so as not to disturb the tuna. Unmold and garnish with shrimp chips.

Smoked Trout Stuffed Cucumber

This recipe evokes early 19th-century Copenhagen at the time of Hans Christian Anderson. If you cut the cucumbers on the bias, they look alarmingly like avocado halves. You can substitute any kind of smoked fish here; whitefish would be great or even smoked herring/kippers. Of course pose as the Little Mermaid when you serve it.

1 unwaxed cucumber
1 cup Cherry Heering liqueur
1 tbsp gelatin

½ cup smoked fish, flaked
1 lime for garnish
Dollop of sour cream

Cut off one end of the cucumber and with a melon baller or long narrow spoon remove all the seeds. With the tines of a fork, scrape down the exterior length of the cucumber to create vertical striations. Sprinkle the interior with salt and turn upside down to drain a little. Dissolve the gelatin in ¼ cup of

liqueur and heat the rest. Add the hot liquid to the gelatin and stir. Let cool and then add the smoked fish and fill the cucumber with the mixture. Put the cucumber upright in a tall glass and let set in the fridge. To serve, slice the cucumber diagonally and arrange on a plate with lime juice and sour cream.

Furikake Shots

This can be made very quickly with a jar of furikake, which is a Japanese seasoning based on nori seaweed sheets and usually katsuobushi flakes, sesame, and other ingredients. It is exquisite and goes on absolutely anything, so why

not in a jello? It can also be made the very slow way, and since I spent many months learning how to make katsuobushi, including at the feet of a master in Japan for a TV show, I figured I would use my own. It involves quartering a skipjack tuna, briefly poaching it, removing the bones, smoking it, drying it, and exposing it to mold (*Aspergillus glaucus*). The result is a rock-hard wedge of pure essence of tuna. This is then shaved into fine evanescent flakes which are used to make dashi, which goes into dozens of Japanese dishes, including miso soup. You can also buy a bag of these flakes in a Japanese grocery.

1 tbsp sesame seeds
3 sheets of nori seaweed
6 large shiitake mushrooms,
    without stems, sautéed in oil
1 handful katsuobushi flakes
1 cup sochu or other clear
    alcohol

2 tbsp gelatin
1 cup dashi stock (instant or
    homemade with katsuobushi,
    kombu seaweed, and a pinch
    of salt)

In a square glass baking dish, make layers of the dry ingredients starting with the sesame, the seaweed crumbled, the mushrooms, then the flakes. Dissolve the gelatin in ½ cup sochu, then heat the rest with the dashi stock. Pour the hot stock over the gelatin. Let it cool, then pour over the other ingredients. Let it set in the fridge and then unmold and slice into finger-sized tidbits.

Lumache, Polenta Fritto, Rucola e Gelo di Cocchi Americano

That means snails, fried polenta, arugula, and a lovely aperitif called Cocchi Americano. It's not entirely clear whether the name comes from Amer meaning bitter or something like an American rooster, but no matter. It's a delightful greenish yellow color and looks very festive festooned with confetti—that is, confetti in its original meaning, confections. In the Renaissance these were spices in a sugar coating, sort of like the mix you see at the door in Indian restaurants. You can use colored dragées too.

2 snails per person, fresh or canned
2 cups polenta
1 cup milk
1 tbsp butter

¼ cup Parmigiano cheese
a few leaves of arugula
1 cup Cocchi Americano aperitif or a white Italian Vermouth
1 packet gelatin

If you are using live snails, as I have done with those in my backyard, the process of cleaning is a bit arduous, but the taste is superior. Essentially you put them in a big lidded plastic bucket with cornmeal. They eat it, and it

cleans out their digestive tract from any poisonous plants. That means you also have to clean out the bucket every day, for about a week. Be careful too, despite what you may have heard about snails, they can be fast and they will try to escape the minute the top is off the bucket. When ready to cook, you plunge them into boiling salted water for about 20 minutes. There's no other way to do it, alas, and if you happen to grow fond of your snails as I have done, just let them loose in the yard and let them eat your plants. But I suggest you persevere. You have to boil and rinse maybe 3 times or more to rid them of the slime. Test one before proceeding. If they're still slimy, boil for a few minutes more and drain again. Then sauté them gently in butter, parsley, a chopped garlic clove, and a pinch of salt. Now if like me you have scared the snails away from your garden permanently, look for frozen, or canned as a last resort. In Europe, you can buy them fresh, but I've never seen them for sale in the US.

Now proceed with the polenta. Boil it in a pot of salted water by sprinkling in a handful at a time and stirring. Lower the heat, and add in milk and butter. Stir more and cover, cooking gently for about 20 minutes. Then add the cheese and incorporate. Pour this onto a flat wooden board and let cool. When completely solidified, cut out rounds with a biscuit cutter or large glass. You can also put it into a plastic container and chill overnight in the fridge. Slice and cut shapes the next day.

Put the polenta in the bottom of your biscuit cutter, or if making many, in a cylindrical mold about the same size. Place a few leaves of arugula (which snails love to eat) on top and then a few snails on top of that. Make the gelatin by dissolving the packet in ¼ cup aperitif, heat the rest, and then mix them. If you're making more of these, just double or triple the amount of gelatin you need. Pour the gelatin over each round. Let set in the fridge. When you have unmolded them, quickly pass a blowtorch over the upper surface to create a sheen and drop on some decorative candies, which will stick however you toss them on. Cut each round in half to serve.

Smoked Mussels, Dates, and Pine Nuts

This looks like something from outer space, and the flavors sound equally bizarre, but I promise you, it's sort of like a devils or angels on horseback combination. The smoky savory fish combines well with the sweet dates, and the bourbon doesn't hurt either.

½ tsp olive oil
3 smoked mussels
3 pitted dates
1 tbsp of toasted pine nuts
1 cup bourbon
1 tbsp gelatin

Start by lightly oiling 3 very small silicone molds, bowl shaped. Place a mussel, date, and some pine nuts in each. Dissolve the gelatin in ¼ cup of the bourbon, and heat the rest, just below boiling. Then pour over the gelatin and mix. Pour that over the molds and let set in the fridge for at least an hour. The key to the weird look is to unmold, then slice each hemisphere of jello in half across the contents. Then stick back together, connecting the two bottom halves, so the cross section shows. You can do this by briefly passing over it with a blowtorch or by scoring with a hot knife and fusing.

Bacalao Stuffed Cabbage in Picpoul Jello

Everyone's had stuffed cabbage made with beef or pork; they were a staple in my house growing up. They're equally interesting stuffed with fish, especially dried salted cod which has an intense flavor and firm structure that can hold up to long braising. The saltiness and sweetness and acidity of the orange and wine make for a surprising but very satisfying combination.

2 small pieces of bacalao	1 cup of white wine such as a
1 small onion	picpoul blanc
¼ cup of golden raisins	1 tbsp gelatin
4 large cabbage leaves	½ cup crème fraiche or sour
juice of one orange	cream

Soak the fish in water for 12 hours or longer, changing the water every few hours. Then chop it finely and add the onion, chopped, and the raisins. Briefly blanch the cabbage leaves in boiling water until tender. Lay them flat on a board, and fill each with the fish mixture. Fold in the bottom of the leaves, then the sides, then roll up into little cigar shapes. Put the rolls in a small pot and squeeze over the orange juice and let simmer gently for about an hour. Get two small plastic containers that will hold two of the rolls each. Dissolve the gelatin in ¼ cup of wine, and heat the rest. Mix the two and pour directly over the rolls in the containers. Let set in the fridge for a few hours. Then unmold, slice each pair of rolls in half, and top with the crème fraiche or sour cream piped on top.

Laks in Aquavit

This is so simple, but I think captures the essence of Nordic aesthetics in gelatinous form. If you're looking for a good aquavit, Linie is excellent and supposedly gets its flavor from having been shipped over the equator. Aalborg is also great, which a bracing caraway flavor, but I haven't seen that around in a long time. Just be careful not to use some fake Viking inspired knock-off made in the US. They are dreadful. Brunost is just brown cheese made from cooked-down whey, sometimes labeled gjetost too. It's sweet and caramelized and tastes like a cross between candy and cheese.

4 very thin slices of wild salmon
salt, sugar, fresh dill
4 Finn Crisp Crackers (ultra-thin rye crackers)
4 thin shavings of brunost

chives cut into neat little sections
1 small gherkin pickle
1 cup aquavit
1 tbsp gelatin
dollop of sour cream

Sprinkle the salmon with the seasoning, wrap tightly in plastic, and put in the fridge for a few days under some other heavy foods, so it's weighted down. Then arrange the crackers in a shallow plastic container top or tray, put the cheese on top, then the salmon, then a thin slice of pickle. Bloom the gelatin in ¼ of the aquavit and heat the rest. Pour the hot liquid over the gelatin and combine the two, let cool, then pour over the crackers. Sprinkle on the chive. Set in the fridge. To serve, cut out neat squares of the jello, slightly larger than the crackers. Arrange on a plate in the shape of a cross like the flag of Scandinavian countries, with the sour cream in the middle. Or if you're serving many people, arrange them on a large platter.

Vatapà in Caipirinha

This begins with a recipe from a cookbook published in Buenos Aires in 1888—the *Cozhineiro Imperial*. It's a dish originally brought with slaves from Africa and then it evolved in Brazil. The main ingredient is a salted cod, which was a staple since medieval times through Europe and then adapted for the slave trade as a sturdy and nutritious food that could last for years without refrigeration. For this very reason you find it across the Atlantic world. Today the recipe is often thickened with bread, but originally used mandioca flour made from manioc or cassava root, which you can find in a Latin supermarket or online. Pairing it with the national drink made perfect sense, and since I was preparing this for Carnival, I went a little overboard with the decoration and hit it with a black light to make it look really festive.

For the Vatapà:

1 4–6-inch piece of bacalao (dried salt cod)
1 small tomato
1 small onion
2 *cumari verde* chilies and a few more for garnish (comes pickled in a jar)

pinch of saffron
¼ cup white vinegar
½ cup okra, cut into rounds
¼ cup dende palm oil
mandioca flour
crushed peanuts
parsley for garnish

For the Caipirinha:

2 limes
2 tbsp sugar

2 cups cachaça liquor
2 packets gelatin

Begin by soaking the cod for a day and changing the water several times. Put the fish in a dry pan and let cook on both sides for a few minutes. This

will help it fall apart, which is what you want. Then add the tomato, onion, and chilies and continue cooking with some water. Add the saffron and vinegar and the okra. Let this stew gently, stirring often. Add the palm oil, and after about 30 minutes thicken with the flour. You can continue cooking this until it forms a solid mass, but I like it still a little chunky. Set this aside to cool.

Cut the limes into wedges and crush them with the sugar using a muddler in a sturdy glass or with a mortar and pestle. Mix in the liquor and then strain. Bloom the gelatin in ¼ cup of the cocktail and heat the rest. Then mix the two. Put the peanuts at the bottom of your mold, arrange the vatapà over them, and pour over the cocktail. Let set in the fridge, then unmold onto a plate garnished with the parsley and more chilies.

The Deep

I was thinking of Chinese flavors with this jello, which is why I went for Red Star Ergoutou liquor (Baijiu) made from sorghum. You can substitute soju/shochu or any clear liquor with about 50% alcohol. Or use a less potent distillate if you prefer. Red Star naturally conjures up the flag of the People's Republic and there's even a patriotic museum in downtown Beijing with life-size figures showing how the product was made historically. It's quite cheap but an acquired taste, something vaguely reminiscent of Juicy Fruit chewing gum. I was very surprised to find that in the Beijing Airport a bottle of water costs about 3 or 4 dollars. A bottle of soda costs about 2. The same-sized bottle of Red Star costs the equivalent of a dollar, so of course that's how you slake your thirst.

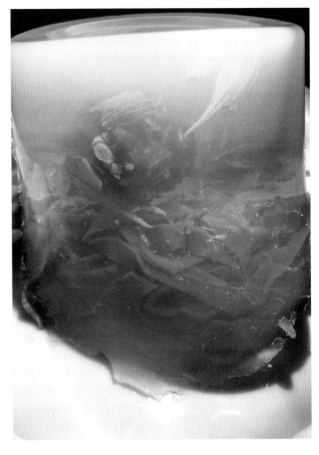

With this you are going for an imaginative seascape, so feel free to use whatever you like. I used small whole crunchy crabs—that are eaten shell and all. For the seafloor, use matcha tea powder to make the noodles.

2 tbsp Green Matcha Tea powder
1 cup flour
¼ tsp salt
2 cups Red Star

2 packets gelatin
1 tbsp sugar
assorted fish snacks such as whole crabs, small dried fish, etc.

Mix the tea and salt with about ½–¾ cups flour. Knead and roll out and cut into wide noodles. Boil these until tender and rinse with cold water. Arrange these at the bottom of a plastic container.

Mix ½ cup liquor with the gelatin to bloom. Heat the rest, being sure to use a wide pot with a lid so the liquor doesn't ignite. Mix the two and let cool. Pour over the noodles and let set in the refrigerator until still liquid but just beginning to gel. Place in your crabs, fish, and whatever decorative bits you like so they're suspended in the gel. Return to the fridge to fully set. Serve. Consume with wild abandon, thrashing like a shark.

Jellied Eels

This is a traditional dish of London's East End. I once had a free day in the city and made a long circuitous perambulation from Piccadilly to F. Cooke's shop in Hoxton, one of the few remaining traditional purveyors left. It was a sparse,

tiled space, and I was the only person there. The man behind the counter had to yell to someone downstairs to bring up a bucket of eels. They don't serve alcohol, but I said I'd be happy with whatever they had, which turned out to be a single can of lukewarm Orange Fanta. The eels were exquisite. A little sour, and slightly sweet, with a loose gelatinous spume surrounding the bony rounds of fish. It never occurred to me to make it at home, until I noticed some frozen conger eels in my local Asian supermarket. Cooking them could not have been easier—a simple long poaching in water with a little vinegar and salt and some onion. That mixture is cooled, strained, and let set in the fridge. It was not quite as good as those in London, but still if you've got a bit of honey, I'll give you a jelly. (Cockney rhyming slang: if you have money, I'll give you a deal. Jellied eel rhymes with deal.)

Gefilte Wild King Salmon

It is not unheard of to make gefilte fish with salmon, but I think the generous effluvia of what in my family growing up was called "snots" will make this an exceptional expression of the classic dish. The word *gefilte* has nothing to do with filter—but rather full or stuffed, which apparently the original dish was, a whole fish with stuffing, baked. How it came to be a poached quenelle, and then something only bought in a jar, remains a mystery. If you use a fish like pike or carp the bones in the stock will create their own gelatinous goo, but in this case, with salmon, a little extra help is necessary.

1 carcass of wild salmon,
  including head, fins, and
  backbone
2 peeled carrots
small onion, peeled and stuck
  with cloves
generous sprig of dill
2 celery stalks with leaves
1 tsp salt
¼ cup potato starch
½ tsp salt or more to taste
1 pack gelatin
½ cup rosé wine

Cut as much of the flesh off the carcass as you can. Ideally, you'll have about 2 cups. Put the remaining bones in a stockpot with the vegetables. Cover barely with water and add salt. Bring to a simmer and let gently cook for about 30 minutes. In the meantime, chop the salmon until you have a smooth paste. Add the potato starch until it just comes together and add salt. (Traditionally matzoh meal and egg would be used, and you can certainly use that here instead.) Then strain the stock through a fine sieve lined with cheesecloth into a clean pot. Use a ladle without disturbing the muck, so you'll have a clear gelatin. Using two spoons, form little football shapes of the salmon and drop them in the just barely simmering clarified stock. Remove with a slotted spoon after about 5 minutes and place in a large jar. Include the cooked carrot, cut into neat rounds. Then bloom

the gelatin in the wine, add two cups of hot stock, and mix. Pour over the fish in the jar and put the lid on. Chill in the fridge; it should last a week or so, but is not really shelf stable, but you can process in a pressure canner if you want to keep some jars in your larder.

Frog Aspic

Frog's legs do not taste like chicken. They're sweeter and faintly fishy, which is a good thing. The few times I've had them freshly netted from a pond, they were astounding. But you can still use frozen legs in a pinch, as I did here. If you prefer to bone them for this dish, that's fine, but I like the way they look intact. Just eat it with a knife and fork. As always, multiply this recipe for the number of guests.

1 pair of frog's legs still attached
salt, pepper, cayenne pepper to season
1 tbsp olive oil
½ cup fresh rosemary flowers

½ cup aqua vitae
½ cup water
1 tbsp gelatin
A few drops lemon juice and pinch of sugar

Season the frog's legs and sear in the olive oil until cooked through. You can also grill them if you prefer. Then place them in a shallow oval tart mold and sprinkle with the flowers. Then mix the aqua vitae or other clear alcohol with the gelatin to bloom, heat the water, and pour over to combine the two. Add the lemon and sugar. Let cool and then pour over the legs. Let set in the fridge. To decorate, remove the jello from the mold and place on a plate. Heat an old steak knife over direct flame until red hot. Singe indentations into the edges of the jello. They don't have to be regular—in fact random clefts make the whole look organic, like some kind of sea creature.

CHAPTER 5

MEAT AND POULTRY

Power Lunch or the BLTini

I had been playing around with jello for a couple of months posting blithely on social media for my own entertainment, when one particular experiment, sort of a joke, struck a chord. Reactions were so positive and so viciously negative that I decided then and there that I had to write a book. The flavors were nothing frightening and side by side, in alternating mouthfuls, no one would be shocked. But putting a BLT inside a martini jello for some reason both escalated me into online stardom among aspic afficionados, but also incurred the wrath of casual observers. Several thousand likes in various places, even more shares, and people hailing me as savior or antichrist (I still cherish the latter) was fairly bizarre. In retrospect it wasn't a big deal, but I do enjoy seeing the image pirated in very surprising places. More importantly: how to make it?

1 lb or so pork belly with skin removed
1 tbsp salt
¼ tsp Instacure #1 (pink curing salt)
1 tbsp sugar
pinch of mace
a few crisp lettuce leaves

the best biggest roundest sweetest tomato you ever saw
½ cup gin (I used Bombay Sapphire)
¼ cup Dry White Vermouth
1 packet gelatin
green pimento stuffed olives
fancy toothpicks or skewers

Coat the pork belly in the dry ingredients and leave in fridge for a week to 10 days. Then remove and smoke slowly over oak for 2–3 hours. The temperature shouldn't be so hot that you can't touch the smoker. Next steam the entire belly for about 30 minutes and cut into ¼-thick inch slices. Or you can slice the smoked belly after smoking and cook it gently in a pan. I find the steamed version softer and more pleasant to eat in gelatin. Thin slices of ordinary bacon doesn't work, but a premade piece of slab bacon steamed would.

Get a flat square vessel such as the bottom of a big paper milk carton or plastic container, arrange the pork belly, lettuce, and tomato on top. Take two skewers and run them through the olive and then into the BLT.

Heat the gin, mix the vermouth and gelatin to dissolve, then pour over the gin and mix the two. Let cool and pour over the BLT right up to the olive. Let set in the fridge. Unmold and cut diagonally. Frighten your friends. Makes two triangles, but of course you can make a whole plateful.

Tower of Meat—Veal Tongue in Aspic

The summer I spent doing research at the Vatican Library I became a regular customer at a small local salumeria in the Prati neighborhood. They had cured meats, sausages, cheeses and the like hanging from the ceiling and a *coppa di testa* that was ethereal. The only comparable thing found in the US is headcheese, which can be very good. This is a perfectly lovely and delicate cousin, and feel free to use chicken or turkey if you prefer. The key is a very firm gelatin so it can be sliced, and a little sourness. Perfect for a light supper.

For a mold, I found a cylindrical plastic bottle works best, just cut off the top.

2 veal's tongues or other meat, about 1 pound

¼ tsp Instacure #1 (pink curing salt)

½ tsp sugar

2 tsp salt

pinch each of whole spices: black pepper, coriander, cumin, caraway, fennel

1 lb calf, pig, or chicken feet or combination of these

2 cups dry white wine

Aromatics: 2 stalks celery, 2 carrots, one onion quartered, sprig of thyme

¼ cup white wine vinegar

Water to cover

2 tsp salt

Begin by curing the tongue. Mix with the other ingredients in a well-sealed plastic bag and place in the refrigerator for a week, turning now and then.

Start the aspic by parboiling the feet for about 3 minutes, then running under cold water and washing well. This will assure a clear aspic. Then return to the pot with fresh cold water, bring to a simmer, and let cook gently for about 4 hours or longer with the aromatics and other ingredients.

Steam the tongue, spices and all, gently for 2 hours. Let cool. Peel and cut the meat into small cubes and set aside.

Strain the aspic using a ladle, pouring the liquid gently through a sieve lined with several layers of cheesecloth. Don't just dump the whole pot through or it will become cloudy. Then return to a smaller pot and reduce by simmering further until you have 3 cups. Don't let the pot boil or you will compromise its firmness. It sounds like a lot of fuss, but it is really simple.

Pour the cubes of meat into your bottle, then pour over the cooled aspic. Let chill and firm up overnight in the fridge. Cut the bottle off with a pair of sturdy scissors and you will have a tower of meat. You can serve it this way for jiggly effect, or slice into ½-inch rounds and arrange beautifully on a platter. Garnish with a fruit that will complement it nicely—I used persimmons, but apples or pears would be great and a dab of mustard. Beer goes perfectly, but so does an icy shot of Jäger.

Perry Pheasant

If you come across a wild pheasant, consider yourself blessed. The one I used was frozen and had been sitting in my grocer's freezer section too long, so they lowered the price from about 35 bucks to 6, quite randomly. Still good. The pairing with pear came to me in a dream.

1 pheasant
salt, pepper, and thyme
1 cup arborio rice
1 cup chicken stock (or pheasant), heated
A handful of shiitake mushrooms without the stems, sliced
1 tbsp butter

1 tsp of sliced truffles
2 tbsp grated parmesan cheese
2 cups perry (cider made from pears)
½ cup pear brandy (40% ABV not sweet liqueur)
2 packs gelatin
1 bosc pear for garnish

Cut up the pheasant exactly as you would a chicken, by removing the legs and wings and slicing along the breastbone to remove each half of the breast with the skin. Save the parts for another dish, and the carcass for stock—which of course you can use here. Season the breasts with salt, pepper, and thyme. Sear them in a hot pan with olive oil until just cooked though. Set aside to cool.

Put the rice in the pan with a little more oil and cook until toasty. At the same time gently sauté the mushrooms in butter in another pan. When the rice is golden but not yet brown, add the stock all at once and stir. Lower the heat and cover; let cook for about 20 minutes. Stir in the truffles and cheese, and let rest until cool.

Place the breasts in shallow oval molds or some other container. I confess, I actually used my granddaughter's segmented plastic baby plate. Put a spoon of rice in small round molds. Then heat the perry, bloom the gelatin in the brandy, and mix the two together. Let cool. Pour over the breasts and the rice in their molds. Let chill. Remove from the molds, arrange on a plate, and garnish with fresh pear.

Bullshot Jello with Marrowbone Shortbread and Pickled Lemon

The bullshot is a classic mid-century cocktail but gained a certain popularity in the 1980s. For some reason I picture Tom Cruise ordering it in a bar. As a cocktail, it's pleasantly savory but strange enough that you won't want to sip too much. As a jello, it replicates the smooth creaminess of roasted marrow without being quite as unctuous. Scooped onto the shortbread with a dab of the lemon, it's a marvel.

3 four-inch sawed marrow bone tubes

1 tsp powdered gelatin

¾ cup vodka

¾ cup homemade beef stock (see recipe)

1 cup flour or more

1 tsp crushed fennel seed

½ tsp salt

¼ tsp sugar

1 pickled meyer lemon*

Briefly blanch the bones in boiling water. Remove from water and push out the interior marrow fat with a small knife into a small pot. Simmer the fat on very low heat until melted. Boil the hollow bones about 15 minutes to clean and scrape off any connective tissue on the exterior. Strain the melted fat though a small sieve and reserve.

Carve down three champagne corks to plug the bottom hole of the bones and so each will stand upright. Be sure they are very tight or they will leak. If you have doubts, dribble a little hot candle wax into the bottom of each. Then dissolve the gelatin in the vodka for 10 minutes and bring the stock to the boil. I have deliberately used very little gelatin to keep the final jello soft. Mix the two liquids. Arrange the bones upright in a container so they don't spill, and pour in the hot gelatin; move to the refrigerator until set.

Mix the flour, marrow fat, fennel, and salt into a short crust pastry with just enough cold water to bring everything together. Roll out ½-inch thick onto a square of parchment paper and cut into long rectangles. Bake about 15 minutes at 350 degrees. Watch carefully so they don't burn. Remove from the oven and let cool.

Arrange everything on a wooden board and increase the recipe if you are serving guests.

*Pickled lemons are very easy to make but take a long time. Cut the unwaxed lemons into rounds, and arrange in a jar sprinkling salt on each layer. Cover with lemon juice and make sure everything is submerged. Cover and wait one year. The lemons will be soft and exquisitely perfumed as a condiment. You can add any spices you like. Eat them peel and all.

Savory Pork Canapés

I admit, aspic is an excellent use for leftovers. Sometimes, exactly as you might fortuitously invent a new sandwich simply by piling on the contents of the fridge, this aspic was discovered. Add whatever you have on hand in equal proportion.

leftover roast pork shoulder cut into cubes

sun-dried tomatoes in olive oil, diced

firm blue cheese, diced

1 carrot diced

1 stalk celery diced

pistachios

| 1 cup vodka | 1 tbsp sugar |
| juice of 1 lime | 1 tbsp gelatin |

Mix the first 6 ingredients and place in a mold. Dissolve the gelatin in ¼ cup of vodka and lime juice, heat the rest, and add the sugar to dissolve. Then pour over the gelatin and mix well. Let cool a little, and pour over the other ingredients. Unmold the jello, and cut into finger shapes. You can dip them in mayo if you like, but they're pretty fantastic just on their own.

Mortadella in Black Cherry White Claw

This is basically just a quick sandwich of some of my favorite things in jello form. I don't know when I tasted a White Claw for the first time, but for a while I was addicted.

3 slices of mortadella, cut into strips
2 slices of dill Havarti, julienned
1 small rutabaga or quarter of a large one
1 carrot
1 tsp white vinegar
1 tsp mayonnaise

½ tsp sugar
½ tsp salt
½ tsp fresh dill, chopped
1 cup Black Cherry White Claw spiked seltzer
1 tbsp gelatin
3 leaves of curly leaf lettuce

Get a small plastic solo cup to use as the mold. Put in layers of mortadella, cheese, and a fresh coleslaw. Grate the rutabaga (raw) and carrot and mix with the vinegar, mayo, sugar, salt, and dill. Let marinate for about an hour if you can, then make the final layer with that. Mix ¼ cup of the seltzer with the gelatin and heat the rest, mix the two. This would be an ideal place to use cold set gelatin so you can retain the fizz. Pour the mixture into the cup. Let set. You should have a little extra gelatin—mold in another cup. Unmold the gelatin by cutting notches in the cup and peeling away. Turn upside down over a bed of lettuce and garnish with the remaining gelatin cut finely to resemble shards of glass.

Rabbit Braised in Mead

This recipe takes a little time and patience, but you can of course go the quick and easy route, using store-bought mead. But here's why you should make it yourself. Let me tell you a story. One day in May I was doing a wash and heard a strange humming sound in the laundry room. I thought little of it until I noticed a good number of bees shuttling in and out of a hole in the brick on the side of the house. I shrugged my shoulders and went away for a few weeks for conferences and research. When I returned there were truckloads of pollen-laden bees in a steady stream hauling their bounty into my wall. I went into the laundry room and put my ear to the wall. It was a ferocious humming such as I never heard on earth. And the wall was warm. Uh oh.

I called several people who seemed to know about bees. "Oh, an infestation, we can get rid of those no problem. But there's bound to be ants attracted to the honey afterwards, so we'll have to do two rounds of pesticides and poisons and antifungal treatments and a few tactical nuclear missiles. . . ." Thank you but no. I don't want to kill the bees. Honestly, I dreamt of putting drawers in the wall and keeping them permanently. I read Virgil and have harbored an affection for bees as long as I can remember. When I was young I used to visit the old bee man in Colt's Neck, New Jersey. He claimed the stings cured his arthritis. But I was happy to buy some jars—buckwheat dark as molasses, wildflower, acacia I think. They were magnificent. Why couldn't I be a bee-keeper too?

I was quickly disabused of this notion on the twelfth call to bee experts. A man told me, this was not a good way to keep bees in the wall, but he could move them and keep them in a happy spot, which just happened to be a few miles away, next door to my children's school. I could come visit the babies any time I liked. Perfect.

He arrived with a dry wall cutter, a few big buckets, and his long bare arms. I asked don't you need a bee suit and all? He replied nope. After an hour or so of sawing, he emerged from the closed laundry room, and said: "Come on in!" To which I replied as any sensible human would do: "Are you kidding me?" He wasn't. I walked in. He said open your arms. A few bees fluttered about, but they didn't seem to mind that there was a gaping hole in the wall, i.e. their hive, and that this guy had just moved the whole thing into a few buckets. At which point he handed me several pounds of hive and said, "taste." I did. I was transported. This could not really be happening. The aroma of oranges filled my entire head. Bees swirled around my head. I chewed the wax, and the flavor grew more intense. I was dizzy with rapture.

By the time I realized where I was, I thought it prudent to get out of there. With my armful of honeycomb. The man did take the bees away very neatly, and they lived happily ever after I am told. But as for me with several pounds of honey: I first strained and fermented it with water into a mead that was just remarkable. And then I distilled about a bottle of that mead into a honey hooch, which I put into a few tiny bottles, sealed with beeswax, and hid them around the house. I have found only one since then.

This is why I implore you to find good local organic raw honey and give this a try. You need no equipment aside from a big jar. Take a pound of raw honey, add twice that amount of filtered water and ½ tsp of champagne yeast. You can actually do it without the yeast entirely, but it's a bit livelier with it. Let that ferment for a few weeks, then filter it. You can have a glass too at this point. If you bottle it, it will get pleasantly effervescent, and it gets better with time.

But now for the rabbit. I wish people could get over their aversion to rabbit. It is so environmentally sound to raise, so easy to cook, and despite what people say it doesn't taste anything like chicken. And if you cook it as such, it will be dry and disappointing. It has to be braised. Rabbit has no fat. If you try to live on it as your sole source of protein, you will starve eventually. I'm not suggesting anyone try that, but if people ate a little more of it and got over the fact that they're so incredibly cute, it would probably be more affordable too.

So just take your rabbit, cut into sections, and cover it with mead. Do not brown the rabbit first—it only toughens the meat and clouds the jello. Add some mushrooms and onions. Add a teaspoon of salt to start—if you need more later you can always add it. Braise it slowly. Never let it boil. Wonderfully, this is an aspic you will never need to skim.

Remove the rabbit when it is tender, about two hours or a little longer. Remove the bones and cut into cubes. Set aside. Strain the broth and reduce it by about half. Then just pour it over the rabbit pieces. It will solidify without anything else. If you want to set it in a fanciful mold, maybe even rabbit shaped, that would be fun, but I think of this as a real peasant dish. Just cut in slices and enjoy, ideally on a picnic with happy bees buzzing around and bunnies hopping to and fro. A slice of aspic, a jug of mead, and thou.

Classic Meatloaf

I experimented with three iterations of the classic American meatloaf in jello in the course of my research. The first was simply ground beef and pork, cel-

ery, shallots, tomato sauce, and a pickled egg in the middle, baked in a loaf pan. I added gelatin to the mixture which is supposed to help retain moisture. It was very good, but I'm not sure the gelatin made much difference since it was eaten hot. With a cold paté of course it's standard, but the gelatin usually sits on top to seal in the meat. Making a layer of meatloaf and a distinct layer of jello out of port was also very good, and obviously served cold. But I think it really worked well with the level of wine and gelatin increased, the two mixed, and then the combination wrapped in bacon and baked. It was a little messy. You have to scrape off the congealed fat when cold, and I found it necessary to pour a little more gelatin into the slices to fill up some empty spaces, but in the end it was awfully good.

1 lb ground beef
1 lb ground pork
2 stalks celery, chopped
2 carrots chopped
1 large shallot chopped
handful of dates, pitted and
    chopped
handful of pistachios, chopped

1 tbsp salt
½ tbsp ground pepper
4 slices of thick bacon
2 cups red wine with serious
    backbone, a zin or cab
2 tbsp gelatin
1 lemon

Line a rectangular tinfoil baking pan with the bacon so the ends hang off the edges. Then mix all the meat, vegetables, fruit, and nuts together loosely and fill the pan. Fold over the ends of the bacon and bake in a 350-degree oven for an hour. Remove from the oven and pour off any fat. Dissolve the gelatin in ½ cup of wine and heat the rest. Mix the two and then poke holes into the meatloaf with a skewer and pour into the meatloaf pan. You will probably have some gelatin leftover; set it aside. Chill the meatloaf in the fridge for a few hours until set. Then unmold it. Scrape off any excess congealed bacon fat and slice it into 1-inch pieces and arrange them on their sides in a pan packed tightly together. Heat the leftover gelatin until just barely melted and pour onto the slices to fill any gaps and put back in the fridge to set again. To serve, separate the pieces and arrange on a plate with some sliced lemons.

Jello Sausage

Using beer as a jello base is more difficult than it sounds. Somehow the hops take over, the flavor of the barley malt is muted, and it tastes flat. Guinness Stout makes an awful jello unless super sweetened. I've found the beer either has to be on the sweet side already and mellow, or mixed with other ingredients to taste as good, or ideally even better than the beer on its own. The novelty here is not the beer, really, it's the molding technique. You can find sausage casings online easily, but if you prefer not to, a plastic cylindrical container might work. The beer I eventually chose is very powerful, fruity, and holds up nicely in gelatinous form.

> About 2 feet of small diameter
>   hog casings
> ½ lb ground pork
> 1 tsp each salt and pepper and
>   dried sage
> 2 cups Heretic Tangerine Ale
> 2 tbsp gelatin
> mustard
> baked beans
> sprig of fresh sage

Rinse the casings thoroughly and soak for about an hour in cold water, then squeeze dry. Gently mix the pork with the seasonings. You can add other spices, or even use loose sausage if you like. Next bloom the gelatin in ½ cup of ale and heat the rest. If you can find cold set gelatin, this would be the ideal place to use it. Let the gelatin cool. Mix the ground pork into the gelatin. Then tie off the end of the casing with a piece of string, and with a funnel pour in the gelatin and sausage mix. Tie off the other end and create segments by tying off sections with string. Poke them once or twice with a pin so they don't burst in cooking.

Next bring a pot of water to a gentle simmer and place in the entire sausage. You just want to poach the pork to cook, though, for about 10 minutes. Remove and let cool, then place in the fridge. When they are firm and set, cut the segments apart, peel off the casing, and serve with the other ingredients. They look more or less like sausages, but are bouncy and laced with beer.

Smoked Goose Breast in Peach Jello

There are those who say you should never try new recipes on company, or for strangers at a party. That's exactly when I do it! I brought this to a good friend's house on the Pacific coast and they ate it all. Goose is one of my favorite foods and so expensive that I rarely buy one. Around the holidays my grocery gets a few in the freezer case, and they sit there until January and February because no one bought them. Then they start lowering the price. Once it went as far as 5 dollars a bird! In any case, buy one when you can and lavish great care to it because it's fine just popped in the oven, but incredible when cooked well.

1 goose, breasts with skin removed from bones	3 apples
	handful of walnuts
1 ½ tbsp salt	4 tbsp peach jam
¼ tbsp Instacure (pink curing salt)	4 cup pinot grigio wine
	4 packs of gelatin
¼ tbsp sugar	¼ tsp almond extract
spices such as cloves and cardamom	

Remove the breast from the bone, keeping the skin intact. Sprinkle with dry ingredients and put in a sealable plastic bag in the fridge, turning now and then, for a week. Then hot smoke the goose breasts for about 30 minutes. They should be firm but cooked through. The cure will leave them pink with a texture like corned beef—so don't overcook, they will never lose that color. Let cool and slice both breasts diagonally and arrange in an oval mold or any shape you like. Arrange the apples and walnuts around the sliced breast.

Pour a cup of the wine into a bowl and mix with the gelatin. In another bowl mix the remaining wine with the peach jam and stir to dissolve. Strain out any remaining solid bits and bring to a boil. Mix all the liquids and pour over the goose. Chill until set. To serve, just allow guests to remove slices, jello, and the rest with a serving knife.

Smoked Turkey Surprise

This is about as close to a classic mid-20th-century jello mold as I have ever come and I will admit when unmolded I was taken aback. The smoky aroma really suffuses through all the other ingredients and it was amazingly good. You could probably use any cocktail to bind this, but I was frankly thinking of the mid-'70s pop sensation Peter Lemongello who was kind of like a cheesy Tom Jones or Engelbert Humperdink on steroids, if you can believe that. He was a turkey, in the very colloquial sense current in that decade.

1 boneless skinless turkey breast (c. 3–4 lb)
1 tbsp salt
1 tbsp brown sugar
1 tsp Instacure #1 (pink curing salt)
1 tsp each of mustard powder, Old Bay seasoning, oregano, and the like
1 oak log and plenty of kindling
½ lb Muenster cheese in cubes
2 stalks celery diced
4 leaves of romaine lettuce
2 cups vodka
2 cups lemonade made with Meyer lemons
4 packets gelatin

Season the turkey with the dry ingredients, and leave in the fridge in a sealed plastic bag for a week. Then bring to room temperature. Light the log in a smoker and place the turkey inside the smoking chamber and blow out the log. It should provide smoke for an hour or two, which is sufficient. If the log goes out, simply light it again. It should be a hot smoke, enough to cook the turkey through. When it comes out, it will taste like the best ham.

When cool, slice the turkey and cut about 2 cups into cubes. Place these in a mold. Then add the cheese, celery, and roughly torn lettuce leaves. Bloom the gelatin in 1 cup of vodka and heat the rest with the lemonade. Then mix the two and pour over into the mold. Chill and set, then turn onto a platter. Serve wedges, if you like with mustard or mayonnaise. You can even serve thin slices on bread as a sandwich.

Quail with Foie Gras and Truffles in Madeira Jello

This recipe was invented partly as a challenge from my dear friend Carrie. She said she had the goods if I came up with the dish. The inspiration came from Charles Ranhofer, who was chef at De!monico's. His creations are so complicated and over the top that even I had to scale it back a bit, and this was very pleasant, even if difficult, to make.

4 quails
1 can goose foie gras, or fresh if you can find it
1 tbsp truffles, I used some from a jar

2 cups madeira, port, or marsala
2 packs gelatin
garnishes such as orange slices, lettuce leaves, candied cherries

First bone the quail, leaving only the wings and leg bones. This is not an easy task, but if you cut out the backbone with scissors first, then carefully cut down along the ribs to release the breast meat, it can be done. Season the quail with salt and pepper and cook on the grill just until medium rare. Over-

cooked quail is dry and livery, so leave a little pink on the flesh. Let them cool completely. Then mix the foie gras with the truffles and fill each cavity, squeezing closed the quail around the filling. Then make the gelatin by dissolving the powder in ½ cup wine, bring the rest to the boil, and mix the two. Let cool and pour over the quail, which are in a mold. I used small oval tart molds that held each quail snugly. Let set, then unmold each jello by dipping just the bottom of each mold in hot water briefly. Arrange on a platter with orange slices or whatever you like. Now, if you are not keen on buying expensive ingredients, this dish can also be made using chicken thighs boned, cooked, and stuffed with decent duck liver pate and mushrooms set in a sweet wine aspic. That would make a lovely cold first course for an elegant meal.

Moose Nose Jelly

One day a TV producer called and asked if I could help with a new show called "Eating History." Two guys would taste a lot of old food, I mean actual old packages of crackers, cereal, cans of meat, beer, war rations, etc. My first thought was someone is going to get sick, no? So I asked why they hadn't thought of old recipes too. I offered to find strange but interesting dishes from the past. A few months later they came up with a few things they wanted me to cook on camera. Seriously gross things like beaver tails—which weren't that bad re-

ally, but not dishes that one could easily find in an old cookbook. One was the moose nose jelly.

I kind of figured it out and had actually been to Alaska the previous summer and looked for the dish, but never suspected a few weeks later, the whole film crew would be at my house or that my friend Nadine in Saskatchewan had a moose head in the freezer and was willing to ship it overnight. That is how this version of the recipe came to pass.

Place your moose head on a large sturdy table. It can weigh 100 lbs, so get friends to help. With the sharpest knife you have—not a cleaver—slice directly down into the nose right at the point where the bridge of the nose ends and softer cartilage begins. When you hit the jawbone, turn your knife to the right and slice parallel to the upper jaw toward the tip of the mouth, removing the entire nose. Incidentally, remove and grill the cheek muscles—they're delicious.

Blanch the nose in boiling water for just a few minutes, and then holding the meat steady with waterproof and heat-resistant gloves, pull the hair out with thick sturdy tweezers. I used a Japanese pair about an inch wide. If they're not coming out, return the nose to the boiling water for another few minutes and try again. (Don't under any circumstances try to singe off the fur—it's thick and when burned smells horrid.) When you've gotten every last hair off the nose, place it in a batch of clean water with a dash of vinegar and a tablespoon of salt. You can add aromatics too like celery, parsnip, onion. Cook as low as you can for about 12 hours. I left the whole stockpot on the barbecue grill over night.

The next morning, carefully remove the nose and cut into cubes. If you see any more hair, be diligent about removing it. Put the nose cubes in a nice mold. Then strain the stock by ladling it through a fine-mesh sieve lined with cheesecloth. Reduce the stock by gently simmering. You might want to test it by putting a little in a plastic cup in the freezer, to make sure it will set. When it sets up to your satisfaction, pour the stock over the nose meat and place in the fridge for several hours to set. Unmold, slice, and taste.

Honestly it was rather mild, a little beefy. A pleasantly soft gelatin, but nothing terribly strange. Old Smokey and Josh, the TV show hosts, ate it happily, except for the stray nose hairs I missed!

Chinese Chicken Salad Aspic

When I was growing up, salads like this were a real thing. Sliced chicken with soy sauce, sesame oil, some celery and peppers, mayonnaise. It's not bad, though there's nothing Chinese about it. I used to bring this as lunch with me when I was working at the Metropolitan Museum of Art in New York. I have no idea what motivated me one day to turn it into jello, but it really, truly is tasty.

1 small chicken breast	1 stalk of celery diced
1 tbsp soy sauce	¼ cup cashews
1 knob of ginger, peeled and diced	¼ cup golden raisins
a drizzle of toasted sesame oil	½ cup mayonnaise
tapioca or corn starch for dusting	2 cups Riesling wine
1 tbsp neutral oil, for frying	2 packets gelatin
1 chopped shallot	Shredded red pepper and ginger as garnish

Slice the chicken breast across the grain into ½-inch slices, then slice again into thin strips. Add the soy, ginger, and sesame oil and let marinate 15 minutes. Dust with corn starch. Then quickly stir fry in the oil. Set aside. Mix with the other solid ingredients and put into a mold. Bloom the gelatin in ½ cup of wine, and heat the rest. Pour the hot liquid over the gelatin, mix the two, and let cool. Pour over the rest, making sure to mix well so the mayo doesn't separate out. Chill, unmold, and serve, garnished with pepper and ginger.

Margarita and Cured Short Rib

Short ribs are one of the classic cuts to braise a long time until soft and unctuous. But they are equally good sliced thin and quickly seared as you find in Korean cuisine, or I think even raw. This is something quite different because it's cured but not cooked. The fat that runs through the meat keeps it soft and flavorful, but it never clouds the gelatin, so it's beautiful to look at too.

¼ pound boneless beef short rib
½ tsp salt
¼ tsp sugar
tiny pinch of Instacure #1 (pink curing salt)
raw corn kernels cut fresh from the cob
1 serrano chili

¾ cup clear beef stock or consommé
¼ cup tequila
lime juice
1 tbsp sugar
1 packet gelatin
a few sprigs of cilantro

Cut the beef into tiny cubes and sprinkle with salt, sugar, and the curing salt. Let sit several hours or overnight. Place these in the bottom of a lightly oiled metal timbale or ceramic ramekin. Sprinkle the corn kernels on top and a little finely chopped chili. Then take the beef stock or consommé and bring it to a gentle boil. Combine the gelatin with the alcohol and other ingredients to bloom, and then pour over the hot stock. Let cool thoroughly. Then pour it over the beef. If you prefer, pour over while hot, and the beef and corn will cook. Let set in the refrigerator, then unmold into small decorative bowls to serve. Garnish with the cilantro.

Tongue in Its Own Aspic

Tongue is one of the most versatile, tender, and intensely delicious meats. It takes long slow cooking, and I understand peeling the outer skin studded with taste buds can be a little surreal. Personally, I like to imagine that when I eat tongue, it's tasting me back. Normally I would cure the tongue with spices, poach or steam it, and serve it cold and thinly sliced, on sturdy rye. Or put it into the classic Spanish olla podrida (i.e., rotten pot), which includes pig feet, sausages, turnips, chickpeas, chestnuts, and garlic. But this recipe is so simple that it really allows the flavor of the tongue to stand out. For this aspic you'll only need the front half; after cooking, save the thicker root end for stew or tacos.

For the Stock:

1 small beef tongue
2 lbs assorted beef bones, joints, ligaments
aromatic vegetables such as onion, celery, carrots, parsley, parsnip
1 tbsp salt

1 tbs whole peppercorns
1 tbsp whole coriander seed
1 cup Old Vine Zinfandel
Giardiniera to garnish (pickled onions, carrots, celery, chili, cauliflower)

Cover the tongue and other stock ingredients with water. Bring to a gentle simmer. Skim off the gunk that floats to the top, and let cook for 2 hours. Remove the tongue and let it cool, then peel off the outer skin. It should come off easily. If not, return the tongue to cook more. Set aside the tongue in the fridge to cool completely. Keep the rest of the stock simmering for another 6–8 hours or longer. I often do this overnight. Strain the stock through a fine-meshed sieve lined with cheesecloth. Then add the wine and let reduce by about half for another few hours.

Slice the tongue and arrange in an oval dish that will just hold the slices. Pour over the reduced stock and let set in the fridge. To serve, put the aspic on a plate and briefly pass a torch over the top to give it a sheen and melt a little of the gelatin onto the plate. Then arrange your pickled vegetables around the tongue.

If you would like to make your own giardiniera, you can lacto ferment the mix of vegetables in a 4–5% brine solution, in a sealed jar for about 2 weeks. Or use diluted vinegar and salt—which is the usual way it's done in Italy. I might also serve this with a good mostarda di frutta, which is not exactly mustard, but a spicy pickled fruit relish from Italy. But regular mustard would be awfully good too.

Kir Normande with Boudin Noir and Pommes Frites

We all know the Kir and Kir royale, which is cassis or black currant liqueur with wine or champagne. It's remarkably good but may actually be upstaged by a similar drink made with cider. Use a tart dry sparkling cider, from Normandy or domestic. The combination seems perfect for a cold winter evening.

8 ounces cider
1 packet of gelatin
1 ounce cassis
1 boudin noir or any blood
   sausage, fried and sliced

A few slices of apple sautéed in
   the drippings
1 shallot sliced and browned in
   butter

Bloom the gelatin in ¼ cup of cider and heat the rest with the cassis, then mix the two. Set aside. Cut off the bottom of a plastic soda or water bottle and arrange the pieces of sausage inside, along with the other ingredients. Pour over the gelatin mixture and let set in the fridge. Turn out onto a plate. Serve this to guests, and no one will have the slightest idea what it might be.

Louisiana Back Bay Bayou Bunny
Bordelaise à la Antoine

This is a *plat composé*—meaning an arranged dish which is covered in aspic so it doesn't dry out, and served cold. It was popular from the mid–19th century to about the mid–20th century. Even Julia Child did a duck covered in aspic in an early episode of *The French Chef.* There are two ways to do it, either spoon the nearly set gelatin over the plate, which takes a lot of patience and frequent setting and returning to the fridge to build up a solid layer. I think it's easier to just gently pour the liquid aspic over the ingredients in a plate that has a rim. The only difficulty is keeping the pieces in place. You can always place the plate in the fridge and then gently spoon the aspic onto it and rearrange if necessary. That's much easier than trying to move it to the fridge. Or leave it on the counter to set before you move it to the fridge. The ingredients I used are just a suggestion; use whatever is best.

1 egg
breadcrumbs
1 tbsp butter
2 pieces of pickled okra
1 pickled chili pepper
1 small carrot chopped
1 stalk celery, chopped
handful of fresh peas
a few chives
fresh herbs for garnish
1 ½ cups white Bordeaux
   wine—made mostly with
   Sémillon grapes
1 tbs gelatin

1 rabbit tenderloin or thigh
   meat
Salt, pepper, thyme
Pinch of mustard powder
Pinch chili powder

You can use chicken breast in this dish if you prefer, but rabbit is more interesting. Season the tenderloin with salt, pepper, and thyme, plus a pinch each of mustard powder and chili powder. Dip it in beaten egg and then into fine bread crumbs. (There's no need to dip it in flour first, by the way.) Fry it gently in the butter, then set aside to cool. Slice on the bias and arrange on a plate. Surround it with all the vegetables and garnishes. Then dissolve the gelatin in ¼ cup wine and heat the rest barely to a boil. Then pour over the gelatin and stir. Let cool and then pour over the dish. This uses a very light gelatin since it doesn't need to support its own weight.

Gelatinous Pie

Using gelatin in a meat pie was a traditional way to keep air out of the contents and help them last longer. The unusual trick is to add the gelatinous stock after baking, so the crust doesn't become soggy. You need a funnel to do it. As the pie cools, the contents solidify, at first just slightly, and if held at room temperature, the whole becomes fairly solid and of course all the more flavorful as well. In old cookbooks this would be called a lear, and in this case you can make the gelatinous stock yourself, or just add gelatin packets to store-bought beef stock.

2 cups flour	1 small chopped onion
1 cup shredded beef suet (Atora is an easily found brand online)	1 diced carrot
	1 diced stalk celery
	1 cup cubed cheddar cheese
pinch of salt	1 cup red wine
1 cup raw rib steak, cubed	1 cup gelatinous beef stock

Mix the flour and suet and a pinch of salt and work into a dough with room temperature water. Divide into one large ball and one small. Roll each out into a large round and a small round. Line a small pie plate with high sides with the larger piece of dough. Mix together all the solid ingredients and fill the pie. Then put on the top and crimp the edges. Poke a large hole in the top of the pie. Bake in a 350-degree oven for about an hour, until the crust is golden brown.

While the pie is baking, put the stock and wine on the stove and simmer very gently until reduced by half. If you need to add gelatin, reserve a little wine and mix it with the gelatin to bloom, then add to the stock at the very end. When the pie is done, put a funnel in the hole at the top and pour in the stock, slowly, so it distributes all around without spilling over. Let rest at room temperature for at least an hour, or longer. Serve in slices.

Lamb in Lambrusco

Apart from the silly wordplay, this looks so much like a kind of cake that the cognitive dissonance is thrilling. Lambrusco is a cheap fizzy red wine from Italy, rather on the sweet side. I think I may be the only person in the US that likes it, but if that were the case, no store would carry it. It only has 8% alcohol or thereabouts, so don't worry about it overpowering this dish. The acidity pairs really nicely with the rich lamb too.

2 lamb shanks
salt, pepper, rosemary, thyme,
    oregano to season
2 tbsp olive oil

2 cups Lambrusco
2 shallots, peeled and quartered
1 cup more Lambrusco
1 tbsp gelatin

Season the lamb shanks a few hours ahead and then brown them in a small pot with the olive oil and the shallot. Pour off the excess fat, and lower the heat all the way down. Add the Lambrusco and simmer for about 2 hours or longer until the meat is very soft. Remove the lamb and discard the bone. Chop

the meat into small pieces. Strain the remaining liquid. Reheat it with ¾ cup more Lambrusco. Bloom the gelatin in the remaining wine and then combine the two. Arrange the lamb in a foil-lined baking dish or round pie plate. Pour over the gelatinous broth. Let set in the fridge and then remove from the pan, cut into wedges, and serve. You might even decorate this with mashed potatoes to complete the illusion.

Veal Marsala Poke Cake

I was once asked to cook some period recipes for a film about 17th-century composer Claudio Monteverdi. I didn't realize I would actually be on camera, but when I got to Cologne where the production was based, the director and I went and bought basically anything I thought I'd need, including an enormous granite mortar. The filming took place on the parapet of a castle overlooking the Eifel forest, using a wood-burning stove. Among the dishes I made was a heart-shaped cake decorated with flowers and filled with veal, candied fruits, and spices, and glazed with a sugary frosting. I know that sounds bizarre, but it was very popular in the 17th century—in fact I took it from a menu for a meal that Monteverdi might have actually tasted. More importantly, it is magnificent. The crew devoured the whole thing. In this recipe I try to recapture that wild baroque exuberance in a traditional poke cake, which is just that—jello poured into holes poked in a cake.

2 cups flour	1 cup cooked ground veal
2 tsp baking powder	½ tsp ground nutmeg
1 cup sugar	1 cup marsala wine
1 stick of butter	1 tbsp gelatin
2 eggs	1 cup powdered sugar
½ cup milk	milk
¼ cup dried barberries	1 cup crushed walnuts, lightly
¼ cup candied citron	toasted

Cream the flour, baking powder, and sugar together with a wooden spoon. Add in the eggs gradually, then the milk. Stir in the berries, citron, veal, and freshly rasped nutmeg. Pour into a greased spring form cake pan and bake in a 350-degree oven for about 40 minutes. Test with a toothpick to make sure it's not uncooked inside (when fully cooked the toothpick will come out clean). Let cool on a metal rack at least an hour. Then mix a quarter of the wine with the gelatin and heat the rest. Combine the two and let cool. Using a chopstick, poke holes into the top of the cake all around. Pour in the gelatin as neatly as you can. Let set in the refrigerator for a few hours. Then mix the powdered sugar with just a little milk until you have a thick, pourable frosting. Drizzle that all over the top and sides of the cake. Then top with the walnuts. If you are feeling even more baroque, festoon with swags: angels blowing trumpets and such.

CHAPTER 6

DAIRY AND EGGS

Jello Egg

This is such a delightful trick, and it goes back at least to the 16th century. You can do it with any jello and with any accompanying embellishments. In this version, the egg itself goes nicely with the whole Japanese flavor profile. Make one egg for each guest.

4 extra-large or jumbo eggs
½ cup sake
¼ tsp soy sauce
½ cup dashi stock with kombu seaweed and katsuobushi flakes

1 packet jello
1 lit candle
1 cucumber
Pickled mackerel, nori sheets, pickled eggplant, umeboshi plums, whatever you like.

Poke holes in both ends of the eggs using a pin. Stir the pin around to break the yolk and scramble the inside a little. Then blow out the insides into a bowl.

To make the dashi stock take a sheet of kombu and put in 2 cups of water and bring to the boil. Turn off the heat and add the dashi flakes. Let rest for 10 minutes. Bloom the gelatin in the sake and soy sauce. Then strain the half cup dashi stock over it and mix thoroughly. Reserve the rest of the stock. Then melt a little candle wax on the bottom hole of the eggshell. With a syringe, inject the gelatin mixture into the eggs. I found cheap plastic syringes in the hardware store. Each egg will hold about 4 tablespoons, so a cup should fill all four eggshells. Drip some candle wax on the other holes and leave in the fridge.

Then mix the egg with a half cup of the dashi stock and a little salt and a pinch of sugar. Cook four very thin omelets and remove to a plate. Tuck in the sides and roll them up tightly. It's not exactly tamagoyaki, but if you have the proper rectangular pan, by all means use it. Wrap a thin strip of nori seaweed around each roll of egg.

To serve, break off the eggshells and place the eggs in small sake cups or egg cups. I actually used a section of cucumber slightly hollowed out to form a stand. Set on a plate with the egg and garnish with whatever lovely Japanese ingredients you like. I chose a little pickled mackerel and eggplant.

As it turns out, the egg-shaped jello not only has surprising physical properties, viz., it bounces, but I discovered that its acoustical properties are equally intriguing. Use it as a mute in the bell of a brass instrument, squish it onto the strings of your guitar or violin and it acts as a damper, or bounce it carefully on the head of a drum. It sticks a little and bounces, creating a complex rhythmic pattern all its own. Thhh-bump, Thhhh-bump, Thhhh-bump. I even let it dance on the hammers of my piano while playing jazz riffs.

Macchiato Espresso Jello with Cream and Almond

First find a mold with patterned indentations on the bottom inside. These will later be the raised pattern in cream on the top, after it's turned out. The more it looks like the top of a coffee cup, the better. I think you could make these in individual coffee cups very successfully too. The recipe is divided into three parts since you make each separately.

Foam layer:

1 cup heavy whipping cream
1 tbsp powdered gelatin

¼ tsp almond extract
¼ cup sugar

Espresso layer:

1 cup rum
2 tbsp powdered gelatin

½ cup sugar or taste
1 cup strong espresso

Base:

1 cup heavy whipping cream
1 tbsp powered gelatin
¼ cup sugar
¼ tsp almond extract

10 crushed almond biscotti
1 bar grated 70% cacao
    chocolate

Mix a quarter of the whipping cream with the gelatin and almond extract to dissolve. Add the sugar and mix thoroughly. Heat the rest of the cream to boiling and pour over the rest. Then carefully pour in the mold just so the indented patterns are filled. Place in the refrigerator to set. Reserve any extra jello and add to the last layer.

Mix ½ cup rum with the powdered gelatin to dissolve. Add sugar, mix thoroughly. Heat the espresso with the rest of the rum until boiling. Mix with the dissolved gelatin. Pour over the first cream layer and let set in the refrigerator about an hour.

Mix a quarter of the cream with gelatin to dissolve. Add sugar and almond extract; mix thoroughly. Add the biscotti and chocolate; mix and pour over the coffee layer. Put in refrigerator to set.

Place the entire mold in a sink full of hot water or a basin for about 30 seconds and quickly turn over onto a large platter. Ideally the cream layer will melt a little into the coffee layer creating a swirled effect like on the top of a coffee cup. This was among the tastiest novice-friendly recipes I made. Serve it to in-laws. If you like them, that is.

Eggs Benedict in Champagne Jello

I can already hear you say: but Eggs Benedict are as perfect as food gets, why would you mess with that? They said the same thing to the inventor of the dish. Legend has it that Lemuel Benedict, a Wall Street stockbroker, asked

for his poached eggs with ham and hollandaise at the Waldorf Hotel in 1894, but on toast! The term "English muffin" was only coined in 1894 in New York by Samuel Bath Thomas (yes, that Thomas). The same combination on toast is practically there already in the 1839 *Kentucky Housewife*. But that's not Eggs Benedict. Others will tell you no, the famous chef Charles Ranhofer whose recipe for Oeufs à la Benedick published in 1893 is the real inventor. But if you look at his book *The Epicure*, the recipe only appears in the 1920 edition, not in the first, as the reprint claims. Perhaps it was Commodore E. C. Benedict? No, say Mr. and Mrs. Le Grand Benedict. And we can still hear a faint echo of Pope Benedict XIII in the 1720s who liked something quite like Eggs Benedict. The first recipe actually only appears in 1889 in A. Meyer's prosaically titled *Eggs and How to Use Them*. My point is, no one invented them or first requested Eggs Benedict. The dish evolved, as it should. Nowadays you find salmon on it or spinach, or any number of new combinations—some I argue are maybe even a little better than the original. In that spirit, I ask you to give this a chance.

This only really works if you poach the eggs and remove them to a cold-water bath to stop cooking and keep them chilled. You can use any cylindrical mold. I used a large can from tomatoes. It was easy to unmold because I could remove the base after it set and gently push out the contents without having to heat it. The edges retained the signature wavy lines of the can, which was nice. Use the lid of the can to gauge the size of the other ingredients. Everything but the muffins are for one serving—multiply everything for the number of people.

Muffins (4):

2 cups flour

1 ½ tbsp salted butter

1 tbsp sugar

½ tsp baking powder

1 egg

½-¾ cup milk

1 tsp cornmeal

Jello:

1 thick slice of ham or Canadian
    Bacon

1 egg to poach

1 egg yolk

¼ stick salted butter

Juice of half a lemon

2 cups of champagne

2 packets of gelatin

Rub the flour and salted butter between your fingers to create little flecks of butter through the flour. Mix in the sugar and baking powder, then the egg. Pour in enough milk to make a soft dough. Divide it into four balls and flatten them into rounds one inch thick, slightly smaller than your can lid. Sprinkle one side with fine cornmeal. Put the 4 rounds into a large nonstick pan on medium-low heat with no grease. When browned, turn them over and continue cooking. Set aside to cool. Then divide horizontally to expose the nooks and crannies.

Cut the bacon exactly the same size as the muffin. Get a shallow pot of simmering water with a few drops of vinegar, and swirl very gently. Carefully crack the egg directly into the water. Just when the whites have come together, transfer with a slotted spoon to a big bowl of water and ice. Continue with all the eggs if making many. If there are ragged edges on the whites, trim them off with scissors.

Put half a muffin at the bottom of the can, then the ham, then the poached egg.

Then whisk together the extra egg yolk and lemon juice in a metal bowl until creamy. Place the bowl over your pot of simmering water and drop in the butter cut into small pieces and whisk until the sauce begins to thicken. Just be sure the water isn't too hot or the eggs will scramble. Transfer the hollandaise to a cool bowl.

Then mix ½ cup of the champagne with the gelatin to dissolve. Heat the rest just to boiling and mix with the gelatin. Let cool, then pour over the eggs in the can. It should just cover the ingredients. Chill the can until set. Then with a can opener, remove the bottom of the can, push out the jello onto a plate, and top with a dollop of the sauce. It will be fairly thick at room temperature; you don't want it hot or it will cause the jello to melt.

The exquisite drama of the dish is when you cut it in half and the yolk oozes from the center and you can see the solid hollow white suspended in the clear champagne jello.

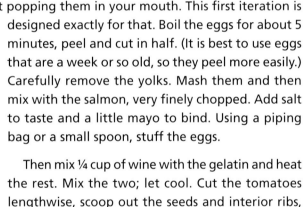

Salmon Mousse Stuffed Quail Eggs in Alsatian Riesling Jello Set in Tomato Halves with Thai Basil then Set in Avocado

6 quail eggs	1 cup Alsatian Riesling
2 ounces of salmon, salted and seasoned for several days	1 packet jello
	6 small Roma tomatoes
dab of mayonnaise	6 avocados

Quail eggs really taste pretty much like regular eggs, but the scale is so thrilling, that it's hard to resist popping them in your mouth. This first iteration is designed exactly for that. Boil the eggs for about 5 minutes, peel and cut in half. (It is best to use eggs that are a week or so old, so they peel more easily.) Carefully remove the yolks. Mash them and then mix with the salmon, very finely chopped. Add salt to taste and a little mayo to bind. Using a piping bag or a small spoon, stuff the eggs.

Then mix ¼ cup of wine with the gelatin and heat the rest. Mix the two; let cool. Cut the tomatoes lengthwise, scoop out the seeds and interior ribs, and salt generously. Turn over on a paper towel to drain a little. Then pour in the gelatin and set the stuffed quail eggs inside the jello. Chill in the fridge.

If you are ambitious and want to serve these as a first course, cut avocados in half, remove the pits, sprinkle on some salt and lime juice, and place the tomato halves inside the hollows. Serve two per person. When you think about it, why stop there? I set the avocado in half a boiled potato. Then set that in more wine jello, set into a baked squash. By the time I was done playing, the jello had taken over the whole town like Strega Nona's pasta.

The Tent of Meeting at Mount Horeb

Milk and honey, both raw, demand a righteous form. Exodus provides. This was made with cold set gelatin, never cooked. It is an unblemished offering unto the Lord. Mix one cup of raw milk and 2 tablespoons of unpasteurized organic honey. Combine with 2 tablespoons of the cold set gelatin and stir until dissolved. Pour into the cut-off top of a plastic oil bottle (previously used for anointing kings). It looks like a tent. Set in the refrigerator until solid. Unmold by gently separating the sides of the jello and removing the cap from the bottle top and sliding out the jello. Rejoice.

If you'd like to play with these basic flavors, I recommend a little rum, or even palm wine seems fitting. A little coffee would go very nicely too, or even some fruit—dried dates especially.

7-UP Cheese Aspic

I have been dared many times to put unspeakable things in jello—including a stapler. But this was a real recipe from 1957 that circulated online, no doubt because it sounded so dreadful. The 7-UP company was not above unscrupulous tactics to sell their product and there are classic ads in which they try to convince mothers to mix it with milk and give it to babies. Somehow this seems even worse. "You'll have guests asking for this special recipe," it claims. Here's the original.

1 package lime gelatin	3 oz. processed cheese, cut into
1 cup hot water	small squares
1 7 oz. bottle 7-Up	½ cup diced celery
1 tsp grated onion	1 tbsp sliced stuffed olives

Dissolve gelatin in hot water. Add chilled 7-Up and onion. Chill until slightly thickened. Fold in remaining ingredients. Turn into one-quart mold; chill until firm. Unmold. Serve on crisp lettuce. Garnish with tomato wedges and cheese cubes. 6 servings.

Even after making and tasting this, I thought it wasn't completely absurd to mix lime juice and cheese, was it? So here is my makeover. It's actually not bad.

Juice of one lime	Castelvetrano olives or good
1 tbsp sugar	pimento stuffed olives
1 cup vodka	chopped
1 packet gelatin	1 stalk celery finely diced
¼ oz. St. André Triple Cream Cheese	

Mix the lime juice, sugar, and a splash of vodka with the gelatin to bloom. Heat the rest of the vodka and mix the two. Let cool. Meanwhile, arrange the cheese, olives, and celery in a small mold and pour over the liquids. Let set in the fridge, unmold, and enjoy.

Deviled Veal Stock Egg

By coincidence the yolk of an egg in Latin texts is called the ovum vitellus—the veal of egg. That might have been what inspired this combination, which is as delicious as arrestingly strange. There are several steps, none too difficult, but a little time consuming. Start with the veal stock. Use the instant pot for the clearest most flavorful base. This makes 4 servings.

2 lb of veal knuckles, sawed into pieces	4 eggs
2 shallots	1 pot of Chinese tea (such as King's Tea from Ten Ren's)
2 small carrots	2 tbsp Kewpie mayonnaise
sprigs of thyme and sage	sprinkle of shichimi togarashi or
1 cup Shaoxing wine	other chili blend
1 tbsp salt	

Place the ingredients for the stock base in the instant pot, just barely covered with water and press the soup button. You can also do this in a pot on very low heat but be sure not to stir the pot or let it boil. You want perfect clarity.

When the stock is finished, simply ladle off the clear liquid into a container, leaving any debris in the bottom of the metal insert. Chill and it should be a lightly set, very flavorful jello.

Next boil the eggs. Not quite so fresh eggs are easier to peel. Remove the shells under running cold water and place into the pot of tea. If you are feeling adventurous, you can lightly crack the shells and put in the tea that way and you might get a lovely pattern on the eggs. In either case, leave in the tea for a day or so.

Then cut off the tops and very carefully scoop out the yolk with a tiny spoon. Mash that with the mayonnaise and a pinch of salt and put into a piping bag with a small star tip. Spoon some of the veal jello into the eggs and arrange them on egg cups. Then squeeze some of the yolk mixture on top in a decorative pattern and top with a tiny nubbin of jello as well. Sprinkle on the chili and briefly torch to char the egg yolk. Chill again in the fridge before service.

CHAPTER 7

FRUIT

Fresh Figs with Laird's Apple Brandy and Pimms

This is very simple and needs nothing more than a description of the technique, but it's so good, especially when you have great fresh figs. As much as I love local mission figs, big yellow striped Turkey figs are even better. Imagine a circle running around the top third of the fig. Then cut sharp diagonal incisions along that circle in a zigzag pattern, deeply enough that you can lift the cap off the top. Scoop out the insides and eat them at once. Then get a quarter cup of apple brandy. You can use applejack, which comes from near where I grew up, in Scobeyville, NJ, but their brandy is the good stuff, not cut with grain neutral spirits. Mix that with a packet of gelatin to dissolve. Then heat to boiling ½ cup of Pimms #1, a very British aperitif that goes wonderfully with the apple. Mix the two thoroughly. Arrange your fig bottoms on a tray so they don't wobble, pour in the gelatin mixture, and replace the caps. Let set in the fridge. The flavor combination is luscious. Serve on fall leaves.

But if you have perfectly ripe mission figs, this alternate version is fabulous. Cut into the side of the fig creating a star pattern and scoop out the insides. Make a jello of port wine and gelatin, nothing else. Then take a small round of goat cheese, mix in a teaspoon of honey and a little dried lavender. If it's too thick, add a touch of sour cream. Squeeze this out of a star-tipped piping bag over the set port jello and serve in all its glorious simplicity.

Screwdriver Creamsicle

My online friend Abbey shared with me her grandmother's handwritten recipe for a kind of fruit salad jello that used artificially flavored Jell-O, canned oranges, and a topping of Cool Whip, flour, eggs, and butter. The flavor sounded interesting, but why not do it with really good fresh ingredients? We cooked each version together electronically across the country. Mine naturally was spiked. For this, use a large mold; it will feed about 8 people.

Top:

    1 cup vodka
    1 cup orange juice
    2 ounces Triple Sec or other
        orange liqueur
    dash of Angostura Bitters
    2 packets gelatin
    1 large navel orange, peeled
        and segmented

Bottom:

    All the same ingredients again but add 2 cups whipped cream instead of orange segments

Mix all the liquids and dissolve the gelatin in about ½ cup of the mixture. Heat the rest and then pour over the heated part and mix the two together. Pour into the bottom of your mold and add the orange segments decoratively. Place in refrigerator to set, but not completely so. Mix the same ingredients again, with gelatin, and let cool completely. Add a few drops of vanilla and/or almond extract. Fold in your whipped cream. Then add to your mold and let it all chill thoroughly. When ready to unmold, dip the whole thing into a basin of hot water for 20–30 seconds. Turn over onto a plate and serve.

Yellow Cherry Conserves and Port Gummies

Use the sweetest cherries you can find—Bing, Rainier, or bright yellow cherries, as I did. The processing was a fortuitous experiment, but I think it works much better than trying to pit them raw. If you can find cherry-shaped molds, all the better.

1 lb cherries	1 cup port wine
2 tbsp sugar	1 ⅓ tbsp gelatin
2 cloves	¼ cup mascarpone
strip of orange peel	1 tsp cocoa powder

Put the cherries, sugar, clove, and peel in an instant pot barely covered with water and cook under high pressure for 10 minutes. You can also simmer them, but risk losing the shape entirely. Remove the cherries from the cooker and reserve the liquid. Cool them so you can gently squeeze out the pits. Again, the idea is to keep them whole. Discard the orange peel and cloves. Gently reduce the cooking liquid until you have a thick syrup. Next either put the cherries in a dehydrator for a day until shriveled but not completely dry, or you can put them in a very low oven overnight. Then pour the syrup over the cherries and let them steep for a few days. Incidentally, these make great cherries for cocktails.

Place a cherry at the center of each cherry-shaped mold. Bloom the gelatin in ¼ cup of the port and heat the rest. Mix the two and then pour over the cherries into the molds. Let set in the fridge. To serve, arrange on a plate, add a dollop of mascarpone, and dust with cocoa powder by putting it in a small strainer and tapping the edge to create an even sprinkle. Toss on a few fresh lavender flowers.

Blackberries in Rosé Jello with Matzo Crackle

Come mid-July, the wild blackberries that grow around the Cosumnes River begin to ripen. It's a short hike into the preserve, and naturally you have to put them in your hat and carry, so that a few get crushed and your hat is stained forever like a badge of honor. These go into pies and tarts and cakes and crumbles in my house. This may be the best. I prepared the two components side by side, but you could also make a kind of pie with the crackle as the chilled base and the jello set directly onto it in a baking dish.

1 pint blackberries	½ cup brown sugar
2 cups rosé	1 cup dark chocolate chopped
1 ½ tbsp gelatin	into small pieces
2 pieces of matzo or unsalted	½ cup cashews chopped
water cracker	sprig of mint
1 stick of butter	

Pick and wash your blackberries; dry thoroughly. Bloom the gelatin in ½ cup of wine. Heat the rest, mix the two, and pour into square molds. Refrigerate. When not quite set, drop in the blackberries so they are suspended in the middle. Return to fridge to completely set, then cut the jello into rectangles with a few berries in each.

Put the matzo on a tinfoil-lined baking sheet. Put the butter and brown sugar in a pot and bring to a boil. Cook for about 3 minutes until thick. Pour over matzo and spread evenly with a spatula. Bake in the oven for 10 minutes at 350 degrees until bubbly. Then sprinkle with the chocolate. The chocolate will melt in a minute or two; spread it evenly and top with the cashews. Chill in the fridge until completely hard. Serve a wedge of the crackle with a piece of the jello and garnish with mint.

Purple Mung Bean Noodle and Mango

Noodles in gelatin sounds like such a good idea. Think of a nice cold noodle soup that has solidified with the gelatinous broth. Nope, it's disgusting. I've wanted it to work so badly. This is the only one I found very tasty, and it may have been more about the bright color than anything else. I am also particularly fond of this purple noodle. I did dozens of noodle-making demos for my last project, before large and small groups without a hitch, but this particular one was the only complete disaster—meant to feed a crowd of maybe 100. Instead of pouring the hot water into the starch, as one should, I poured the starch into the water. After cooking it, the dough eventually formed but once extruded into boiling water, it completely disintegrated. So keep in mind, starch is like animal gelatin in this respect; if you boil a long time, it will never be able to hold together.

1 cup mung bean starch (available at Asian groceries or online)
1 tsp Purple Butterfly pea flower powder
2 cups rum
juice of 2 limes
2 tbsp sugar
2 tbsp gelatin
½ mango, peeled and sliced
sprinkle of smoked paprika

Get a pot of water boiling. Then mix the starch and purple powder. Slowly add a spoonful of boiling water at a time and mix vigorously. Keep adding water until you have a firm dough. Don't add too much. While still hot, knead the dough between the palms of your hands. It hurts, but it's worth it. Then form a cylinder and place in the chamber of a noodle extruder or a ricer. Squeeze the noodles directly into the boiling water. Cook through until still chewy. Drain and rinse with cold water. Place the noodles in a bowl. Dissolve the gelatin in ¼ cup of the rum with the lime juice and heat the rest. Add the

sugar to the pot and stir until dissolved. Pour over the gelatin. Let cool and then pour over the noodles. Let set in the fridge and then unmold on a plate garnished with mango slices and dusted with the paprika.

Starfruit in Pomegranate and Rum

Star fruit or carambola is the prettiest fruit on earth. It doesn't always taste great, but I think that's because the ones we get are picked unripe or are just a variety that will survive shipping. But every now and then you find a perfectly ripe specimen that is both fragrant and succulent. You could say the same for mangos, papaya, cherimoya—most tropical fruits. Wait till you get a great one to make this recipe.

1 ripe star fruit sliced
½ cup rum
1 ½ cups pomegranate juice
and a few seeds from 1 pomegranate
1 ½ tbsp gelatin

Lay the slices of star fruit in a glass dish. Dissolve the gelatin in the rum. Whack the pomegranate all over with the back of a wooden spoon. Then over a bowl cut it open and squeeze out the juice with your hands. Strain the juice if you need to and reserve a few whole seeds. Heat the juice and then add it to the gelatin mixture. Let cool and pour over the star fruit and garnish with a few seeds. There's no need to unmold this; just use a cake knife to serve wedges, garnished perhaps with a little sweetened whipped cream.

Screwdriver with White Chocolate Ganache Center

This was such a fortuitous leap of imagination. I'm not a dessert person, and I'd actually never made a ganache before, then putting it all together at the last minute and having the center still molten when cut open—it was pure beginner's luck. You need the best oranges—these came from Babcia Betty's tree in Modesto.

2 oranges yielding a cup of juice
¼ cup vodka
1 tbsp gelatin

1 cup white chocolate chips
½ cup heavy cream
half a banana, sliced

Juice the oranges with a reamer so you have a cup. Mix ¼ cup of vodka with the gelatin to bloom and then heat the orange juice and pour over the mixture. Then pour into small hemispherical silicon molds. Set in the fridge for at least a few hours until very firm.

Then in a pot over low heat, heat the cream and slowly drop in the chips while stirring until completely melted. Let cool until thick but still flowing. Take out the hemispheres of jello and with a melon baller scoop out the center of each. Then briefly pass a blowtorch over the tops and pour the ganache into each and put the two halves together, making sure they're stuck. Quickly put on plates and garnish with slices of banana. If you get them to the table in time, they will ooze when people cut them. Or you can do it upon service with a red-hot steak knife. It squeals with delight when the knife hits the cold jello.

Grappa and Macédoine of Fruit

This makes a quick and simple dessert. Its dramatic appeal derives entirely from the mold. Use a small silicon shape so you can serve one or two per person, or even shapes made with a cookie cutter would be interesting. I used a grappa made of Nebbiolo grapes, but any good Italian grappa undiluted and unsweetened will work.

1 cup of fruits such as
grapefruit, blueberries,
cherries
2 tbsp sugar
few drops of vanilla extract
few drops of grappa
1 cup grappa
1 tbsp gelatin
5% Greek yogurt
½ tsp lemon zest

Toss the fruit in sugar, vanilla, and just a little grappa and let marinate for an hour or so. Mix ¼ cup of grappa with the gelatin to bloom; heat the rest, carefully in a wide pot—you don't want it to ignite. Mix the two, then pour into molds, and set in the fridge. Unmold onto a dessert plate. Spoon the fruit next to it with a dollop of yogurt and sprinkle lemon zest on top.

Coconut Agar Jello

Coconuts were prized possessions in medieval Europe, valued more for the shell than the contents. I doubt many people in Europe had even tasted fresh coconut until the colonial era, but they definitely imported and carved coconut shells. You can saw off the top of a coconut and either use as is, or I often then sand and polish it to smoothness. It makes a really beautiful bowl.

1 coconut
2 tsp agar
1 cup coconut milk (not water) canned or fresh
3 tbsp raw sugar or date palm sugar

1 cup rum
2 drops vanilla extract
1 banana
1 mango

Saw off the top of the coconut, leaving the meat inside. Drink the water. In a small pot, dissolve the agar in the coconut milk and heat. Boil for about 3 minutes. Add the sugar to dissolve, extract, and then the rum. Let cool. Pour this into your coconut and add pieces of mango and banana. Let it set in the fridge.

If you want to make fresh coconut milk, you need a device they use in Southeast Asia that looks like a sharp claw on the end of a thick bamboo stick. It scrapes out the coconut meat. You can do it with a spoon too, but it's a lot of work. Chop the coconut meat up and pour over boiling water to cover. Let it sit until room temperature. Then pour the whole thing through a cloth and wring out to remove all the moisture. You have coconut milk.

Pineapple Gin Popsicle

You all know fresh pineapple contains an enzyme called bromelain that prevents gelatin from setting. The first time I tried this, I forgot that. The jello set initially, but when I pulled it out of the fridge, I could see the jello disintegrating before my eyes, at which point my son and I gobbled it down as quickly as we could. This version deactivates the enzyme with cooking. Use wide plastic cups as the mold.

1 fresh pineapple
1 tbsp brown sugar
2 cups St. George Terroir Gin or
    something with really piney
    aroma
2 tbsp gelatin
lavender and rosemary flowers
Luxardo cherries
wooden skewers

With a large sharp knife cut off the top and bottom of the pineapple. Then remove the outer peel and any dark spots. Then put the pineapple on its side and cut into 1-inch rounds. If you have a round cookie cutter or coring device, cut out the hard inner core or just use a knife. Sprinkle the circles with brown sugar and place on a hot grill until lightly charred, about 5 or 6 minutes. Let these cool, then place in the bottom of your cups. Mix ½ cup gin with the gelatin to bloom. Heat the rest, then mix them. Pour directly over the pineapple, just to cover. Sprinkle with flowers and put a cherry in the middle. To unmold, snip the rim of the cup with scissors and pull back the plastic to loosen the pineapple rounds. Then put two skewers into the side of each round and pass around.

Fruit Cake Jello

I know people joke about fruit cake, and pass it back and forth each year as Christmas presents. But I really like it, even when it's leaden. I think this gelatinous version is even better; in fact, it may be my favorite jello of the entire lot. You want the gelatin really sturdy for this one, so it's more of a dried fruity gummy than a soft jello, and the texture of the fruit melds perfectly.

Making it could not be simpler: arrange dried fruits and nuts in a rectangular plastic container. I used dried cherries, raisins, figs, prunes, cranberries, candied citron, walnuts, and pistachios. Anything will work, but the more tart and brighter the fruit, I think the better. Then make a batch of bourbon Old Fashioned cocktail. Just put a few dashes of angostura bitters in a glass, a teaspoon of sugar, a little bit of water just to loosen it up—muddle these together with a twist of lemon and pour over really good bourbon. I added two full cups, but you can use more water and less bourbon too if you prefer. Mix 2 ½ tbsp gelatin with ½ cup of the drink. Heat the rest, pour over the gelatin, and mix the two together. Then pour over the fruit. Let set in the fridge, unmold, and slice into long sticks that people can pick up and eat. It rather reminds me of Turkish Lokum—but I'll give you a separate recipe for that.

Lokum

You may have tried what they call Turkish Delight—which are little gelatinous squares of fruit-flavored candy, sometimes rose, pistachio, or other flavors. These are complete frivolity, appropriate only for pasty-faced British children-villains named Edmund. The original sweet is far more interesting, dark and mysteri-

ous, and might be worth selling your soul for. My grandfather who was from Kastoria in northern Greece would buy a section of the snake-shaped lokum at a Middle Eastern shop on Atlantic Avenue in Brooklyn, and so did my father. I hadn't tasted it in decades until a recent trip to New York, at which point I vowed to figure out how to make it. While not a gelatin per se, it is very close to some of the creations here, so I had to include it.

Take a quart of grape juice, either store bought or even better, squeezed from fresh wine grapes. Whisking in a half cup of wheat starch or cornstarch will work fine as well, with a pinch of cream of tartar, a splash of rosewater. Cook this in a wide pan, stirring constantly on low heat for about an hour and a half. I know this sounds crazy, but listen to something diverting, good bouzouki music, and you will end up dancing. When it is almost thick, add a handful of pistachios. Then with a rubber spatula, scrape the mass onto a sheet of parchment paper dusted well with powdered sugar and roll into a long snake. It will cool and solidify eventually, at room temperature. Slice off sections or serve the entire log for a party with plenty of rakı.

Sherry Raspberry Blintz

This was among the best tasting jellos I have ever made. The combination of flavors is spot on, and if you want to serve this to children, I'd just use grape juice.

2 tbsp unflavored gelatin
2 cups Hartley and Gibson Fino Sherry
1 tbsp raspberry jelly without seeds
2 tbsp cream cheese

2 tbsp cottage cheese
4 tbsp powdered sugar
½ tsp almond extract
8 crushed amaretti
lemon zest

Bloom gelatin in ½ cup sherry and add jelly. Bring remaining sherry to a boil and add to the mixture. Let cool; pour into two large teflon frying pans to create jello crepes. Mix cheeses and sugar and extract and spread on the jello. Carefully roll jello around cheeses and move to a plate. Garnish with crushed amaretti and lemon zest.

Lemon Saffron Sake Jello

These little wedges are intensely bright and sour. The simplicity is its real appeal, and the sake adds a very gentle kick. The shape is made by setting the jello in small oval tart molds and then quartering that and lining up the slices. The Tajín is a combination of chili, lime, and salt and is great for its visual effect and pungency. Be careful though—it's very addictive.

1 cup sake
1 tbsp sugar
juice of 1 lemon
¼ tsp lemon extract
1 pack gelatin
pinch of saffron threads,
    crushed
sliced strawberry, melon balls,
    raspberries, and whatever
    you have on hand
sprinkle of Tajín powder

Mix the first three ingredients to dissolve the sugar. Then set aside a quarter cup to bloom the gelatin. Heat the rest with the saffron. Mix the two and pour into the molds. Then drop in the pieces of fruit. Let set, unmold, and cut into quarters. Arrange on a plate and sprinkle with the powder.

Grapefruit Greyhound Jello

You've all seen the trick of hollowing out a citrus peel and filling it with sherbet or jello. This goes a step farther. I wanted it to look as close as possible to the actual fruit cut in half and taste much like it too. Greyhound is the name of the cocktail. If you add salt to the rim, it's a Salty Dog.

2 pink grapefruits	a little sugar
2 shots of vodka	1 red hot
splash of bitters	

Start with one grapefruit. Peel one down through the white pith, getting as close as possible to the flesh without cutting into it. Then, holding the

grapefruit in one hand, with the sharpest paring knife you have, cut out each individual segment leaving behind all the membranes. Do this over a bowl so you don't lose the juice. The segments are called *suprêmes de pamplemousse*. It takes a little practice, but it's worth it. Then cut your other grapefruit in half and scoop out all the flesh, leaving a sturdy hollow shell of the peel. Squeeze all the juice from the membranes and whatever dripped from your slices, and add a couple of shots of vodka and a splash of bitters, and a little sugar to taste.

Then take toothpicks and skewer the slices inside the grapefruit peel, right through the peel, exactly where they would have gone before. Then dissolve a packet of gelatin in a little of your cocktail and heat the rest. Mix the two, stir, and let cool thoroughly. Pour over the grapefruit right up to the top. Put in the fridge to set and then garnish with a red hot or whatever you like.

Negroni with Charred Cara Cara Orange

The Negroni is arguably the perfect drink. Perhaps not in winter, but then there's the Boulevardier, switching out the gin for bourbon. Whenever I have a negroni, I think of a particular al fresco table at a bar in Genoa, just slightly above the winding medieval streets of the city's core. A little farinata—a kind of chickpea pancake baked until crunchy on the outside, and a few other bits to nibble on. It all goes perfectly. This is a gelatinous version of that vibe.

⅓ cup each Gin, Red Vermouth, Campari
1 Cara Cara Orange or other type
1 cup chickpea flour
2 tbsp olive oil
squares of blue cheese
slices of salami

Start with equal parts gin, red vermouth, and Campari. Cut thin slices of the cara cara orange, and char over an open flame. Make a jello of your cocktail in a shallow bowl, and place the orange wedge inside.

Garnish with farinata crisps. This is not how it's traditionally made, but it's easier and doesn't require heating the oven. Boil a small pot of water and while constantly stirring, sprinkle in the chickpea flour. Add a pinch of salt. Turn the heat on low and continue cooking. Cook about 10 minutes or more until very thick, then pour out into a shallow casserole. Let cool several hours in the fridge. Then cut out rounds or whatever shape you like and fry these gently in olive oil until crispy; sprinkle with salt. This can also be done with cornmeal polenta if you like.

Arrange the crisps around the jello with cheese, salami, some random bits of herbage. Lovely.

Karelian Pie

I was told in no uncertain terms that this is not Karelian pie, which is an appellation with protected designation status under EU law. A Finnish friend suggested I call it mustikkakukko, which sounds great to me! It is only reminiscent of the original in its oval shape, as there's no rice in it, but rather a fruit jello. I think if you can find cloud berries or lingonberries or even sea buckthorn, that would be amazing. The array of berries available at the outdoor market in Helsinki and the adjacent striped brick Vanha Kauppahalli made me think

of this. I used squeezed local blackberries because that's what was available. I think even blueberry or cherry juice would be superb. If you want to make several servings, just multiply the recipe per person.

1 cup rye flour
½ stick butter
pinch of ginger
2 tbsp sugar
ice cold water

1 cup berry juice
¼ cup aquavit
1 packet gelatin
slices of pickled watermelon
   rind for garnish

Make the crust by mixing the first 4 ingredients and adding enough cold water just until the dough comes together. Roll it out and place in a small oval tart tin. The original pie is folded over without a mold, but that won't work with jello. Pinch the edges so you have an elegant rim. Bake for about 20–30 minutes at 350 degrees until cooked through but not burned. Let the shell cool completely.

Mix the aquavit with the gelatin and heat the juice. Pour the juice over the gelatin and mix the two. Let cool. Then pour into the crust and put in the fridge to set completely. To serve, garnish with slivers of the watermelon rind or berries if you have them, and remove from the tart pans.

Tiny Watermelon Jello

The watermelon is native to Africa and supposedly in the wild was so bitter that people only collected it for the water it contained, or the seeds. Egyptian pharaohs, including Tut, were buried with the seeds so they could have these portable canteens in the afterlife. Think of this as a variant on the original.

Anything you can scoop out, you can also fill with jello. When I spied tiny watermelons in a Cambodian grocery store, the idea was irresistible. I don't think they were what are called mouse melons or Mexican gherkins (*Melothria scabra*), which are tiny. Those I found were about the size of an orange, they fit in the palm of your hand. Whatever they were, the insides taste more like a cucumber, so use the juice of a regular watermelon to complete the deception. Spiked with a little liqueur, it was delightful.

4 little watermelons that hold about ¼ cup of filling	2 tbsp Maraschino liqueur
2 cups of watermelon juice	1 packet gelatin
2 tbsp Campari	a pinch of white and black sesame seeds

Slice off the top of each melon and scoop out the insides. Cut a few slices of a regular watermelon and squeeze by hand until you have 2 cups of juice. Heat the juice and reduce by one half. Don't worry if the liquid separates into clear water and red bits. Dissolve the gelatin in the two liqueurs and then add the hot juice. Mix and fill the melons. Lining them up in a plastic container will prevent them from tipping over. When almost set, drop in a few white and black sesame seeds. Serve with tiny spoons.

Peach with Hypocris Custard Gelatin

To stick with my idea that if it can be hollowed, it can be filled with jello, the peach offers so many possibilities. Hypocris (or more typically Hippocras) was a kind of medieval spiced wine, filtered through a bag to clarify. But by the early modern period there was also a neat trick to make the liquid completely clear that uses milk. This was an early version of the milk punch, recorded in the manuscript cookbook of one Lettice Pudsey in the 17th century. I happened to be making it for a video series, an episode of which featured Lettice, so I had several bottles on hand. The cookbook first came to my attention while giving some talks at the Folger Shakespeare Library in Washington, DC, where it is housed. I worked there my senior year in college, so it was so nice to return decades later. My college English professor even came to hear my talk.

For the Hypocris:

3 pints of dry white wine	3 slices of ginger
1 pint of sherry	1 tsp crushed coriander
1 cup sugar (the original recipe calls for 4!)	1 tbsp whole cloves
	2 cups milk
3 slices of whole nutmeg	

For the Jello:

3 ripe but slightly firm peaches	1 egg, yolk and white separated
1 vanilla bean	sprigs of tarragon
1 cup heavy cream	1 packet gelatin

Crush all the spices but don't reduce them to a powder. You want whole pieces. Soak the spices in the wines overnight, or better yet, for a few days. Bring the milk to a gentle boil and pour directly into the spiced wine. It will curdle and look dreadful—don't worry. Let it rest for about an hour, and you'll see all the debris gather into the raft of muck. You can even do this with red wine and it strips out most of the color, leaving it light pink. Then with a ladle gently pour the wine through a fine-mesh sieve lined with several layers of cheesecloth. You should have perfectly clear hypocris.

Cut the peaches in half from top to bottom, remove the pit, and scoop out some of the flesh so you have enough room to hold some jello. Then gently heat your cream with the vanilla bean that has been split and the seeds scraped out. Reduce by about half and remove the vanilla pod. Then whip the egg yolk and add a drop of cream to temper, whisking the whole time. Keep adding the rest of the cream. Whip the egg white until you have soft peaks.

Dissolve the gelatin in a half cup of the hypocris. Add that to the warm custard and then fold in the egg whites. You should have a thick creamy aromatic mass. With a rubber spatula, fill the peach halves and let set. When ready to serve, slice the peach halves into quarters or thirds and serve with a sprig of the tarragon.

Peach Lambic Waffle

You know how cooking everything on a waffle iron became popular a few years ago? I admit I made some crazy stuff on it: sandwiches, burgers, pasta. As crazy as this one sounds, it turned out very well, and the texture is nothing you might expect—chewy and crunchy at the same time.

1 cup flour	1 packet gelatin
1 egg	1 tsp butter
1 tsp baking powder	½ cup cream cheese
1 cup peach lambic beer from Belgium	½ cup sour cream
	2 tbsp sugar

Mix together the first three ingredients. Bloom the gelatin in the beer and mix that in. Heat up your waffle iron and spread with a little butter. Pour in the batter and close the top. Cook until golden brown and then remove carefully. The waffle will probably split horizontally, and that's what you want. Repeat until you've used all the batter. Then mix the filling ingredients and spread on the inside of each waffle half. Roll them into tubes and cut on the diagonal. Serve with strawberries, or peaches if in season.

Cranberry Juice Jello for Thanksgiving

Cranberry is one of the few fruits that will solidify entirely on its own with cooking. Quince will also do it, hence quince paste. Thanks to the pectin, which is usually added to fruit to make jam and jelly in the American sense of those words, we have that singularly exquisite phenomenon of cranberry sauce in a can, presented seemingly as a jello and eaten as such. This recipe is more of a traditional sauce, but in actual gelatinous form. You can use any mold you like; I used a Bundt-like form I made in my basement pottery studio. Judge the quantity your mold will hold and adjust accordingly for 1 cup of liquid per packet of gelatin, or slightly less gelatin if you like it softer.

2 cups applejack	slices of apple, blood orange and whole cranberries
3 or 4 packets of gelatin	more cranberries for garnish
2 cups cranberry juice cocktail (sweetened)	powdered sugar
	1 egg white

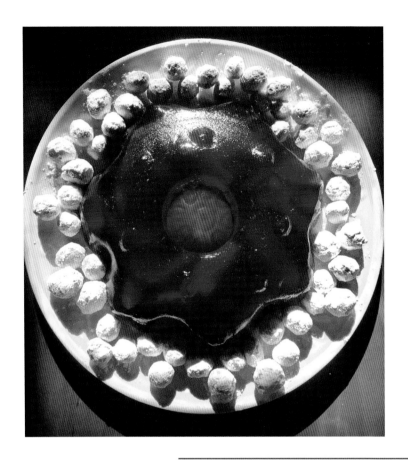

Bloom the gelatin in 1 cup of the applejack. Mix the other cup with the juice and bring to a boil. Then add it to the gelatin. Pour into a lightly greased mold. Let chill until not quite set. Put in the fruit and let it sink inside the jello, but not sink all the way to the bottom of the mold. Chill thoroughly. You can also add crushed walnuts, or any other fruit you like.

Prepare the garnish by dipping the cranberries into the egg white and then rolling in the powdered sugar. Place on a plate to dry completely. They will become crunchy and deliciously sour. When ready to serve, unmold the jello onto a large platter. Surround with the candied cranberries. Just don't store them together, or the moisture in the jello will dissolve the sugar on the berries.

Dates Stuffed with Chestnuts Wrapped in Bacon and Set in Rosé Jello

This recipe will immediately make you think of Angels or Devils on Horseback, a popular midcentury hors d'oeuvre involving either oysters or chicken livers wrapped in bacon. This one still has the bacon but shoots for a more delicate flavor profile that will stand up to being served cold. The bacon of course won't be crispy, but it offers just the right chew to contrast with the other ingredients. You can boil your fresh chestnuts, but I've found them sold in a package lately already cooked, which is also very nice.

1 cup peeled and chopped
   chestnuts
1 dozen dates

6 slices of bacon
2 cups rosé wine
2 packets gelatin

Chop the chestnuts coarsely. Slit each date down the side and remove the pit. Stuff the chestnuts inside. Cut each slice of bacon in half and cook very slowly until the fat is rendered, but still pliable. Drain on paper towels. Wrap each stuffed date with the bacon and secure with a toothpick. Dissolve the gelatin in ½ cup wine and bring the rest to the boil. Mix the two. Pour into small cup-shape molds large enough to hold each wrapped date, but not too big. Set each date in the jello, leaving the toothpick intact. Let set in the refrigerator for an hour or more. Unmold each jello and slice in half. Arrange on a plate exposing the interior. They look rather disturbing, which I like.

Crème de Cassis Gummies

I approach the topic of gummies with some ambivalence. As you will have noticed, I am hesitant to use artificial flavors and colors in my creations. It is partly an irrational fear; I know I eat such things unwittingly all the time. In fact, although I'm not fond of cake or chocolate or even ice cream that much, I love gummy candy—sour cherries, peaches, worms. It's partly the texture and partly the sourness. If I want something to nibble on during a long airplane flight, a small bag will keep me entertained for hours. I couldn't do a whole book on gelatin and just leave out gummies. On the other hand, I could make them more interesting. I know people toss gummies in alcohol, but I don't see the appeal. I want the booze in the gummy to start.

The principle is simple. You add a lot more gelatin, and you let it sit out for a few days to get really chewy. I learned this lesson years ago, before I ever had any interest in gelatin. I was at a food ethnography conference in Heidelberg (there really are such things). The conference meets somewhere different in Europe every other year, and part of the fun is going to see a local food manufacturer. There was olive oil in Greece, a wheat farm in Finland, a dairy in Southern Sweden. This year we were taken by bus to a gelatin factory: Gelita. It was an enormous complex in Eberbach on the banks of the Neckar River. Somehow, I had imagined we would see whole pigs being tossed into vats and a malodorous stench arising from the rendering carcasses and bones. In fact, exactly the opposite was the case. It was all clean, efficient, and dare I say, sweet smelling? The simmering machines were beautiful. The people working there were cheery and welcoming. The clear sheets that emerged from the end were like translucent little windowpanes with impressed hatch marks. I couldn't resist picking up a few that had fallen on the floor. At the end of the fabulous tour, we were taken into a plush conference space, had a pleasant meal, and listened to gelatin executives make presentations, and we were offered infinite quantities of gummy bears to gorge on in a variety of flavors that was astonishing. This company supplies the sheets to Haribo.

After that I would not even attempt to replicate what you can buy in a package if you want gummy bears. Leave that to the experts. The gelatin alone will cost you more than to just buy gummies. But maybe something they can't sell. I have friends on social media who make cannabis gummies, and part of me really wishes I liked weed. But here is something with a little kick.

1 cup real Crème de Cassis liqueur	1 tbsp lime juice
3 packets gelatin	Small silicone mold lightly sprayed with oil
1 tbsp corn syrup	

Mix ¼ cup of cassis with the gelatin and stir until it becomes a thick dark paste. Heat the rest with the syrup and lime juice. The corn syrup will prevent it from being grainy. Mix the two thoroughly and then carefully pour with a spoon into the molds and let set in the refrigerator for a few hours. Unmold the gummies and place them on a parchment sheet and leave out for a few days until you like the texture. They will get stiffer fairly quickly. Then put them in a plastic bag and enjoy at your leisure. How about on a plane?

You can substitute any good liqueur here. Gummies really need the sweetness and some acidity, but otherwise use Grand Marnier, Drambuie, Benedictine—I think just about any liqueur would be splendid.

Cooked Peach and Candied Walnut

When the peaches you bought at the market are overripe, remove the pits and slice them skin and all, put them in a nonstick pan, and toss on sugar and maybe a little vanilla extract. Gently cook them, not so they fall apart but release their juice. Let that reduce slowly until they are thick and place in a jar. The quantity you make is of course entirely whatever you have on hand. Or proceed with this recipe using a commercial whole fruit preserve. The charm I think is using a fluted mold that makes the slices look like pie—this was a plastic container from an order of take-out chow mein.

1 cup peach preserves
1 cup walnuts
½ cup unrefined sugar
¼ tsp ground cinnamon
pinch of salt
1 cup water

juice of one lemon
½ cup sugar
2 drops lemon extract
¼ cup gin
1 packet of gelatin

In a nonstick pan put the walnuts, sugar, cinnamon, and salt. Heat on low until the sugar melts, then stir to coat the nuts. Don't touch them, but put aside on a plate to cool. Put the peach preserve and walnuts in a mold. Put the water on the stove to boil and combine all the other ingredients to let the gelatin bloom. Then add the boiling water and pour into the mold. Let set in the refrigerator. Slice into wedges and serve, perhaps with ice cream.

Superbowl Orange Tequila Bundt

Every year, friends throw a big Superbowl party that has been ongoing for over 20 years. I have no interest in the game, honestly, but the people and the food are always very interesting. It's a chance to try out new recipes on a big crowd and see their reactions. The past several years, I've been bringing a kind of savory dump pie—which means you make a crust of Doritos or Flamin' Hot Cheetos with butter, and then throw in onions, cheddar, bacon, pepperoni, ham, chilies, and literally whatever happens to be in the fridge, bind it with eggs, and bake it. It always gets eaten. This Big Honking Jello was rather like that: I put in layers of whatever was in the house and it turned out fabulous. I encourage you to do the same. Use a bundt pan as the mold.

2 oranges, peeled and segments separated
1 cup orange flavored sparkling water
8 tbsp sugar—divided into 4 parts
almond extract—a few drops in each layer

8 packets of gelatin
1 bottle of tequila, divided into 4 parts
1 cup Greek yogurt
1 cup orange juice
½ cup crème de cassis

This will contain 4 layers, each of which is set separately. It's a good idea to set out four different bowls and align the ingredients so you can quickly add the next layer once each is set. Place 2 packets of gelatin in each bowl and plan to add about 2 cups of liquid to each. Also add sugar and almond extract as you please to each bowl. Start by assembling the orange segments slightly overlapping around the bottom of the mold. Pour over a gelatin made of sparkling water and quarter of the bottle of tequila, then set the gelatin with a little of the liquid, heat the rest, then mix them. For the next layer, mix in yogurt and another quarter of the tequila, sugar, and pour over the just-set layer with oranges. The third layer make with the orange juice, tequila, and sugar. For the last layer, use the remaining tequila, crème de cassis, and sugar. For parties, I usually put a big warning notice nearby—eat at your own risk, no children S.V.P. You can of course use less booze or none at all if you prefer. Just substitute more orange juice.

CHAPTER 8

OUTRAGEOUS COMBINATIONS

Cantaloupe with Roast Duck and Celeriac Salad Spritz

This is sort of like a tower of a meal in three courses. I happened to see an enormous celeriac, i.e. celery root, in the market and bought it on a whim. I'd tried it before and was generally disappointed, but this one was so aromatic, crisp, and delicious that I shredded it all for the salad which lasted several weeks. It makes buckets and was good to the end.

2 slices ripe cantaloupe, cut into small cubes

1 leftover roast duck parts cut into cubes (these were legs)

1 cup celery root, shredded

1 cup mayonnaise

2 tbsp white wine vinegar

2 tbsp sugar

1 tbsp dried dill (or more fresh)

2 cups dry white wine

1 cup lime-flavored seltzer water

3 packs gelatin

a raspberry for garnish

First make the salad by peeling and shredding the celeriac on a box grater. Mix with the mayo, vinegar, sugar, and dill; set aside in the fridge. Then mix your spritz, dissolving the gelatin in 1 cup, heating the rest and mixing the two. Let cool. Mix one third of the gelatin with about a cup of salad. (Save the rest for the week and serve every single day to your family; eventually they will look at you derisively when it appears.) Put this at the bottom of a cylindrical

mold or whatever shape you like. Place in the freezer to set quickly. Then add duck with another third of the gelatin. Let that set and finally make the last layer with the cantaloupe. Unmold and serve in slices. Although you can eat each part separately, they go very nicely together with a little bit of each in every bite.

Dance of the Green Faerie

Absinthe is without any doubt the finest beverage ever invented. I won't make any claims for its supposed hallucinogenic effects, or whether thujone has anything to do with it, but I can vouch for its tendency to heighten the sensations and even jumble them up in unusual ways. This is called synesthesia, an actual condition in which people can hear flavor, see textures, smell color. Enough absinthe and you will understand what this means, and following Oscar Wilde's advice, that would be after "the first glass of absinthe you see things as you wish they were" and after the second when "you see things as they are not" but before the third when you see things as they really are.

This is pure edible poetry. The sound must be Claire de Lune or some other very dreamy piece by Debussy. Or maybe even Erik Satie—they were both absinthe addicts. If you can, have someone read the poetry of Rimbaud or Verlaine.

To make this you need a tall thin plastic cup or a mold that will yield a shape that will cause the jello to wobble and teeter. Mix ¼ to ½ cup of absinthe (the strongest you can find) and half a cup of water. Add a tablespoon of white sugar. Bloom a packet of jello in the absinthe and heat the sugar water (not the absinthe or it will ignite), then mix the two and set in the mold. Chill, then unmold onto a plate. It will be a pale green luminescent color and surprisingly not cloudy and opaque, but you might capture a hint of the green swirls or louche. Lower the lights and shine a spotlight on the jello and jiggle it to the Debussy and be transported.

Painted Jello

In college, I played Sir Toby Belch in a production of *Twelfth Night*. Type casting. The play was set in the 17th century, and so for the part I grew some facial hair, wore a long wig, and carried a sword. The part was written for me. The costume manager also fit me with a magnificent fat suit. It was tailored so beautifully, even with a belly button dimple, that it looked absolutely real. So much so that after the first day's rehearsal in the suit, my fellow performers seeing me backstage in street clothes said—oh, you're really not that size!

The next day the director ordered the suit be changed. He had the costume manager lengthen it, making it bulge weirdly under my belt, so it didn't fit well, and the dimple was gone. It was actually uncomfortable and difficult to

move in. I thought at the time he was trying to make it more realistic and just failed. I asked him if the suit could be put back, and the director immediately refused.

I never understood what was going on until 35 years later. If art imitates life exactly, it ceases to be art. Think of reality television. A statue that is perfectly lifelike is imitation, nothing more. Art must not look real in some way, either to make a point or to express something beyond the everyday. Had I worn the first fat suit, the audience would have thought that was my body. With the misshapen one it was a reminder that I was playing a part, this was not real. It is a farce. I was a caricature of a real drunken uncle.

The same logic lies within those beautiful plates of fake Japanese food one sees in restaurant windows. They are meant to explain to customers what's for sale, but more importantly, they dazzle the senses—because they don't look real. They look like wax. If they looked real, people would think, eew—why did they leave that bowl of soup in the window? Andy Warhol's images of soup cans, if utterly realistic, would have said nothing, but in repetition, in a series of prints, meant to look similar to but not exactly, that's something different, beyond reality, but mocking it.

So it was that I set out to replicate sushi from jello. I had just started playing with painting techniques and by accident discovered that you could get an eerie translucence if the color was only on the outside of the jello. I played with it more by using black rice instead of white. I don't think it was as good as my performance as Sir Toby, but it was fun and tasted good.

Here's how: Make a jello of sake and a little sugar and ponzu or lemon juice. Two cups sake to two packets gelatin. Let it set in a square casserole or container and then cut it into thin rectangles. Smooth the edges of the cuts with a hot knife so it looks more like cut fish. Then using natural vegetable dyes or regular food coloring diluted with vodka, paint some striations on the top to replicate those of ahi tuna. Then fill in the rest with red dye painted on the sides and between the lines. Cook a batch of black rice or regular sushi rice, let cool by fanning. Then form small rectangles and place the jello on top. Serve with pickled ginger and wasabi.

Generation Z Cocktail

Both my children technically qualify as members of this generation. This is the kind of stuff they like. I made it jokingly and I admit it sounds like an absolute abomination, but the flavors meld beautifully. It's the incongruence of really great ingredients and junk that wins me over, dude. Eat this while texting.

1 handful Flamin' Hot Limón
    Cheetos
a few sprigs of cilantro
6 fresh cranberry beans,
    boiled in salted water and
    marinated in olive oil and
    vinegar
1 stick of string cheese
2 jalapeño stuffed olives
about half a can of Black Cherry
    White Claw Spiked Seltzer
1.5 tbsp cold set gelatin
2 ounces ground beef
pinch each of salt, oregano,
    paprika, cumin
a wedge of avocado sprinkled
    with salt and lime juice

For this you need a squat disposable clear 9-ounce plastic cup. Put the Cheetos in first, then the cilantro, the beans, cheese shredded, olives. Mix the seltzer with 1 tbs gelatin. The reason to use cold set is so you can capture the bubbles. Pour into the cup.

You will see the Cheetos fizz and color the gelatin. Let this set for about 20–30 minutes. Season and fry your ground beef, let cool. Crumble on top of the cup. Then take the remaining half tablespoon of gelatin and add about half a cup of seltzer and pour on top of the beef. Put back in the fridge to set. Unmold gently, place on a plate, and top with the avocado. The pleasant illusion is that the upper rim will look like glass; the bubbles will make it look like it's frosty.

You can easily switch out the ingredients to suit your taste. Lime seltzer would be great, or grapefruit. Sausage meat would be nice or even crumbled bacon.

Trifle

A traditional English dish known as trifle, which perhaps suggests how seriously it is taken, usually consists of custard, fruits, ladies' fingers or cake, and fortified wine. The appeal is that it is served in a glass vessel so you can see each layer separated. It developed from a simpler recipe called a fool in the 16th century. Many versions contain gelatin, as does Hannah Glasse's version in the mid–18th century. The advantage of the gelatin is that it keeps the fruit from wobbling around and the whole thing from collapsing when scooped out. Here we will not trifle with the original version, but rather a sardonic subversion. Diners will expect something sweet and instead they encounter a very savory cake indeed.

1 cup cherry juice
1 cup 100 proof bourbon
2 packets gelatin
ladyfingers (or savoiardi biscuits)

¼ lb cured and cooked pork belly cut into small cubes
¼ lb blue cheese
mascarpone—enough to make the cheese spreadable
freshly ground pepper

Mix ½ cup cherry juice with the gelatin to bloom. Heat the rest with the bourbon and then combine the two. Line a deep glass bowl with the lady fingers and soak with the gelatin. Add some pork belly and then add another layer of biscuits. Spread on the cheese mixture. Sprinkle with pepper. Repeat, creating many layers, alternating soaked biscuits with pork and cheese. Then pour the rest of the gelatin on top. It should cover everything. If it doesn't, just make more of the gelatin to do so. Cover and let chill in the fridge. Serve in the bowl cut into wedges—as an appetizer I hope.

Basil Seed and Rice Whiskey

At a point in my research I was experimenting with substances that are naturally gelatinous, or become so with minor coaxing. There is a whole class of Jelly fungus called colloquially witches' butter in the field and identified by scientists in several orders of *heterobasidiomycete* in the subphylum *Agaricomycotina*. Apparently most of them are perfectly edible if not all tasty, and a few are put regularly in soup. Someday I hope to find a mycologist to help me identify these in the wild, but I did find them in a Chinese grocery (see the recipe for Tremella). Spirulina seemed perhaps a little more promising, as the prized pond muck much esteemed by the Aztecs and now available in pill form in health food stores.

Finally I decided that it should be seeds that swell. Chia is delightful. But Basil seeds are really exciting, mostly because they look like some kind of insect or monster egg, especially when set in gelatin. When I posted an image of this, hundreds of people commented on social media that it triggered an apparently not uncommon terror of dark holes called Trypophobia. I apologize reader if it has had the same effect on you. If not, do try making it—it is perfectly lurid.

1 cup basil seed
2 cups rice whiskey
2 packets gelatin

Cover the basil seed with water and let soak several hours or overnight until swollen. Drain any excess water in a colander. Then mix ½ cup of whiskey with the gelatin, stir, and let bloom. Boil the rest and mix together, stirring. Place the gooey basil seeds in a bowl and cover with the gelatin. Let set for at least two hours. Unmold and cut into wedges, arrange decoratively. It does really look like frog spawn. The flavor of the seeds themselves isn't very pronounced, so you'll be able to taste the whiskey with every bite. You can of course substitute any liquor.

Kohakutou

In Japan there is a beautiful form of agar cut into crystal shapes and left out to harden on the outside, remaining soft inside. It's made with much more sugar than would normally go into a gelatin, so the outside recrystallizes

when exposed to air for a few days. Usually they're purplish and red and ideally translucent, but the name in Japanese means amber sugar, so it seemed fitting to make it with raw unprocessed sugar to get that color. And here wine forms the base rather than water.

> 1 ½ tbs agar powder
> 1 cup Sauvignon Blanc Wine
>   from New Zealand
> 1 ⅓ cup raw sugar
> 3 drops peppermint extract
> 1 tsp oil
> 3 drops green food coloring

In a pot dissolve the agar in the wine, stirring thoroughly. Bring to a boil and then add in the sugar and flavoring. Pour into an oiled glass baking dish. Add a few drops of green food coloring if you like and swirl around into patterns. Let the gelatin set at room temperature for a few hours. Then cut into shapes like shards of glass, crystals, beads of amber. It will be very sticky so you might want to wear plastic gloves. Then set these shapes on a rack over a baking sheet and leave to dry for several days. You will need to turn them over from time to time or arrange them so the greatest surface area is exposed to air. When hardened eat them, or store in an airtight box so they don't continue to dry. I strung mine outside like a wind chime.

Phosphate Jello Cubes

This is not only a neat party trick, but it is deliciously refreshing, surprising, and the cubes will not water down your cocktail. Use a large square glass baking dish to set the jello and you should have plenty of cubes for about 4 cocktails. I used vodka and tonic but these could go into straight whiskey or even rum and coke. Phosphate was actually used as a souring agent in early instant gelatin, as it was in fountain drinks.

3 tbsp Superclear Gelatin
  (Custom Collagen)
3 cups water
1 cup vodka

1 cup sugar
1 tbsp acid phosphate or citric
  acid powder

Dissolve the gelatin in a cup of water and then add the phosphate. Heat the water, vodka, and sugar just below boiling, then add the sugar. Next pour that over the gelatin mixture, let cool. Pour into your glass dish and spoon off every last bit of foam that may have arisen. Let set in the fridge for about 2–3 hours. Then with a hot knife, cut out squares. With a very small spatula, carefully scoop them out onto a plate. Touch them up with the very hot knife if you need to, so they look like lovely sparkling ice cubes. Place a few in each glass and pour over your favorite cocktail. Don't tell anyone what is going on, just hand out spoons to go with each glass.

Aged Peeps

I admit, this is extraordinarily silly. But art made from peeps is nothing new. The originality of this recipe is precisely its organoleptic properties, which I assure you are mind blowing. First, peeps are terrible right out of the package. They're  too soft, the flavor is a little acrid, and the sweetness is cloying. But with aging, peeps take on a chewy texture, the sweetness is somehow muted, and that yellow dye flavor takes on a strange alluring aroma. I keep them at least a year, in the opened package, in a cool dark place. This recipe goes one step beyond. Just set the aged peeps—classic yellow chicks—in small cylindrical molds face down. A plastic cup works perfectly. And squish their faces a little into the mold. Pour over a gelatin made from vodka with a drizzle of rosewater and no sugar; be sure it's cool or the peeps will melt. When you pour it over you will see little bubbles emerge from the surface of the peeps. Eventually the gelatin will capture and freeze the bubbles in place. Chill thoroughly and unmold without using hot water. I cut the plastic cup and peeled it off. You will notice first that the dye makes the whole jello yellow. Now bite in. The outside is jiggly and the inside perfectly crunchy. Loudly so in fact, and shatteringly delicious. Much more so than if you freeze the peeps, because then all the flavors are muted. I have absolutely no idea how or why this happens, but I imagine it's probably similar to a freeze-dried peep.

Arnold Palmer Squared

You've probably heard of the drink named for Arnold Palmer which is half lemonade and half iced tea. Did you know that there is also a sandwich, half tuna and half egg salad? It's a beautiful combination. So why not throw all these together, bound with jello instead of bread, and toss in a little booze too?

2 packets of gelatin
½ cup vodka
1 teabag
2 tsp sugar
juice of 1 lemon
thin slice of ahi tuna
pinch of tarragon
1 tsp olive oil
1 egg
1 gherkin pickle

Bloom one packet of gelatin in ¼ c vodka. Make a cup of strong tea and add a teaspoon of sugar. Pour it over the gelatin and let chill in a rectangular container. Bloom the second pack of gelatin in the lemon juice. Heat ¾ of a cup of water with another ¼ c vodka, add sugar. Pour over the gelatin and set aside at room temperature. Salt the tuna and sear it quickly in a pan with the olive oil. Let cool a little and then place it on top of the chilled ice tea gelatin. Return to the fridge. Boil an egg, starting in cold water and bringing to the boil then cooking for 3–4 minutes. Run under cold water, peel, and slice in half. It should be pleasantly soft and slightly runny. If you like it firmer, go to 6 minutes. Pour the ice tea on top of the set lemon and tuna layer and gently place the egg on top. The gelatin should just reach the top of the egg. Garnish with slices of gherkin. If people don't get the joke, just yell FOUR!

Jello Dumplings

Xiao Long Bao is among the most delightfully intriguing foods on earth. It is basically soup in a dumpling; you bite off the top and sip out the soup and then eat the rest of the noodle casing. I have had some magnificent ones in Hong Kong, but I couldn't help feeling that it would have been better if you could gobble the whole thing down soup and noodle together. Well you can.

The trick to making the original recipe is using gelatinous soup, encasing a lump in a circle of dough with a twisted top knot and then steaming, so the gelatin melts into soup inside while the noodle cooks. But what if you were to engineer that basic idea and serve the noodle cold with jello inside? The key is a paper-thin noodle wrapper that will cook in a few seconds:

Start with a basic boozy jello. Use a cup of good vodka to 1 tbs gelatin. To mellow the flavor, add 1 tsp powdered sugar and 1 tsp lime juice. Let it set in a casserole.

Then take 1 cup of flour and a quarter tsp of salt and slowly sprinkle in about half a cup of water, stirring with a fork until you have a stiff dough. You may have to add more water or a little more flour. Trust me, you can't measure this precisely. It will always be different depending on the weather, your flour, and the whim of the kitchen gods. Let the dough rest about 5 minutes. Then, on a floured board, knead the dough for about 10 minutes, adding more flour if necessary to prevent sticking. Roll this out into the thinnest sheet you can, always adding more flour if needed. With a glass, cut circles out of the dough.

To form the dumplings, you can go for the traditional shape or whatever seems best to you. The former is made by taking a spoonful of the firm jello, placing it in the middle of each round then gathering in the edges moving around in a circle and pinching every millimeter or so at the top. It should have precisely 18 folds. This takes some skill. I prefer to just fold the circle of dough over into a half moon, pressing down to seal the edge, then make small pleats in that edge and set it down so the ruffle is on top.

As you fold them, put each dumpling on a floured tray in the fridge. When done with them all, bring a pot of salted water to the boil. Drop in the dumplings and cook about a minute (do taste for doneness) and scoop each one out and place in a big bowl of ice water. Drain the bowl and place the dumplings in the fridge to let the jello reset.

At this point you can of course go with complementary flavors: soy sauce, black vinegar, and some sliced scallions and a little ginger, maybe a drop of sesame oil. But with the vodka I went in a totally different direction—a kind of salsa to dip these in, something like the flavor combination of a Bloody Mary. Chop tomatoes, chili, cilantro, celery, green onion and add lime juice and a splash of Worcestershire and a hit of smoky hot sauce.

The Hand

Virtually anything can become a mold for jello and one of the easiest is a disposable vinyl glove. Once molded, you can paint on fingernails, or blood from the severed wrist, or even inject it with colors if you have the tools to make gelatin flower art. A really deft hand could probably inject veins into it with a proper syringe and needle. If you use a standard large glove it will hold about 3 cups of liquid. After this was unmolded it looked very much like slices of hot dog inside the hand, which elicited a frisson of delight.

For the hand:

3 cups white wine	1 tbsp raw sugar
3 packs of gelatin	3 drops vanilla extract

For the filling:

1 cup heavy cream	1 drop almond extract
1 tbsp gelatin	2–3 drops food coloring
1 tsp raw sugar	

Dissolve the gelatin in 1 cup of the wine. Heat the rest, adding the sugar and extract. Combine the two and stir to make sure the sugar is dissolved. Let cool to room temperature. Put the end of a funnel into the opening of the glove and tie around with a rubber band. Spoon in the gelatin. Then extract the funnel and tighten the rubber band to close the opening. Place the hand on a plate and put in the fridge to set for several hours.

Very carefully cut off the glove with sharp scissors, but leave the bottom of the glove in place under the hand for support. Then for the filling, bloom the gelatin in ¼ c of cream and heat the rest. Add the sugar and extract and stir until dissolved. Let cool a bit, so still liquid but not too hot or it will melt the hand, and not too cool or it will solidify. Add some food coloring. Fill your syringe and inject

fanciful shapes into the flesh. Scrape off any excess carefully with a spoon or a wet paper towel. Put into the fridge to set again for half an hour or so. Then turn the hand over, be careful lest the fingers fall off—it's best to put a plate right on top and flip it over. Peel off the plastic remains of the glove and you should have a lovely see-through hand. Touch it up if there are stray remains of the injections and wave a blow torch over it to give some sheen.

When you serve it, be sure to give it a high-five, but don't bite the hand that feeds you. It will be finger-licking good if you use this hands-on approach.

Jägermeister Worms

I spent one summer doing research on fasting in the charming town of Wolfen-büttel at the magnificent Herzog August Bibliotek. The entire place smelled of Jägermeister, which is made there, and I grew extremely fond of it. Imagine waking up in the morning, reading in the library, going to sleep—with that same bracing herbal aroma. It can be a little intense; you wouldn't want a big slice of it, so I came up with these silly worms. I used an empty Kewpie Mayo bottle, but you could use any squirty bottle, or even a plastic ketchup bottle.

Mix ½ cup of the Jag with 2 packages of gelatin, and heat another 1 ½ cups. Mix the two and funnel into your plastic bottle. Put this on ice for about 15 minutes, to just barely set. Then squeeze the bottle onto a plate to form little squiggly worms. You can use this technique with any other jello too.

Onigiri in Tonka Bean Jello

Tonka beans have one of the most seductive and alluring aromas in the entire plant world, something akin to vanilla, but spicy and almost savory too with almond and clove notes. They're not allowed to be sold in the US because they're the source of coumarin, the heart medicine, and can be dangerous in large quantities. In the rest of the world they put the beans in liqueurs, pipe tobacco, and even perfume. A friend managed to get some and asked if I wanted a handful to play with and naturally I said please! Among the various things I did with them was tossed a few into a bottle of vodka and forgot about it for about a year. The vodka turned amber, became ridiculously aromatic, and even stranger, held up to light seemed to have flecks of mica suspended in it.

1 cup Japanese sushi rice	1 tsp sugar
2 sheets of nori seaweed	1 packet gelatin
1 cup tonka bean vodka or purchased liqueur	2 pickled red umeboshi plums

Rinse and cook the rice in 1 ¼ cups of water. Start on high heat and then when it comes to the boil simmer on very low for 20 minutes. When cool enough to handle, form into flat triangles. Place a strip of the seaweed at the bottom and fold around the rice. Put each onigiri piece into a rectangular mold that is just slightly larger. Or you can also line them up in a plastic container, just slightly separated. Bloom the gelatin in ¼ c of the vodka and heat the rest with the sugar. (If using liqueur, omit the sugar.) Mix the two and let cool. Then pour over the onigiri. The tops of the rice triangle should be peering out above the jello coating. Let chill until set. Then unmold onto a plate and garnish with a circle of the plums. To get a smooth surface on the jello, I also charred it, and the rice, a little with a blow torch. That seems to have really brought out the aroma of the tonka.

Fernet for Friday the 13th

For this day, and Halloween would be good too, you want to serve something composed of pure unmitigated evil. I think Fernet Branca comes as close as you can get in liquid form, except maybe fresh human blood—which would even coagulate into jello on its own. Anyway, this began as an experiment. I heard that extreme bitter flavors are tamed by salt. It is true. Fernet jello on its own is inedible, but with black Gangetic salt that smells like brimstone and rotten eggs, it actually becomes interesting, even more so with the black garlic.

1 cup Fernet Branca
1 tbsp gelatin
sprinkle of black salt (found in
    Indian groceries or online)

a few cloves of black garlic
sprig of dead lavender

In ¼ cup of liquor bloom the gelatin. Heat the rest. Mix the two and set in a round mold. If you had a little skull-shaped mold that would be great. Chill to set. Unmold and arrange with the other ingredients. Don't let children touch this obviously and if there are squeamish adults around, maybe warn them too.

Konjac

You will often hear this described as a kind of gelatin. Not exactly. The only similarity is in the chewy bounce and clarity, but they are so different in texture that no one could mistake the two. Moreover, konjac or konyakku in Japanese, or glucomannan in powdered form, cannot be digested by the human body. It has virtually no calories. It makes a really interesting noodle called shirataki, but you can also make odd shapes by cutting with scissors. I used a pair of pinking shears with this one. If you want to add alcohol to the recipe, it won't form properly, so I suggest soaking it afterwards in a cocktail. Unlike any other gelatin, it must be kept in liquid and will never dissolve.

1 ½ tbsp glucomannan powder
2 ½ cups water
¼ tsp calcium hydroxide (*Cal*
    can be found in Mexican
    groceries or online)

1 cup vodka
½ cup orange juice
dash of amarena cherry syrup

Mix the glucomannan in a pot with the water, whisk, and let dissolve for 10 minutes. Cook on medium heat for 4 minutes. Let cool. Mix the *cal* in a tablespoon of water and let dissolve. Then mix the two. You will then have a solid mass of dough. Remove from the pot and form or cut into any shape you like. Or press into a mold or onto a textured surface. Boil the shapes for 30 minutes. Then when hot plunge directly into any cocktail. I've used a screwdriver here. Place in the fridge for a few days so a little of the alcohol is absorbed.

Froot Loop Negroni

The Froot Loops mysteriously appeared in my house one day. I warned my son that anything I find in the cabinet is likely to end up in jello. He did not heed the warning. I have a weird fascination for breakfast cereals. I never on any occasion eat them for breakfast, but as candy, they can be fun. I had a roommate in college who used to eat Cap'n Crunch with beer. Those of you old enough to remember the TV commercial rivalry of Quisp and Quake will, like me, wish you could still find a box to make into marshmallow treats. Do they still make Trix? Or Count Chocula? I mention all these because any would be appropriate for this recipe. Use an 8- or 10-inch pie plate to set this.

Enough Foot Loops to cover the bottom of a pie plate plus a few more	1 cup Red Vermouth
	3 packets gelatin
	1 cup dried white mulberries
1 cup Campari	¼ cup decorative red sugar
1 cup gin	

Carefully place a single layer of Froot Loops laying flat and covering the bottom of the pie plate so the colors are distributed evenly.

Mix the ingredients for the cocktail, dissolve the gelatin in 1 cup of the mixture at room temperature. Boil the rest and immediately mix the two. Let cool a little then carefully spoon over the cereal, being sure not to disturb your arrangement. You will notice that as the cereal absorbs the liquid it doesn't

expand but rather shrinks. Curiouser and curiouser. This is why you need more Loops to fill in the gaps. After a few minutes of fussing and when the jello beings to set, place the mulberries gently on top of the cereal. If you can't find them, golden raisins would be nice or other dried fruit chopped up. The idea is that you are creating another layer of texture and flavor to add depth to the combination. I was tempted to add another layer of milk to replicate a breakfast bowl, but the idea of milk and a negroni just didn't sound that good.

Chill the jello and then when set, dip the bottom briefly into hot water, turn it upside down into a large plate, and sprinkle the sides with the red sugar to look like a pie crust rim. Put back into the fridge to set again until ready to serve. It looks stunning and tastes just as good. Surprisingly.

Viniq Ham and Carrots

When my older son was moving, he found a bottle of this lurid purple liqueur flecked with what seems to be sparkly eye shadow in hypnotizing swirls. He was about to throw it away but asked me if I was interested. For jello, yes. I can't say I like the stuff too much; it's very sweet. Vodka, Moscato, and natural fruit flavors is how they describe it. Mixed with other ingredients, it's interesting. Remarkably, the visual effect remains in the jello.

2 cups Purple Viniq	handful of baby carrots
2 tbsp gelatin	4 slices of ham
1 cup champagne	carrot tops for garnish, or
1 tbsp gelatin	parsley

Dissolve the gelatin in ½ cup of the liqueur and heat the rest. Observe carefully how it swirls as it heats. Mix the two and pour into a bowl-shaped mold. Likewise dissolve the third pack of gelatin in ¼ cup of champagne and heat

the rest. Mix the two and set in a smaller bowl or mold. Let them set in the fridge. Unmold the champagne and place at the center of a plate. Unmold the larger one and slice in wedges and arrange around the center so it looks like an aster or purple daisy. Then shred the ham and slice the carrots and arrange all around. This close-up doesn't show them around the edge of the plate. Garnish garishly with greens. If you wave a flashlight over the plate while serving, you will gain the greatest visual effect.

DIY Jello Pizza

A pizza that can be made in a few minutes or a few years. I offer both options and much in between. In any case, you will need a wad of dough, some salami, some wine on the sweet side, and some pickled lemons. You can bake the dough into a flat round, make the wine into jello, chop it up, and place on top and then cover with the other toppings. But if you would like to make this the pure unfettered expression of your own creative élan, here's how. Ideally you have a few grape vines; if not, plant them and then start this recipe a few years later. Likewise with a lemon tree.

For the wine: With your hands, crush the ripe unwashed organic grapes in a large well-scoured stockpot. The amount you want to make is entirely up to you. I rarely get more than about 5 gallons, and sometimes much less. That's a manageable amount. Every day for two weeks press down the skins that will have floated to the top. In a few days you will smell alcohol, see and hear bubbles, and the proliferation of life in the pot will made you swoon. Fermentation will take around two weeks, but keep tasting, you want nearly all the natural sugar fermented.

Then pass the wine through a fine-meshed sieve lined with several layers of cheesecloth into another large stockpot. Once you have just grape skins and seeds left, twist the top of the cheesecloth closed and squeeze out as much of the remaining liquid as you can. Don't worry about clarity at this point. Then pour the liquid into bottles using a funnel and close with corks. Let the wine sit for a few weeks in a cool place and you'll notice the sediment sink to the bottom. When you're ready to use, just decant the clear liquid and leave the sediment in the bottle. My only word of caution: a little fermentation will continue in the bottles, so put them in a place where you won't be upset if a bottle blows its cork. I once kept mine in the kitchen where it exploded into a fountain directly onto a panama hat, which bears the stains to this day.

To make this wine into a jello, just mix ¼ cup with a packet of gelatin, heat the rest and let set in the fridge in a container. Then chop it finely and keep chilled.

For the salami: Get about 2 lbs of pork shoulder with a decent amount of fat and chop it finely by hand. I don't recommend a meat grinder which smears the fat and ruins the final texture of the salami. To this add 1 tablespoon sea salt, 1 tablespoon raw sugar, ½ tsp Instacure #2 (#1 will not work), and a nice pinch each of coarsely ground pepper, paprika, oregano. Then take some well-soaked and rinsed hog casings somewhere about 1 ¼-1 ½ inch in diameter. Tie off one end and with your fingers fill the casings, pressing down on the filling, but not too tightly so you split the casing. Tie a piece of hemp twine with several knots to seal the top end. Then with a pin, poke many tiny holes in the sides of the casing. Hang in a cool and dry place with good air circulation. I have found a wine fridge to be perfect. In about a month, they should be ready to eat. Remove the casing and slice.

For the lemons: Get untreated organic lemons, or if you have a tree, that's ideal. Slice them into rounds, sprinkle salt on each round, and layer in a crock or glass jar. You can add cinnamon stick and other spices if you like. Then add more lemon juice so they are completely covered. Wait a year, then remove and enjoy. You eat the whole thing, rind and all, as a condiment or cook it with a chicken. Luscious.

For the dough: Take a cup of flour and a cup of spring water. Mix them in a large bowl and cover with a dishtowel. The next morning add a few spoons more of each. Continue for two weeks, at which point it will be bubbly and smell sour. At this point, name it. That way you'll think of it as a pet that needs to be fed every day. My last starter was St. Agatha. You can of course borrow some sourdough, but I see no reason to do that, since it's so easy to make and whatever you borrow is going to adapt to your local bacteria and yeast anyway. Just keep it on the counter and feed her every morning. If you bake a bread once a week or so, you will never need to throw any of it away.

For this recipe, take about a cup and add another cup of water and enough flour to create a smooth and firm dough, about the size of your fist. Add about ½ tsp salt and knead for 10 minutes. Let rise for an hour or so. Then roll the dough into a flat disc on a well-floured wooden board. Place it on a hot non-stick pan over high heat for 20 seconds, then turn over for another 45 or so. Then take the flatbread and place it directly on the open flame of your range, turning over for a few seconds on each side until lightly charred. It may even puff up, which is very exciting. If you don't have an open flame, use a blowtorch or throw into an oven at 500 degrees for a few minutes. When done, place the bread between two plates until ready to serve. Of course you can make many of these in a session.

Assemble by placing the chopped jello right on top of the bread, adding the salami and lemon cut into bits. It's not real pizza per se, but it is lovely.

Prognostication

As I have been pointing out, jello is among the best examples of a food that goes in and out of fashion—most recently very much out. It never disappeared entirely, and there were always enthusiasts, but there are many ways to gauge the popularity of a food or lack thereof. Simply look at cookbooks and articles in magazines and newspapers. You'll always find a few gelatin recipes here and there, but when they proliferate, you can be sure that a recipe is at least on the mind of authors and probably readers too. An n-gram search for the word gelatin, which tracks books, magazines, and newspapers in google, reveals a multi-peaked mountain that rises dramatically in 1901, the highest peak in 1922, and then in 1941. It drops gradually from there to the present. These data are not easy to interpret; they might just reflect the number of ads placed, in which case these would be points when companies thought they needed to advertise more—so in fact, low points in popularity. Spelling complicates the issue, because gelatine with an e peaks around 1880, but is still around as an alternate spelling. The n-gram pattern for Jell-O is even more confounding—it forms three peaks in 1900 around when the product was introduced, 1929, a low point in sales according to the company's own statements, and then a massive spike in 2012—which everyone recognizes as the nadir of Jell-O sales. Again, I think this reflects the public lack of enthusiasm much more than the opposite.

What this does suggest, though, is a peak in the Victorian era around the 1880s, and another glorious era in the 1950s to early 1970s, when they didn't need to advertise so much. It would be great to parse out cookbooks from other printed materials. It would take a stupendous amount of time to statistically chart the number of gelatin recipes in cookbooks published in the last century. But I can say, albeit anecdotally, that the late 19th century and the mid–20th century were golden ages. Scanning over menus across the past century reveals the same pattern.

Incidentally, the word "aspic" on an n-gram search looks more like the Sierra Nevada range. And this wouldn't be skewed by advertisements because it's a recipe. There's a peak in 1848, a huge spike in 1900, then craggy ups and downs to the present, including weirdly a little peak in 2011 that makes no sense. The term "Perfection Salad" is much easier to explain. There nothing before 1906–7, then a rise straight up to 1938, then a drop right down again back to nearly 0 in 1980. Another huge peak around 2009 reflects Laura Shapiro's book of the same name.

With time, one could refine the search by type of publication too. Perhaps cookbooks and articles aimed toward a specific type of consumer featured jello more or less dramatically while other types remained more consistent, reflecting preferences in fashionable high-end cooking. In other words, jello might disappear from *Gourmet* magazine in predictable patterns, while not at all from *Taste of Home*—which might reflect better the population at large rather than the elitist publications. In the same way, expensive restaurants would show clear patterns of gelatin offerings, but diners and Denny's, maybe not.

Online recipes might be a little more accurate when thinking about an ingredient or recipe, but you would have to carefully trace them by date of publication. All this would make a fascinating research project for a dedicated and technically savvy student.

Sales would be much a better indication of popularity, and it would be great to have some reliable data sets. But that's guarded company information. They leak a little here and there, but not enough to be precise. I also pay attention to grocery shelves. In my supermarket, there's a sizeable section just devoted to jello, but I also note not much moves there. For the large boxes of unflavored gelatin, I'm pretty sure I'm the only customer. That would almost certainly be different in places like Utah and Iowa where jello remains popular.

Without scientific precision it is equally difficult to predict the future with any accuracy. Trends can be as fickle as the economy, and sometimes every pattern is randomly influenced by chance events—wars or epidemics. But if we look at this from a cultural perspective, assessing the prevalent values that would inform gelatin consumption more in certain periods, then it is clear. Periods that favor scientific innovation, creativity even at the expense of being gaudy, and exotic imported ingredients, then the heydays of gelatin are the late Middle Ages, the Enlightenment, the Victorian Era, and the mid–20th century. That would mean popularity trails off in the later Renaissance, in the early 19th century, the Roaring Twenties flapper age, and the early 21st century. These were periods that distrusted science and looked for more natural foods. Incidentally they're also periods in art history with the same values: the Romantic period, the Era of Muckraking and the Pure Food Act, and the Hippie Era.

If you had asked me when I started this project where fashionable cuisine was headed, I would have said high-end restaurants are coming back, exotic and imported food will become treasured again, science will return to the kitchen, and many people will forget about the all-natural, organic, kale-laden cuisine of the early 21st century. A single virus threw off that prediction completely. As I write, the restaurant industry is in danger of collapsing. People are baking sourdough bread, pickling, and tackling new DIY projects because they're stuck at home. Trends popular for the past few decades are resurging, but I don't think it will last. I can't predict when or how this all will end, but I think it will usher in a new culinary aesthetic with a vengeance. The economy will pick up again, people will be spending money. New scientifically engineered foods will hit the market, as of course they have been in general lately. People will trust science in the food supply again. People will look to jello as a creative outlet. It will be an evolved jello—maybe without artificial flavoring and dyes, but with new forms as yet unheard of, mixing new ingredients. Hopefully, precisely the sort I've been imagining in this book.

Acknowledgments

First and above all, I would like to thank the thousands of people in the *Show Me Your Aspics* Facebook group who gave unflagging support and patiently witnessed this entire project unfold. In addition, all the other aspicious groups, *Aspics with Threatening Auras*, *Aspics with Inviting Auras*, etc.

The following no doubt incomplete list of names is intended to express my debt of gratitude to the many individuals who sent me molds or ingredients, cooked with me online or in person, answered questions, gave me sound advice and encouragement, or simply cheered me on while I slogged through the world of jello. To those of you whose ideas I stole accidentally, or even worse, those I forgot in this list, my sincere apologies.

Carrie Tillie, Madeleine Kemeny, Asc Helvetius, Kali Fish, Karen Ellery, Cecelia Watson, Irene Martinez, Siew Heng Boon, Elle Mactans, Abbey Kasemer, Kaye Shetron, David Shields, Stephanie Renee, Danielle Dioneff, Ruby McCoy, Angie Peregrine-Khan, Stephanie Walker, Laura Brehaut, Susan Fox, Gaia Galene, Lauren Chappers, Brooke Bowes, John Doughty, Brooklette Robertson, Amber Juno, Madeline Namtihw, Cecelia Leong-Salobir, Rachel Thoo, Martha Esersky Lorden, Maggie Topkis, Sheila Crye, Sarah Prentice, Sabina Catazzo, Nathalie Dupree, Steve Mo Fye, Eden Rain, Faye Levi, Rosi Song, Cristasha Reardon, Crystal Puckett, Tree Valentino, Diana Sbaitri, Ceci Vaughn, Jesse Knust, Craig Jones, Elizabeth Reno, Laura Duncan Wilgus, Marija Walter, Emma Heins, Julia Skinner, June Jacobs, Dee Brimley, Jade Rende, Corinne Brons, Jennifer Spencer, Margaret Kelly, Lambkin Hale Knight, Tori Jill Nehoc, Jessica Krcmarik, Harley Camp, Rachael S. Mamane, Katie Red Jimenez, Dawn Amber, Paul Ustach, Holly Brynjulfson, Katie Pippin, Nicole Ramos, Samantha Reynolds, Deirdre O'Reilly, Tracy Johnson, Chani Bee, Ndona Kukau Mayangi, Suza Kanon, Amanda Weischedel, Jacobien ter Veld, Sheila Ratcliffe, David M. Rosenstein, Bob del Grosso, Alison Zhang,

Krishnendu Ray, Med Oliver, Desiree Lopez, Elisabeth Luard, Leigh Chavez Bush, Lisa McShine, Peter Hertzmann, Stuart Cristol-Deman, Jim Comer, Randi Kenyon, Roz McLean, EK Snowden, Urtatim al-Qurtubiyya, James Englehardt, Kim Hildebrandt, Dave Poppen, Kevin Paulsen, Ariel Stirling, Laura Kelley, Nicki Tarulevicz, Andrew Martin, Beth Forrest, Alicia Reay, Elizabeth Andoh, Sandra Mian, Mark Dornfeld, Amanda Lynne Ramsey, Regula Ysewijn, Margot Finn, Marie-Christine Boutet, Karen Peters, Darling Ren, Willa Zhen, SJ Pienaar, F. Page Steinhardt, Lauren Ausmus, Galefridus Perefrinus, Lauren Sevrin, Lisa Falls, Claire Piper, Rose Harriott, Matthew Amster-Burton, Adrienne Millon Hemsley, Jim Dodge, Aiko Tanaka, Sasha Grigorieva, Jeremy Umansky, Greg de Saint Maurice, Kathleen Butler, Danika Tkacik

Bibliography

Alighieri, Dante. *Inferno*. NY: Hackett, 2009.

Bate, John, Edward Deaves, James Jenkin, Samuel Nicoll, and C. K. Ogden. *The mysteries of nature and art. In foure severall parts. The first of water works. The second of fire works. The third of drawing, washing, limming, painting, and engraving. The fourth of sundry experiments*. London: Thomas Harper, 1635.

Belanger, Victoria. *Hello, Jell-O*. Berkeley: Ten Speed, 2012.

Berni, Francesco. *Tutte le Opera di Berni*. Venice: Curtio Navo, 1538.

Blum, Deborah. *The Poison Squad*. NY: Penguin. 2019.

Bompas, Sam and Harry Parr. *Jelly Mongers*. NY: Sterling, 2011.

Brears, Peter. *Jellies and Their Moulds*. Totnes, Devon: Prospect Books, 2010.

Charles B. Knox Gelatine Co. *Dainty Desserts for Dainty People*. Johnstown, NY: Knox Gelatine, 1915.

Chaucer, Geoffrey. "Rosemounde." *Complete Works*. Hastings: Delphi, 2012.

Cox's Gelatine Recipes. NY: Cox Gelatine Co, 1930.

Cox's Manual of Gelatine Cookery. Edinburgh: J. & G. Cox, 1910.

Digby, Kenelm. *The Closet of Sir Kenelm Digby Opened*. London: E.C. for H. Brome, 1669.

Duffin, Christopher J. "Ichthyocolla." *Pharmaceutical Historian* 49, no. 4 (2019): 116–122.

Escoffier, Auguste. (1903) *The Escoffier Cookbook*. Reprint NY: Crown Publishers, 1975.

Evelyn, John. "Diary." In *Memoires Illustrative of the Life and Writings of John Evelyn*, edited by John Bray. London: Henry Colburn, 1819.

Farmer, Fannie. *Food and Cookery for the Sick and Convalescent*. Boston: Little, Brown, 1904.

Favorite Brand Name Recipes: Jell-O Celebrating 100 Years. Lincolnwood, IL: Publications International, Ltd, 1997.

General Foods Corporation. *Album of Jellied Salads and Aspics*. NY: General Foods, 1953.

General Foods Corporation. *Joys of Jell-O 4th edition*. White Plains, NY: General Foods Co., 1965.

Gentleman of Fortune. *Complete Modern London Spy*, 1772.

Glasse, Hannah. *Art of Cookery Made Plain and Easy.* London: 1747.

Graves, Robert. A Pocket Conspectus. London: J. Murray and J.S. Highley, 1799.

Guybert, Philibert. *Le medecin charitable.* Paris: 1659.

Harder, Jules. *The Physiology of Taste: Herder's Book of Practical American Cookery.* San Francisco: Self-published,1885.

"Hartshorn." http://www.angelfire.com/md3/openhearthcooking/aaHartshorn.html.

Holbrook, Kate "Jell-O Medium" *Mormon Studies Review* 5 (2018): 53–59.

Horowitz, Roger. *Kosher U.S.A.: How Coke Became Kosher and Other Tales of Modern Food*. NY: Columbia University Press, 2016.

Hugget, Jane. *A Propre New Booke of Cokerye*. Bristol: Stuart Press, 1995.

Huxham, John. *Essay on Fevers.* 1750, 2nd ed.

Knox Gelatine Cookbook. NY: Rutledge, 1977.

Lemery, Louis. *Traicté des aliments.* Paris: Pierre Witte, 1705.

Liber de Coquina, Marianne Mulon, tr. in "Deux Traités Inédits d'Art Culinaire Medieval." *Bulletin Philologique et Historique* 1 (année 1968): 369–435.

Marshall, Agnes B. *Mrs. A. B. Marshall's Larger Cookery Book of Extra Recipes*. London: Marshall's School of Cookery, 1902. https://archive.org/details/b21537999/page/n9/mode/2up

Marsilius de Sancta Sophia. *Opus Aureum* (De Febribus) Lyon: Fradin,1517 ed. https://books.google.com/books/about/Opus_aureum_ac_praeclarum_de_recenti_mem.html?id=LR26YgEACAAJ

Martino of Como. *The Art of Cooking: The First Modern Cookery Book*. Tr. Jeremy Parzen. Berkeley: UC Press, 2005.

Messisbugo, Christoforo. *Banchetti*. Ferrara: Bughlhat, 1549.

Meyer, Ethel S. *A Practical Dictionary of Cookery.* London: 1898.

Papin, Denis. *A New Digester or Engine for Softening Bones*. London: Henry Bonwicke, 1681.

Plat, Hugh. *Delightes for Ladies.* London: Humphry Lownes,1603.

Platina, Bartolomeo Sacchi. *On Right Pleasure and Good Health* (*De honesta voluptate*). Tr. Mary Ella Milham. Tempe, AZ: Medieval and Renaissance Texts and Studies, 1998.

Purchas, Samuel. *Purchas His Pilgrims*. London:William Stansby, 1625.

Rabisha, William. *The Whole Body of Cookery Dissected*. London: George Calvert, 1682.

Raffald, Elizabeth. *The Experienced English Housekeeper*. Manchester: J. Harrop, 1769.

Rossetti, Giovanni Battista. *Dello Scalco*. Ferrara: Mammarello, 1584.

Rowbottom, Allie. *Jello Girls*. New York: Little, Brown and Company, 2018.

Scappi, Bartolomeo. *Opera*. Venice: Tramezzino, 1570.

Shapiro, Laura. *Perfection Salad*. Berkeley: UC Press, 2008.

Sinclair, Upton. *The Jungle*. Amazon Classics, 2017.

Spackman, Christy. "Mormonism's Jell-O Mold." https://slate.com/human-interest/2012/08/jell-o-and-mormonism-the-stereotypes-surprising-origins.html.

Taillevent, Guillaume Tirel. *Viandier*. Translated by Terence Scully. Ottowa: University of Ottowa Press, 1998.

"The Seaweed Site: Information on Marine Algae." http://www.seaweed.ie/uses_general/carrageenans.php.

Tomasik, Timothy, and Ken Albala, eds. *The Most Excellent Book of Cookery (Livre fort excellente de cuysine)*. Totnes, Devon: Prospect Books, 2014.

Wyman, Carolyn. *Jell-O: A Biography*. San Diego: Harvest, 2001.

Index

KEN ALBALA is a professor of history at the University of the Pacific. He is the author of *Noodle Soup: Recipes, Techniques, Obsession* and many other academic monographs, reference works, translations, cookbooks, and food history video series.

The University of Illinois Press
is a founding member of the
Association of University Presses.

———————————————

Text designed by Jim Proefrock
Composed in 9.75/14 Frutiger 55 Roman
with Mercurius Black display
at the University of Illinois Press
Manufactured by Versa Press, Inc.

University of Illinois Press
1325 South Oak Street
Champaign, IL 61820-6903
www.press.uillinois.edu